D0832678

Jean Conil's

CUISINE VÉGÉTARIENNE FRANÇAISE

Gourmet French Vegetarian Recipes

From the finest *haute cuisine* to traditional country fare — a unique collection of dishes which combine French flair with natural wholefood ingredients.

Jean Conil's CUISINE VÉGÉTARIENNE FRANÇAISE

Jean Conil
with Fay Franklin

Colour photography and illustrations by Paul Turner

THORSONS PUBLISHERS LIMITED
Wellingborough, Northamptonshire

To the new generation who understands that health is the only wealth that really matters.

First published 1985

British Library Cataloguing in Publication Data

Conil, Jean
Jean Conil's cuisine végétarienne Française: gourmet French vegetarian recipes.
1. Vegetarian cookery 2. Cookery, French
I. Title II. Franklin, Fay
641.5'636'0944 TX837

ISBN 0-7225-0999-5

Printed and bound in Great Britain

Contents

Acknowledgements

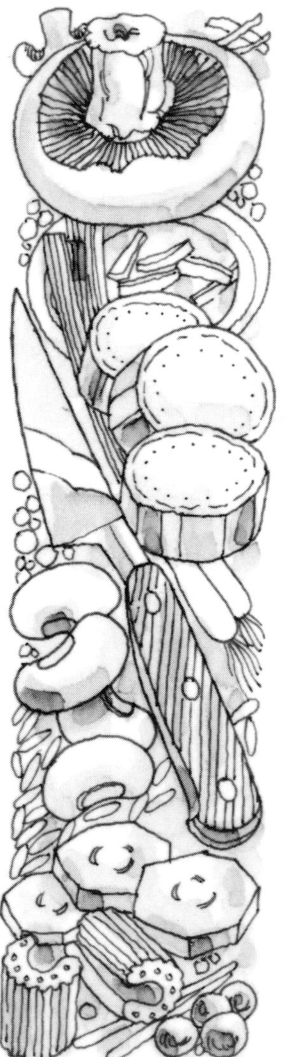

The author and editor would like to thank the Chairman of the Arts Club, Mr Stuart Rose CBE, for his kind co-operation throughout the preparation of this book; Mr Paul Cockerton of Hyam and Cockerton (Hotel and Catering Suppliers) Limited, for generously supplying fresh fruit and vegetables for photography; and Paul Turner and Sue Pressley of Stonecastle Graphics for a most enjoyable, professional and successful photography session.

I should like to express my thanks to the members of the Arts Club whose appreciation of good food has helped to shape this book. I am especially grateful to my patrons the Baron and Baroness de Juniac for allowing me the pleasure of cooking for the French Ambassador and other discerning gourmets. My thanks go, too, to the members of my staff who worked so hard in helping me prepare the food for photography: my two senior Spanish chefs, Tony Ordono Damaso, my sauce cook, and Julio Alvarez, my sous chef; and particularly my adopted French pupil Bruno Meunier, who no doubt has all the makings of a great chef in due course; also my nephew Stephane Margnon, a French university student who took time off from his studies to act as steward during the photography session; Jérome McCarthy, who always prepares the salads and hors d'oeuvres with such artistic flair; and last, but not least, my Moroccan chef, Ahmed. I am most grateful, too, to André Eldon-Edington, Secretary of the Arts Club, for his encouragement and support, and to Frank Wheeler, one of the best supporters of the Society of Master Chefs and the culinary profession. My gratitude, especially, to my family: my son, Christopher Conil — a Master Baker in his own right — and my wife, Mary, and daughter, Patricia, for always sampling my cooking with so much enthusiasm. And I am much indebted to my editor, Fay Franklin, whose talent, guidance and encouragement have helped me to a true understanding of vegetarianism.

JEAN CONIL

I am most grateful to Master Chef Jean Conil for the privilege and pleasure of working on this book with him. It has been inspirational, educational and enjoyable — feelings which I hope our readers will share. My thanks go to the following people, all of whom have been instrumental in bringing this about: David Young and John Hardaker, for their confidence in me; Frances Clapham, for the skills with which to fulfil it; Nadine Pageaud, for her assistance and enthusiasm; Sally Freestone, my Production 'team mate'; and, of course, my husband Simon and my parents, for everything.

FAY FRANKLIN

Foreword

I am absolutely thrilled to have been asked to write the foreword to this exciting new book on French vegetarian cooking by my fellow countryman Master Chef Jean Conil.

Everyone, I would imagine, has encountered this great Chef, whether on television or the radio, or has followed a recipe from one of his many books. Whenever good food is mentioned, look closer, you will find the influence of Jean Conil.

It seems to me that the story of his life is a history of cooking in itself: as a child he played with pots and pans instead of toys in the kitchen of his father's restaurants in Boulogne-sur-Mer and, later, Paris. He learned the tricks of the trade as an enchanting game and never imagined himself anywhere but in the cookery business. His prodigious imagination and flair astonished and impressed his elders, and the great Escoffier, by then retired, who was a regular visitor to Jean's father's *Brasserie Ducastaing*, encouraged and helped him to train as a chef with letters of recommendation which enabled him to learn his trade in some of the best restaurants in Paris. After two years in the French navy, as an Officer's cook, he came to England as Petty Officer Chef to the British Admirals. After the war, instead of returning to France and the security of a family business, he was encouraged to remain in London and became favourite *commis* chef to two of the Savoy's greatest chefs — Dutrey and Alban — who were his mentors. Later, at Fortnum and Mason, his customers included aristocrats and royalty: another feather in his 'Chef's toque'. For the past six years he has been delighting the members at London's very exclusive Arts Club — and everyone knows what demanding gourmets artists can be! For Jean Conil it has been a perfect niche, as he is a gastronomical writer of great talent, as well as a very talented chef.

I was very privileged when he kindly asked me to attend a banquet to celebrate the fiftieth anniversary of his cooking life — and one can indeed say life, because Jean Conil's life truly is his art. To that party came all the greatest chefs, all the most important hoteliers, and I was delighted to be seated next to Anton Mosimann, who has given the Dorchester Restaurant the fine reputation it now has, and who, like me, was there to honour the career of Master Chef Jean Conil.

Ever since the 1950s, Jean has been a leading light in a handful of visionary chefs who have been promoting a healthier way of eating which sacrifices none of the pleasures of the table — a concept which later became known all over the world as *nouvelle cuisine*, and which has caused something of a revolution in the finest restaurants. We French, with our centuries of *haute cuisine*, have very clear ideas about food. There is no question but that a completely new approach to cooking and eating has to be very special to strike such a chord in the heart of our nation, and there is no doubt

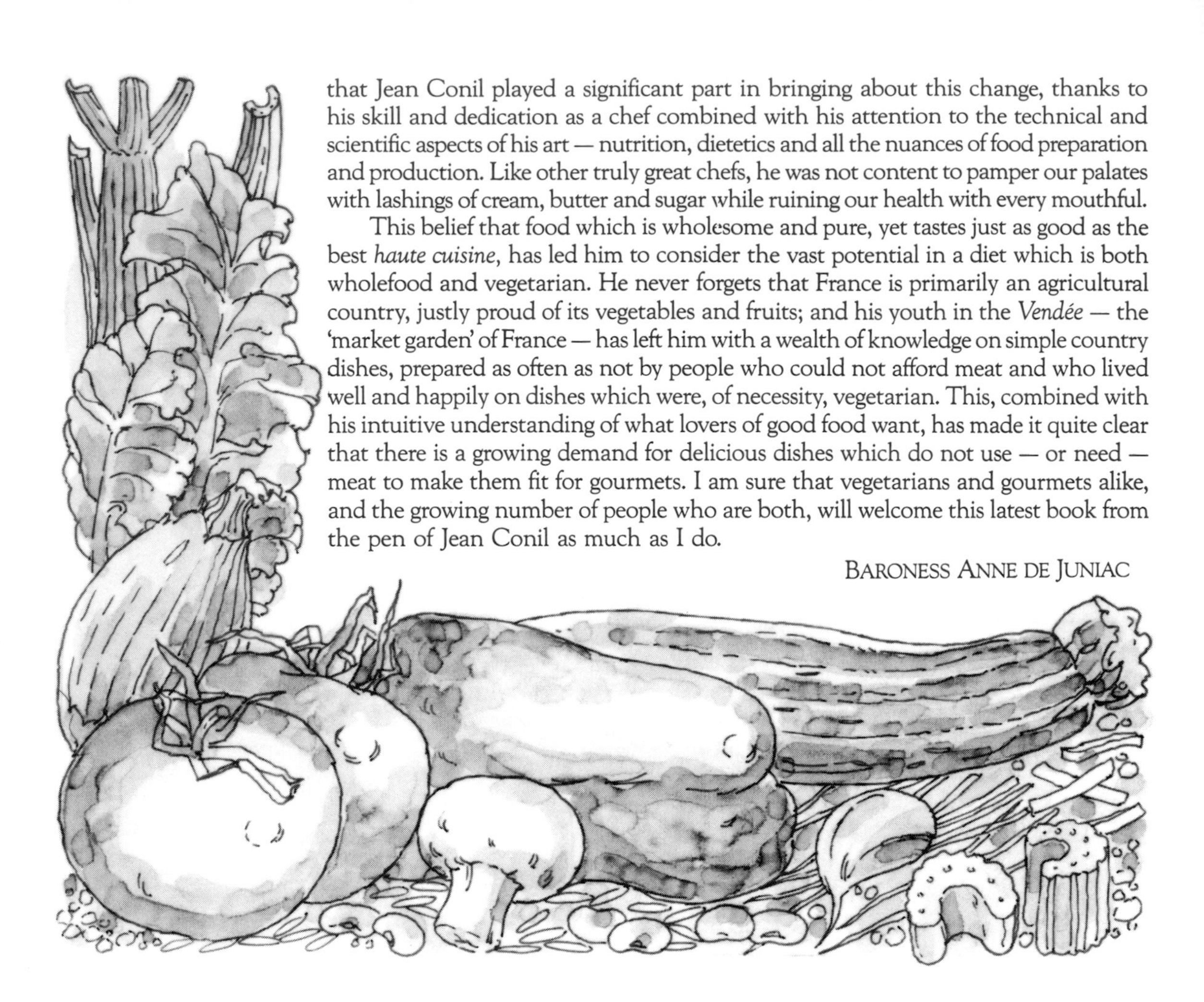

that Jean Conil played a significant part in bringing about this change, thanks to his skill and dedication as a chef combined with his attention to the technical and scientific aspects of his art — nutrition, dietetics and all the nuances of food preparation and production. Like other truly great chefs, he was not content to pamper our palates with lashings of cream, butter and sugar while ruining our health with every mouthful.

This belief that food which is wholesome and pure, yet tastes just as good as the best *haute cuisine*, has led him to consider the vast potential in a diet which is both wholefood and vegetarian. He never forgets that France is primarily an agricultural country, justly proud of its vegetables and fruits; and his youth in the *Vendée* — the 'market garden' of France — has left him with a wealth of knowledge on simple country dishes, prepared as often as not by people who could not afford meat and who lived well and happily on dishes which were, of necessity, vegetarian. This, combined with his intuitive understanding of what lovers of good food want, has made it quite clear that there is a growing demand for delicious dishes which do not use — or need — meat to make them fit for gourmets. I am sure that vegetarians and gourmets alike, and the growing number of people who are both, will welcome this latest book from the pen of Jean Conil as much as I do.

BARONESS ANNE DE JUNIAC

Introduction

At no time during the history of French gastronomy has there been such a rationalization of our eating habits as has occurred over the past decade. Not since the Revolution was sparked into action by the people's demands for bread has food caused such an upheaval in the French way of life. But this time the demand of the people has not been for bread, but for a healthier, simpler fare, avoiding the rich and extravagant concoctions on which classical *haute cuisine* has placed such emphasis. The *nouvelle cuisine,* as this new approach to cooking has become known, has reached a peak over the past ten years, but it is in fact the culmination of a growing response by chefs to the changing mood of their customers, which has been taking place over twenty to thirty years, as attitudes towards nutrition have changed, and as people have become more and more aware of the food they eat and the lifestyle they adopt. This response by my profession has taken many forms. Some chefs have gradually modified the great, classic dishes, to present their public with food which is still beautiful to behold and pleasurable to eat yet at the same time far more healthy than before; some have claimed the invention of this 'new look' food, refining it to a point where the food on the plate has become a miniature work of art — lovely to look at but which has lost all meaning as food in itself; many more have felt the moment as a free-for-all, with *haute cuisine* being sent to the guillotine to be replaced with whatever is their particular style or gimmick.

French vegetarian cooking is not a gimmick, nor is it for followers of any latest fad. It is a sincere move towards meeting the demands of customers and cooks who wish to eat well and live well, to enjoy long and health-filled lives. It is for this reason that vegetarianism has made its first inroads into our great culinary profession. France is a nation where food plays an important part in all aspects of daily life — it is not considered hedonistic to enjoy *les plaisirs de la table,* but perfectly legitimate and necessary for the enjoyment of life. Yet this attitude has, in the past, led to senseless over-indulgence, greed and illness. From being a nation in revolt against starvation we are fast becoming a nation in revolt against a bounty which is out of hand. In Napoleonic times an English blockade forced the French to begin the cultivation of sugar beet, because cane from the West Indies was not available. Now we are faced with an overconsumption of refined sugar — over 100 lb (50kg), as opposed to 15 lb (7kg) 150 years ago, per head per annum. And our meat and butter mountains, milk lakes and other monuments to the vagaries of international agricultural policy indicate that, while our farmers are hard-working, skilled agronomists, they are being steered in the wrong direction and their energies are going to waste. All over the world, not just in France, land given over to meat production to feed the Northern hemisphere could

be growing crops to feed the world. I am not trying to say by this that this book is attempting to change the world, but I do hope that, by perhaps convincing some of the many doubters in our society that it is perfectly possible to eat well without eating meat, and by using resources which can be grown cost-effectively and easily, it may change minds here and there — or at least provide food for thought!

French vegetarian cooking is really not such a radical step as it might at first sound. The French have always treated the vegetables which garnished the meat on their plates with far more flair and respect than most other Western countries. The British are famed for their overcooked greens and potatoes, the Americans sometimes seem to have borrowed *pommes frites* from us and nothing else! Yet a French gourmet has always appreciated a perfectly-cooked spear of asparagus, a tiny, fresh mangetout pea or a well-dressed salad with as much enthusiasm as a *chateaubriand* steak or fine *charcuterie*. I think everyone would agree, too, that the produce of our dairies is the finest to be found anywhere. Our cheeses are famed throughout the world and our *crème fraîche* and *fromage frais* are invaluable in *cuisine*, be it *nouvelle* or *haute*. So, from the point of view of classic French cookery, the love of food which is vegetarian in essence has always been present.

And it is the country people of France, the 'peasants' who revolted centuries ago, now living off our bountiful land, who have contributed other aspects of a healthy, meatless diet. Often unable to afford much meat themselves, they have long enjoyed dishes which use pulses and grains, humble root vegetables and 'wild' plants such as dandelions, to make dishes which are nourishing, sustaining and delicious. Take all this into consideration and it is not so surprising, after all, to find a Master Chef, especially one who hails from the French countryside, arguing the merits — in terms of both health and enjoyment — of meatless dishes!

There is another aspect to making this a most enjoyable way of eating, which should not be left out. In the past France, like Britain, was a colonist nation. Just as Britain has 'absorbed', for example, the kedgeree of India, so we have taken into our cuisine many influences of the regions we colonized in past centuries. And of recent years, our palates have been entranced by the delicate and flavoursome cooking to be found in the Vietnamese restaurants which have been started in France by refugees from that country. This national cuisine is currently very fashionable in Paris especially, and reflects all I have been saying about the wealth of imagination and respect paid to vegetables by those who rely upon them for their staple diet. I travelled to tropical regions during my time in the French navy, and the wonderful exotic fruits and vegetables to be found there fired my imagination as a chef — the scents, colours and flavours of a whole new world of ingredients have never left me, and you will find some recipes in this book which reflect the harmony of French cooking and that of her former colonies. Of course, until a very few years ago, a book which included ingredients such as pawpaw, or even aubergines (eggplants) and peppers would have been considered very adventurous and beyond the scope, in terms of cost and availability, of the average consumer. Now, thanks to the international 'larder' of foods open to us, the range of produce available to the vegetarian gourmet is as wide as anyone could wish for. As a chef, with a natural love of experimenting with exciting new ingredients, I have welcomed this scope and tried to use it to best advantage in my recipes.

As a food technologist, too, I can only welcome this move towards a more rational way of eating, and I have always been fascinated by the many sources of alternative protein available to us, which Oriental nations have long exploited in the form of tofu and other soya products, and which Western society is only just beginning to discover. But I feel we are taking the wrong approach to these products, sometimes — seeing them as meat extenders, meat substitutes to be shaped and flavoured and disguised. Certainly there is no harm in this, and many people welcome the chance

to stretch their budget, or carry on enjoying burgers and other 'meat'-based dishes without actually using meat, but it does not reflect the concept of enjoying these products for themselves. There is no question that a soya bean is a dull thing on its own, but in the hands of a good cook, and in its tofu, miso or tempeh form, it can be used to make all sorts of flavoursome, protein-packed dishes. Its use for thousands of years in Oriental cooking is testament to that, and there is, too, the point that these nations are now leading the world in all sorts of technological advances, as well as the influence of their peaceful practices of meditation, yoga, and drug-free medicines being absorbed into our blossoming 'alternative' culture. Perhaps it is time we extended our appreciation of their cuisine to take in more of their products.

As a Frenchman, it is in my nature to abhor waste. This ranges from the news reports of food being left to rot in the fields, or sold off cheaply to Eastern countries to keep prices up in the West, to the archetypal French concept of the stock pot, whereby no food scraps need be wasted unless they are bad, and in which food which would have been thrown into the bin is transformed into a rich, nutritious base for soups, sauces and many other purposes. This natural inclination of mine is so well met by the concepts I have been explaining. On every scale, meeting the needs of a vegetarian diet naturally avoids the sort of waste we have become so used to in this century.

As I said before, I hope this will be a book to change minds, and thereby — just a little, perhaps — to change the world. The advent of *nouvelle cuisine* has indicated that all the re-education of people's ideas will only start the ball rolling, but once people find out that something which is good for you can actually be pleasurable too, then an idea becomes a movement and changes really come about. So this is a book for everyone. I hope that vegetarians will be pleased to try my recipes, and I trust that they will welcome a rather fresh and different approach to their chosen diet. I hope that wholefooders will welcome a book which uses only natural products to make dishes which are as light, delicate and enjoyable as anything that could be created with the refined ingredients. I trust that meat-eaters will at last feel able to invite their vegetarian friends to dinner without worrying about what to give them, and when they are invited back, I trust they will be sure of a wonderful meal in return. Whatever you normally eat, I hope you will leave the table after a dish taken from this book feeling totally content. Enjoy this gourmet vegetarian book in the confidence that these long-tried recipes have made the grade with some of the most fastidious palates in the world — people for whom eating is one of the great pleasures of life and who, because they were enjoying their meal so much, probably never even noticed that it did not involve meat. The ingredients used stood up, and still do, as a wealth of flavour, colour, texture and character in their own right. As a creative person myself, who loves to modify a recipe, to experiment, test and taste, and come up with new ideas, I hope you will see this book as only the beginning. If you try a recipe and enjoy it, consider how it might be if you substituted a particular favourite vegetable of yours for one I have suggested, or a different cheese perhaps, for the one in the recipe, or a different type of bean . . . from just one dish you can create a whole range of different ones, just by experimenting, which is, after all, the pleasure of cooking.

French vegetarianism is here to stay. I predict that before too long every chef will have built upon it, created his own variations on it, and soon we will have the greatest repertoire of exciting natural dishes the world has ever seen — just mark my words!

JEAN CONIL
President of the Society of Master Chefs 1985

Note: All recipes serve six people, except where stated otherwise.

1 Les Pâtés de Légumes

Vegetable Pâtés and Dips

For centuries, the French have been the chief protagonists of these light, creamy vegetable purées but, although the professional culinary world revolves around rigid French technical disciplines, any great chef of today would consider it ludicrous not to include in the repertoire the wealth of delicious purées which have been developed, over the centuries, in the Third World. Both the French and British Empires brought back with them, in their day, many delicious and attractive dishes, but it is only recently that modern cuisine has adopted them as nutritious 'new' snacks, starters and *hors d'oeuvres*. In keeping with modern trends, their preparation is simplicity itself.

In this section I will be introducing pâtés, most of which can be served as dips with raw vegetables, to suit the fashion of today. Many are traditional, others have been evolved and improved in the kitchens of the Arts Club in London, where my fastidious clientele are always quick to contribute their suggestions.

In this era of the Common Market and the huge international trade in food, most exotic vegetables and fruits are now familiar sights in every supermarket. New horticultural techniques, too, enable countries with a cool climate to grow 'tropical' vegetables. Kiwi fruit, for example, is no longer the stranger it was when first featured by some chefs in all manner of dishes as little more than an overrated ornament.

In France, lighter purées are generally known as *mousses* or *mousselines*, depending on whether they are served hot or cold, whether prepared with cream or whipped egg white. In these recipes, the basis of the purée is primarily the pulp of the main ingredient, be it vegetable, fruit or pulse. According to the consistency and texture, the mixture is either thickened with a starchy paste or arrowroot, cornflour (cornstarch) or potato flour, or thinned out with cream, depending on the desired result, effect and intended use.

Dips and pâtés made with beans such as lentils or chick peas (garbanzos) should not need thickening. If you are making a dip of aubergines (eggplants) you may be interested to know that specialist food stores (in Britain, Arabic stores in particular) sell a product made especially for that purpose from salep starch. Tahini (sesame seed paste) can also be used. For nutritional purposes, and for a delicacy of taste, I often advocate the use of soft white cheese, either cream or low-fat, and eggs, so that the final *pâté de légumes* is smooth in texture without being either too firm or too sloppy.

La Parmentière (Rich Potato Mousse) in this chapter is not my invention. It is, in fact, Turkish. However, *pommes purées* have become as close to the hearts of the French people as to those of the Irish, who claim this versatile tuber as their own. I have named my own version of this dish for Antoine-Auguste Parmentier, who gives his name to many potato dishes in honour of his 'conversion' of the French to this previously despised vegetable. Since then gourmets have always appreciated the flavour of a hot new potato served with a Vinaigrette Sauce. This potato dip has a similar flavour, and is a favourite dish in those North African states which were once part of the French colonies and thus shared a unique interchange of gastronomic cultures. So, as with all the dishes in this chapter, you may try it with confidence. Many of my customers have, and have asked for more!

La Tapéna aux Olives Noires

Black Olive Tapénade

In Greece the olive tree is a symbol of wisdom, abundance and, as everyone knows, peace. In cooking, the olive is a fruit which lends itself to many inventive uses. By far the best, to my mind, is that delicious Mediterranean pâté known as Tapénade. It is usually made with anchovies but my version, with walnuts, is far more delicate in flavour.

Imperial (Metric)	American
½ lb (225g) large black olives, stoned*	**2 cups large black olives, stoned***
½ lb (225g) shelled walnuts	**1⅔ cups shelled English walnuts**
2 oz (50g) large pickled capers	**4 tablespoons large pickled capers**
4 hard-boiled egg yolks**	**4 hard-boiled egg yolks****
4 raw egg yolks	**4 raw egg yolks**
1 small green chilli	**1 small green chili**
2 cloves garlic	**2 cloves garlic**
1 pinch grated nutmeg *or* **mace**	**1 pinch grated nutmeg** *or* **mace**
2 tablespoons soya sauce	**2 tablespoons soy sauce**
2 tablespoons wine vinegar	**2 tablespoons wine vinegar**
1 tablespoon yeast extract	**1 tablespoon yeast extract**
2 fl oz (60ml) olive oil	**¼ cup olive oil**
Pinch dried tarragon	**Pinch dried tarragon**
1 teaspoon raw cane sugar *or* **black treacle**	**1 teaspoon raw cane sugar** *or* **molasses**
Freshly ground black pepper	**Freshly ground black pepper**

1 Combine all the ingredients in a blender and liquidize to a paste. Alternatively, mince the ingredients to a coarse paste. Then beat the mixture to blend the ingredients thoroughly.

2 This pâté will keep well, stored in the fridge. Serve on wholemeal toast or as a filling for tomatoes or cucumber. For a lighter mixture, add 4 fl oz (120ml/½ cup) whipped cream. The dish can then be served as a dip.

* Most good kitchen supplies shops sell a device for removing the stones from small fruits such as olives or cherries.

** The whites can be used too, if liked.

Pâté de Flageolet Bretonne

Flageolet Bean Dip from Brittany

Serves 4

Flageolets are the youngest seeds from the finest variety of haricot beans, gathered and shelled while they are still a pale, delicate shade of green. Dried flageolet beans are sold in most health food shops, and tinned pre-cooked flageolets are also available.

Dried flageolets must be soaked overnight. After soaking, wash them in fresh water before cooking. Some tap water contains minerals which tend to make beans tough. Adding a little bicarbonate of soda (baking soda) to the soaking water will help, but best results will be achieved using distilled water.

If you are in a hurry, most beans take only 20 minutes to cook in a pressure cooker. The traditional method of baking beans in a casserole takes from 1½ to 2 hours — chick peas (garbanzos) can take as long as 3½ hours. For this reason, even the finest chefs today rarely bake their own beans, preferring to take the short cut of using tinned beans which are available in convenient 'catering' sizes as well as the standard sized tins.

Imperial (Metric)	American
2 cloves garlic, peeled	**2 cloves garlic, peeled**
Juice of ½ lemon	**Juice of ½ lemon**
½ lb (225g) tinned flageolet beans, drained	**1 cup canned flageolet beans, drained**
4 fl oz (120ml) olive oil *or* **melted French butter**	**½ cup olive oil** *or* **melted French butter**
Pinch cayenne pepper	**Pinch cayenne pepper**
Pinch ground coriander	**Pinch ground coriander**
1 small onion, finely chopped	**1 small onion, finely chopped**
1 tablespoon tomato purée	**1 tablespoon tomato paste**
1 teaspoon sea salt	**1 teaspoon sea salt**
Freshly ground black pepper	**Freshly ground black pepper**
½ teaspoon raw cane sugar	**½ teaspoon raw cane sugar**

1. Liquidize the garlic with the lemon juice.
2. Place all the ingredients in the blender and liquidize to a smooth purée.
3. Chill the pâté for an hour and serve with rice crackers, Matzos or water biscuits and a garnish of strips of root vegetables, radishes, cauliflower florets, quartered mushrooms, strips of cucumber, celery and chicory (endive) leaves.

Note: Red or black kidney beans, cannellini beans, butter (Lima) beans and chick peas (garbanzos) can be prepared in the same way.

If the mixture is too stiff, add a little whipped cream. If it is too soft, add a little cream cheese.

Pâté de Légumes will keep well in the fridge, and can be frozen. It can be spread on bread or toast, or used in sandwiches.

La Parmentière

Rich Potato Mousse

Serves 4

Floury, late-season potatoes are the best type for this dip, although sweet potatoes are good, too. French gourmets simply adore hot potato salad served with a Vinaigrette dressing and this dip, when served hot, evokes just that delicious flavour. In Turkey, where this dish is known as *Patates Ezmezi*, it is a great favourite, served cold as a starter.

Imperial (Metric)	American
1 lb (450g) potatoes, peeled and quartered	**1 pound potatoes, peeled and quartered**
Sea salt	**Sea salt**
2 egg yolks	**2 egg yolks**
2 oz (50g) butter	**4 tablespoons butter**
Juice and rind of 1 lemon	**Juice and rind of 1 lemon**
1 clove garlic, chopped	**1 clove garlic, chopped**
1 small onion, chopped	**1 small onion, chopped**
2 fl oz (60ml) natural yogurt	**¼ cup plain yogurt**
1 oz (25g) freshly chopped dill, parsley *or* **chervil**	**2 tablespoons freshly chopped dill, parsley** *or* **chervil**
8 black olives	**8 black olives**

1. Place the potatoes in a large pan with plenty of salted water. Boil until tender, about 20 to 25 minutes. Drain and reheat very gently, to dry the potatoes, for a further 5 minutes, but take care not to let them scorch.
2. Pass the potatoes through a sieve to obtain a fine purée.
3. Add the egg yolks and butter to the purée and reheat in the pan for 5 minutes, stirring gently. Do not beat the mixture. Add the lemon juice.
4. Liquidize the garlic and onion with the lemon rind and fresh herbs, blended with the yogurt. Add this mixture to the potato purée.
5. Place the mixture in small bowls and chill for 1 hour, or serve hot with a garnish of black olives. The best accompaniment for this delicate purée is celery sticks, crispy Melba toast or pitta bread.

La Crécy

Carrot and Swede (Rutabaga) Purée

The sugar content of carrots is 4.5 per cent. This explains why they are sometimes used in sweet dishes, such as American Carrot Cake and some Christmas Pudding recipes. They can be sautéd at the start of a soup, stew or sauce to caramelize their sugar, which will give the dish a rich and distinctive flavour. Syrups, jams and even wine can be made from carrots, too. The carrot reached its height of popularity and fashion in Elizabethan times when the green tops as well as the tubers themselves were boiled as vegetables . . . and ladies wore them as decorations in their hats!

This dish, as with many which contain carrots, is named for the town in France which is reputed to grow the finest carrots in the world. I have created a flavoursome gourmet dish from a purée well-known in France as a dish for infants and invalids. At Vichy, the spa at which liver diseases are often treated, carrots are served at every meal because of their carotene content, from which the body makes vitamin A. Young carrots are very tender, but old carrots will benefit from being cooked in Vichy water.

Imperial (Metric)	American
½ lb (225g) young carrots, peeled and sliced	**8 ounces young carrots, peeled and sliced**
½ lb (225g) swede, peeled and cut into thin slices	**8 ounces rutabaga, peeled and cut into thin slices**
½ lb (225g) floury potatoes, peeled and cut into small cubes	**8 ounces floury potatoes, peeled and cut into small cubes**
1 teaspoon sea salt	**1 teaspoon sea salt**
½ oz (15g) fresh ginger, peeled	**1 tablespoon fresh ginger, peeled**
Juice and grated rind of ½ orange and 1 lemon	**Juice and grated rind of ½ orange and 1 lemon**
6 fl oz (180ml) natural yogurt	**¾ cup plain yogurt**
2 beaten eggs	**2 beaten eggs**
1 teaspoon honey	**1 teaspoon honey**
Pinch cayenne pepper	**Pinch cayenne pepper**

1. Rinse the vegetables and place them in a large saucepan with plenty of cold salted water. Boil until tender. Drain, and then reheat the vegetables for 4 minutes over a gentle heat, to evaporate any moisture.
2. Pass the mixture through a sieve and return the purée to the saucepan. Reheat.
3. Liquidize the ginger with the lemon and orange juice and rind, and add the yogurt, eggs and honey.
4. Stir this juice mixture into the hot purée, mixing it thoroughly for about 4 minutes so that the eggs cook gently and bind the mixture together. Season with cayenne pepper.
5. Cool, and place the mixture in individual serving bowls. Serve chilled, with *croûtons* of fried bread, crackers or *crudités*.

Le Caviar des Champignons de Prairie

Field Mushroom 'Caviar'

Illustrated opposite page 32.

The field mushroom (*Agaricus campestris*) is the best variety to use for this dish. It has a better flavour for grilling or use in cooked dishes than the white cultivated variety. This pâté is developed from a filling known in classical cuisine as *Duxelles*. Traditionally, *Duxelles* accompanies meat and fish dishes, but this pâté has a flavour and character which warrants being served as a dish in itself. It is a great favourite with gourmets, and is best savoured quite simply with hot fried wholemeal bread.

Imperial (Metric)	American
1 lb (450g) field mushrooms with stalks	**1 pound field mushrooms with stalks**
4 oz (100g) butter	**½ cup butter**
6 oz (150g) chopped onion	**1 cup chopped onion**
2 oz (50g) wholemeal breadcrumbs	**1 cup wholewheat breadcrumbs**
1 clove garlic, peeled	**1 clove garlic, peeled**
Juice of ½ lemon	**Juice of ½ lemon**
3 fl oz (90ml) Marsala, sherry *or* **dry Vermouth**	**⅓ cup Marsala, sherry** *or* **dry Vermouth**
2 tablespoons freshly chopped parsley	**2 tablespoons freshly chopped parsley**
1 tablespoon cornflour	**1 tablespoon cornstarch**
4 fl oz (120ml) double *or* **sour cream**	**½ cup heavy** *or* **sour cream**
1 teaspoon sea salt	**1 teaspoon sea salt**
Large pinch freshly ground black pepper	**Large pinch freshly ground black pepper**
4 oz (100g) curd cheese	**½ cup curd cheese**
Large pinch ground mace	**Large pinch ground mace**
Pinch ground thyme	**Pinch ground thyme**

1 Trim the ends of the mushroom stalks, leaving as much as possible. Wash the mushrooms and wipe dry. Chop them finely.
2 Heat the butter in a pan and gently sauté the onion until light brown. Add the chopped mushrooms. Literally boil them down until almost all their moisture has evaporated, then add the breadcrumbs.
3 Liquidize the garlic with the lemon juice, Marsala or sherry and parsley. Stir this mixture into the mushrooms and boil for 5 minutes.
4 Blend the cornflour (cornstarch) and cream together in a bowl and stir this into the mushroom purée to thicken it. Simmer for 5 minutes, season and cool.
5 In a bowl, beat the mushroom purée well with the curd cheese. Add the mace and the thyme and stir thoroughly.
6 Arrange on individual serving plates. Chill and serve with hot fried bread cut into triangles or fingers.

Note: For a white pâté, use cultivated white mushrooms, but make sure to wash them well and blanch them in water and lemon juice before use. This delicately-flavoured pâté makes an ideal filling for tomatoes, courgettes (zucchini) or little pastry cases.

For a Mediterranean flavour, decorate your pâté with black olives, walnut halves and marinated button mushrooms.

Le Pâté de Fromage Blanc au Carvi

Cheesy Potato and Onion Pâté with Caraway Seeds

The root of the caraway plant is similar in appearance to, and has a better flavour than, parsnips. Mixed with milk, and made into a bread-like pudding, it is said to have been the *Chara* of Julius Caesar, eaten by the soldiers of Valerius. Shakespeare mentions it in *Henry IV*, when Squire Shallow invites Falstaff to 'a pippin and a dish of caraways'. The seeds have long been used in Central Europe and eastern France as a flavouring for syrups, liqueurs and, of course, rye bread as well as for the less well-known Munster cheese. I also use caraway seeds to good effect in goulashes and beetroot soups.

Imperial (Metric)	American
½ lb (225g) potatoes, peeled and cubed	**8 ounces potatoes, peeled and cubed**
4 oz (100g) onions, peeled and thinly sliced	**4 ounces onions, peeled and thinly sliced**
2 oz (50g) butter	**4 tablespoons butter**
½ oz (15g) caraway seeds	**1 tablespoon caraway seeds**
2 eggs	**2 eggs**
½ lb (225g) curd cheese	**1 cup curd cheese**
Sea salt	**Sea salt**
Freshly ground black pepper	**Freshly ground black pepper**

1 Rinse the potatoes and place in a pan with the onions. Add water to the level of the vegetables. Boil for 15 minutes until soft. Drain and pass through a sieve over a bowl to purée.

2 Heat the butter in a pan and gently stir-fry the caraway seeds to enhance their flavour. This should take no more than a minute or two. Add the seeds to the potato purée.

3 Beat the eggs and blend in a bowl with the curd cheese. Add this mixture to the purée, which should still be hot. Season to taste. Cool and transfer to individual serving bowls. Chill and serve with celery sticks, wedges of pear or apple, crackers or toasted rye bread.

Variations:

A different flavour can be obtained by using sesame seeds, celery seeds, cumin seeds, anise seeds or fennel seeds.

The mixture can also be used as a filling for pastries. Fill pastry cases and bake at 400°F/200°C (Gas Mark 6) for 15 minutes, or use puff pastry with this filling to make potato turnovers.

Le Pâté de Roquefort au Celeri-Rave

Roquefort Cheese Pâté with Celeriac

This celebrated cheese has been made in the little village of Roquefort for over 2,000 years. Pliny mentions it in his writings. It is one of the finest cheeses in the world and is copied by all the many Western countries with varying degrees of success. The best is England's kingly Stilton, followed by the various blue cheeses of Denmark and Italy's pungent Gorgonzola. Any of these blue cheeses could be used in this recipe. The blue streaks in these cheeses are due to the introduction of *penicillium glaucum*, a mould obtained from wheat and barley. All blue cheeses contain around 25 per cent protein. This recipe is an ideal way of using up any odds and ends of cheese left over from a dinner party.

Imperial (Metric)	American
½ lb (225g) celeriac, peeled and sliced	**8 ounces celeriac, peeled and sliced**
4 oz (100g) cream cheese	**½ cup cream cheese**
½ lb (225g) Roquefort cheese	**1 cup Roquefort cheese**
1 good pinch grated nutmeg and celery seeds	**1 good pinch grated nutmeg and celery seeds**
Freshly ground black pepper	**Freshly ground black pepper**
1 teaspoon sea salt	**1 teaspoon sea salt**
1 tablespoon freshly chopped parsley *or* **coriander leaves**	**1 tablespoon freshly chopped parsley** *or* **cilantro**
3 fl oz (90ml) ruby port	**⅓ cup ruby port**

1. Boil the celeriac in enough water to just cover for 10 minutes, or until soft. Drain and purée through a sieve over a bowl.
2. Blend the purée with the cream cheese and the Roquefort. Reheat to bubbling point and either liquidize or pass through the sieve again.
3. When the mixture is cold, season and blend in the chopped parsley. Add the port and mix well.
4. Serve in individual ramekins or bowls. Garnish with celery and serve with hot wholemeal toast.

Note: Celeriac is the name given to the root of a celery-flavoured umbelliferous plant. The flavour of celeriac is well complemented by other strong flavours, such as that of the blue cheese. The French are very fond of it in a salad. The root is peeled and washed, then sliced and immersed in cold water with lemon juice to keep it white. The slices are cut into thin strips or shredded and blended with a mustardy mayonnaise. This makes a delicious salad on its own or as part of an *hors d'oeuvre*. The seeds and leaves of the plant are used as a flavouring in soups and stews.

Le Pâté Aux Noix de Puislaurent

Walnut Pâté

The finest walnuts come from southern France, Italy and Spain. They can be bought ready-shelled, but go rancid very quickly so are best bought whole to guarantee freshness. To develop the best flavour from shelled kernels, fry them for 1 minute in walnut or olive oil, then drain on kitchen paper. I have created this recipe around the unique flavour of pickled walnuts. These owe their delicious savoury taste to the unhardened shell of the nut and to the pickling spices. Pickled walnuts are a traditional British condiment which is given a new lease of life with this French approach.

Legend has it that, in the 'Golden Age', when men lived on acorns the Gods lived upon walnuts!

Imperial (Metric)	American
¼ pint (140ml) vegetable oil, preferably walnut	**⅔ cup vegetable oil, preferably walnut**
4 oz (100g) chopped celery	**½ cup chopped celery**
4 oz (100g) onions, finely chopped	**4 ounces onions, finely chopped**
4 oz (100g) carrots, finely chopped	**4 ounces carrots, finely chopped**
2 oz (50g) mushrooms, chopped	**2 ounces mushrooms, chopped**
½ lb (225g) walnut kernels	**2 cups English walnut kernels**
½ lb (225g) brown rice	**1 cup brown rice**
1 pint (600ml) water	**2½ cups water**
Juice and grated rind of 1 lemon	**Juice and grated rind of 1 lemon**
2 cloves garlic	**2 cloves garlic**
1 tablespoon yeast extract	**1 tablespoon yeast extract**
2 eggs, beaten	**2 eggs, beaten**
2 oz (50g) pickled walnuts	**2 ounces pickled English walnuts**
2 oz (50g) curd cheese	**¼ cup curd cheese**
1 teaspoon clear honey	**1 teaspoon clear honey**
2 fl oz (60ml) Marsala	**¼ cup Marsala**
Sea salt and freshly ground black pepper	**Sea salt and freshly ground black pepper**
A good pinch each of ground mace and ginger	**A good pinch each of ground mace and ginger**

1. Heat the oil in a saucepan and stir-fry the vegetables and walnut kernels for about 5 minutes. Add the brown rice and fry for a further 4 minutes.
2. Stir in the water and boil gently for about 45 minutes, until the rice is soft (this should be done with a lid on the pan, so that the water does not evaporate before the rice is cooked). When cooked, if there is any liquid left, drain and reserve it.
3. Mince or liquidize the rice, vegetables and nuts to a purée.
4. Place in a blender the liquid from the rice (if any — there should certainly be no more than ¼ pint/140ml/⅔ cup), the lemon juice and rind, the garlic, the yeast extract, the eggs, the pickled walnuts and 1 tablespoon of the pickling juice, the curd cheese, honey and Marsala. Liquidize.
5. Combine the rice and vegetable purée with this liquidized mixture, stir together well and season. Pour the mixture into a well-oiled oblong tin (to hold at least 1½ pounds/700g) and bake at 400°F/200°C (Gas Mark 6) for 45 minutes. Cool and chill.
6. To serve, cut the pâté into thick slices, and garnish with celery and spring onions (scallions). Serve with crackers or toasted wholemeal French bread.

Pâté de Lentilles d'Ésaü

Lentil Pâté

The red pottage for which Esau sold his birthright is said to have been made from split red lentils. Whether whole or split, or reduced to a flour, lentils are exceedingly nutritious. In the old days, though, they were not always very hygienic and needed thorough inspection before cooking — nevertheless it was common to break a tooth on a bit of stone still lurking in the dish. Today, modern methods remove most of the impurities before packing, but care should still be taken to check for grit if you are at all doubtful.

Imperial (Metric)	American
½ lb (225g) red lentils	**1 cup red lentils**
6 oz (150g) potatoes, peeled and sliced	**6 ounces potatoes, peeled and sliced**
6 oz (150g) onions, chopped	**6 ounces onions, chopped**
6 oz (150g) carrots, peeled and sliced	**6 ounces carrots, peeled and sliced**
1 good pinch dried thyme	**1 good pinch dried thyme**
3 eggs	**3 eggs**
1 good pinch ground cumin	**1 good pinch ground cumin**
2 teaspoons sea salt	**2 teaspoons sea salt**
1 teaspoon raw cane sugar	**1 teaspoon raw cane sugar**
Freshly ground black pepper	**Freshly ground black pepper**
2 cloves garlic, peeled	**2 cloves garlic, peeled**
2 oz (50g) butter *or* **oil**	**¼ cup butter** *or* **oil**

1 Check the lentils over for impurities. Wash, drain and soak for a minimum of 6 hours, or overnight.
2 Drain the lentils, and place in a pan. Just cover with cold water and add the potatoes, onions, carrots and thyme. Boil for 25 minutes. Drain and then dry off the vegetables and lentils over a very low heat for about 4 minutes.
3 Mash the vegetables and lentils using a *mouli-légumes* or a potato masher.
4 Beat the eggs with the spice, salt, sugar and pepper in a large bowl. Add the coarse purée to this mixture.
5 Liquidize the garlic with the butter or oil and stir this into the mixture.
6 Place the mixture in an earthenware dish and bake for 20 minutes at 400°F/200°C (Gas Mark 6) until golden-brown on top. Cool, chill and serve with wholemeal bread.

Le Pâté aux Deux Chou-Fleurs

Broccoli and Cauliflower Pâté

Cauliflower is so easily spoilt by overcooking that many people have to be reintroduced to it in its 'gourmet' form, raw with dips or marinated in Vinaigrette or lightly steamed until just tender. Tasting it this way for the first time is a delightful experience. Broccoli is much the same. Its delicate flavour should be treated with care and is enhanced when served with Vinaigrette or Hollandaise Sauce like asparagus. Cauliflower and broccoli complement each other well, particularly in this subtly flavoured pâté.

Imperial (Metric)	American
4 fl oz (120ml) peanut oil	**½ cup peanut oil**
½ lb (225g) cauliflower, divided into florets and rinsed	**8 ounces cauliflower, divided into florets and rinsed**
4 oz (100g) onion, chopped	**4 ounces onion, chopped**
1 green and 1 red pepper, de-seeded and chopped	**1 green and 1 red pepper, de-seeded and chopped**
½ lb (225g) potato, peeled, washed and cut into small cubes	**8 ounces potato, peeled, washed and cut into small cubes**
1 good pinch each ginger, mace, turmeric, black pepper and paprika	**1 good pinch each ginger, mace, turmeric, black pepper and paprika**
2 oz (50g) tomato purée	**4 tablespoons tomato paste**
½ lb (225g) broccoli	**8 ounces broccoli**
Juice and grated rind of 1 lemon	**Juice and grated rind of 1 lemon**
2 cloves garlic, peeled	**2 cloves garlic, peeled**
5 oz (150g) curd cheese	**⅔ cup curd cheese**
4 eggs	**4 eggs**
Sea salt to taste	**Sea salt to taste**
2 oz (50g) grated cheese	**½ cup grated cheese**

1. Heat the oil and stir-fry the cauliflower with the onion, peppers and potato cubes for 5 minutes. Sprinkle on the spices, add the tomato purée (paste) and mix well. Add about 1 pint (600ml/2½ cups) water and boil for 15 to 20 minutes until the vegetables are cooked.
2. Drain the vegetables, reserving the cooking liquid in a bowl.
3. In this liquid, boil the broccoli for 12 minutes.
4. Drain the liquid into a blender goblet. Add to it the lemon juice and rind, the garlic and curd cheese. Liquidize to a thin purée. Blend this into the cauliflower and potato mixture.
5. Beat the eggs and stir them into the mixture. Add salt to taste.
6. Dice or roughly chop the broccoli and stir it into the mixture. This gives a nice contrast of colours and textures. Place this mixture in an earthenware container of 1 pint (600ml/2½ cups) capacity and sprinkle the grated cheese on the top.
7. Bake at 400°F/200°C (Gas Mark 6) for 45 minutes. Cool and chill. Serve with fresh wholemeal bread or hot toast.

Le Pâté Clamart

Green Pea, Lettuce and Onion Pâté

In England, pease pudding and mushy peas are traditional favourites yet, for some reason, 'fresh' peas are expected to be a vivid green and usually tasting of nothing but mint. In France we put flavour before colour and hence our *Petits Pois à la Française* (page 111), gently cooked with tiny onions, lettuce and butter, is a classic vegetable dish. I have combined the traditional pea purée of England with this famous French recipe to create a dish to delight all nations!

Imperial (Metric)	American
½ lb (225g) shelled peas	**1⅓ cups shelled peas**
½ lettuce, shredded	**½ lettuce, shredded**
4 oz (100g) button onions, peeled and blanched	**4 ounces button onions, peeled and blanched**
2 oz (50g) butter	**¼ cup butter**
2 oz (50g) wholemeal flour	**½ cup wholewheat flour**
2 eggs	**2 eggs**
4 oz (100g) curd cheese	**½ cup curd cheese**
Sea salt and freshly ground black pepper	**Sea salt and freshly ground black pepper**
1 teaspoon raw cane sugar *or* **honey**	**1 teaspoon raw cane sugar** *or* **honey**

1. In a saucepan put the peas, lettuce and onions with enough water to just cover. Boil until the peas are tender — about 20 minutes. Drain, reserving the liquor.
2. Reheat the cooking liquid to boiling point and thicken it with a butter paste, made by creaming the softened butter with the flour and adding it bit by bit to the boiling liquid. Whisk the sauce so that it is perfectly smooth and allow it to cool for 5 minutes.
3. Beat the eggs and blend them with the curd cheese.
4. Mince or mash the peas, lettuce and onion mixture to a purée with the sauce, and stir this into the egg mixture. Add seasoning and the sugar.
5. Reheat the mixture until it begins to bubble, stirring constantly. The heat will cook the eggs, binding the pâté. Cool and chill and serve with wholemeal bread, or serve hot on sippets of fried wholemeal bread.

Variation:
Fresh spinach leaves can be substituted for the lettuce.

Le Pâté Aux Cacahuettes

Peanut Dip

Serves 4

The peanut is very useful in a vegetarian diet because of its high protein content — over 25 per cent. It is also high in fat and this oil, when extracted, is an important part of many styles of cooking. The nuts are familiar to everyone, when ground, as peanut butter, but ground peanuts can also be used to make soups and sauces. It is very easy to make a peanut paste at home. Simply rinse the nuts if salted, liquidize with half their weight in oil and there is your paste. Roasted peanuts are best for this because of the extra flavour. Nutritionally, the amino acids in peanut protein are unbalanced. They can be balanced by serving them with a grain, such as wholemeal bread, or with a little cheese, egg or cream.

Imperial (Metric)	American
½ lb (225g) roasted peanuts, rinsed if salted	**1½ cups roasted peanuts, rinsed if salted**
2 ripe bananas, peeled and sliced	**2 ripe bananas, peeled and sliced**
½ small onion, chopped	**½ small onion, chopped**
Juice and grated rind of 1 lemon	**Juice and grated rind of 1 lemon**
1 tablespoon tomato purée	**1 tablespoon tomato paste**
½ teaspoon honey *or* **raw cane sugar**	**½ teaspoon honey** *or* **raw cane sugar**
3 fl oz (90ml) natural yogurt	**⅓ cup plain yogurt**
3 oz (75g) wholemeal breadcrumbs	**1½ cups wholewheat breadcrumbs**
4 oz (100g) softened vegetable margarine *or* **butter**	**½ cup softened vegetable margarine** *or* **butter**
Sea salt to taste	**Sea salt to taste**
Freshly ground black pepper to taste	**Freshly ground black pepper to taste**

1 Grind the peanuts.
2 Liquidize the bananas, onion, lemon juice and rind, tomato purée (paste), honey and yogurt.
3 Combine all the ingredients in a bowl, tasting before seasoning is added, and mix well.
4 Spoon the mixture into individual serving bowls and chill for 1 hour. Serve with crackers or celery, or use as a spread.

Note: A little milk powder can be added to the mixture to give a thicker consistency.

2 *Les Hors d'Oeuvres*

Hors d'Oeuvres

Originally, the *Hors d'Oeuvre* formed a part of a many-coursed gastronomic meal. Today, this rigid discipline of courses is rarely adhered to, and the dishes in this chapter may be eaten as a starter, singly or as a selection, or as a main course in themselves.

The Greeks called them *mezze* and the Romans *promulsis*, but the nineteenth-century French refinement of the *hors d'oeuvre*, where variety, quality and high standards of preparation are of prime importance, is the name which always comes immediately to people's minds. The main characteristics are much the same as for most good food: visual appeal; delicious flavours; stimulating ingredients; freshness and a simple, easy-to-eat appearance. Simplicity, contrasting ingredients and presentation are the key points.

The preparation of your vegetables will make all the difference to the dishes in this chapter, because the eye and the palate will almost certainly come fresh to them and a harsh flavour or a wilted leaf will be quickly noticed. Dressings or sauces for *hors d'oeuvres* must not be too acid or too oily. Tomato salads should be dressed only at the last minute, to prevent them from getting watery, as should green salads to prevent them from going limp. All green salads should be cleaned in plenty of cold water. The water should be acidulated with a little wine vinegar or lemon juice (one spoonful per gallon/4 litres of water) to be sure of removing any grit or insects. A short soak is enough for lettuce, longer for cauliflower and cabbage, and spinach should be washed and rinsed in three changes of water. There is a basic rule for all root vegetables: wash them before peeling and wash them after. Never keep carrots, turnips, swedes (rutabaga), parsnips or onions soaking in water, as they will lose much of their sugar content and thus their flavour — a quick rinse is enough. If you leave chopped onions for a while they will develop a stronger flavour, which is sometimes desirable, but when washed and rinsed quickly they will be whitened and milder in flavour. Make sure that all your leaf vegetables, such as lettuce, cress, chicory and endive, are crisp by placing them briefly in the salad drawer of the fridge after washing and draining.

For this chapter I have selected a dozen *Hors d'Oeuvres* which can be served and enjoyed as a single starter, or made up into combinations *ad infinitum*. Globe artichokes are always a favourite, and my asparagus tartlets are ideal for a small dinner party. The stuffed tomatoes with eggs are perfect for a light luncheon or a late breakfast, and the marinated vegetables can accompany the cheese course instead of being served as a starter. My concept of stuffing pears with cream cheese and serving in a Ravigote Sauce can be varied by using peaches or pineapple rings. Whichever of these dishes you choose, be sure to make the most of their versatility.

Les Oeufs à la Paloise

Hard-Boiled Eggs on a Bed of Apple Mayonnaise, Coated in a Mint Mayonnaise

Serves 4

Mayonnaise is that wonder-sauce created in Spain and developed into hundreds of variations by the cooks of the world. Rich in protein and vitamins A and D, when made with olive oil — or, better still, walnut oil — it is the peak of gastronomic pleasure. Combined with fresh and fragrant herbs, such as basil, mint or chives, it takes on an entirely different character and makes a delightful change. Blended with the acidic tang of an apple purée it becomes a sauce unique in terms of perfect flavour.

Imperial (Metric) For the basic mayonnaise:	American For the basic mayonnaise:
3 egg yolks	**3 egg yolks**
1 teaspoon sea salt	**1 teaspoon sea salt**
Good pinch freshly ground black pepper	**Good pinch freshly ground black pepper**
1 teaspoon Dijon mustard	**1 teaspoon Dijon mustard**
½ pint olive *or* walnut oil, tepid	**1⅓ cups olive *or* walnut oil, tepid**
1 tablespoon white wine vinegar, tepid	**1 tablespoon white wine vinegar, tepid**

1 In a bowl, place the egg yolks, the salt and pepper and the mustard. Start whisking to blend all the ingredients.
2 Start to add the oil, a drop at a time at first, very gently whisking all the time, in a steady rotary fashion, always in the same direction.
3 As the mayonnaise starts to thicken you can increase the flow of oil slightly, to a steady thin stream, until it has all been absorbed and the sauce is very thick. Add the vinegar to thin it down slightly.

Imperial (Metric) For the salad:	American For the salad:
4 lettuce leaves	**4 lettuce leaves**
2 Golden Delicious apples, peeled if wished and sliced or diced	**2 Golden Delicious apples, peeled if wished and sliced or diced**
Juice of 1 lemon	**Juice of 1 lemon**
1 orange, peeled and segmented	**1 orange, peeled and segmented**
1 Golden Delicious apple, peeled, sliced, cooked and puréed	**1 Golden Delicious apple, peeled, sliced, cooked and puréed**
4 tablespoons natural yogurt	**4 tablespoons plain yogurt**
1 tablespoon freshly chopped mint	**1 tablespoon freshly chopped mint**
1 teaspoon raw cane sugar	**1 teaspoon raw cane sugar**
4 hard-boiled eggs	**4 hard-boiled eggs**

1 Place one leaf of freshly rinsed lettuce in each of four large cocktail glasses. Arrange over them a few pieces of apple, dipped briefly in lemon juice, and two segments of orange.
2 Divide the mayonnaise into two parts. To one part add 1 tablespoon cold apple purée. Coat the apple slices in the glasses with this mixture. To the other part, add the yogurt and the mint, crushed in with the sugar.
3 Halve the shelled hard-boiled eggs. Place two halves in each glass on top of the apple mixture. Coat the eggs with the minted mayonnaise. Chill and serve.

Artichaut, Sauce Gribiche

Globe Artichokes in a French Dressing Enriched with Eggs

Serves 4
Illustrated opposite page 33.

The globe artichoke is one of the oldest cultivated vegetables. The base is the most solid edible part, but the leaves have a small portion of flesh where they attach to the body of the plant. When boiled in acidulated water to prevent discolouration, this part of the leaf is tender and quite delicious. All kinds of dressing can be served, in which to dip the leaf before eating. A full-sized artichoke has an inedible, thistly part above its heart, which must be carefully removed. In Italy, where young artichokes are eaten, the whole plant can be used as the inedible part, the choke, has not yet formed.

Imperial (Metric) For the Sauce Gribiche:	American For the Sauce Gribiche:
4 hard-boiled eggs	**4 hard-boiled eggs**
1 teaspoon sea salt	**1 teaspoon sea salt**
Freshly ground black pepper	**Freshly ground black pepper**
3 tablespoons white wine vinegar	**3 tablespoons white wine vinegar**
4 fl oz (120ml) olive oil	**½ cup olive oil**
1 teaspoon Dijon mustard	**1 teaspoon Dijon mustard**
1 teaspoon each of the following, all finely chopped: tarragon, chervil, parsley, capers, gherkins	**1 teaspoon each of the following, all finely chopped: tarragon, chervil, parsley, capers, gherkins**
1 spring onion, chopped	**1 scallion, chopped**

1 Separate the egg yolks from the whites and place the yolks in a blender with the salt, pepper, vinegar, oil and mustard, and liquidize the ingredients to a smooth sauce.
2 Finely chop the egg whites and mix them in a bowl with the sauce, the chopped herbs, gherkins, capers and chopped spring onion (scallion).

Imperial (Metric) For the globe artichokes:	American For the globe artichokes:
4 globe artichokes	**4 globe artichokes**
4 slices lemon	**4 slices lemon**
2 tablespoons olive oil	**2 tablespoons olive oil**
1 tablespoon wholemeal flour	**1 tablespoon wholewheat flour**
Juice of 1 lemon	**Juice of 1 lemon**
Sea salt	**Sea salt**

1 Hold the globe artichoke firmly with one hand and snap the stem sharply downwards with the other. Using a very sharp stainless steel knife, in a curving motion cut off all the bottom leaves to trim the base of the artichoke neatly without exposing the white flesh. Attach a slice of lemon to this bottom part, tied on with string. Repeat this with the other artichokes.
2 Neatly trim 1 inch (2cm) off the top of the upper leaves with a pair of scissors, to ease the removal of the choke after cooking.
3 To prevent the artichokes discolouring, prepare a blanching liquid. Cream together the oil and the flour with the lemon juice. Add this to 3 pints (1.7 litres/7½ cups) water, with a good pinch of salt.

Bring this to the boil and drop in the artichokes. Cook for 35 minutes.

4 When the artichokes are cooked, refresh under running water until cold. Place each artichoke in an individual serving dish, having first carefully removed the choke so that the heart is exposed. Serve the Gribiche Sauce separately.

Note: Globe artichokes have a better flavour served cold rather than hot, but if you wish to try them hot for a change, serve with a sharper sauce, such as Béarnaise (page 36) or Ravigote (page 40).

Tomates Farçies aux Oeufs Brouillés Tartare

Tomatoes Stuffed with Scrambled Eggs, Capers and Gherkins

Serves 4

Large, tasty red tomatoes are needed for this dish — not the insipid kind too often offered for sale in shops. For a change, or as an alternative in the same *hors d'oeuvre*, tomatoes could be stuffed with *Caviar des Champignons de Prairie* (page 20), a nut or vegetable mixture, or cream cheese (if this is used, 1 egg and 1 ounce/25g wholemeal flour should be added per 6 ounces/180g cheese). Raw tomatoes could be stuffed with the same mixture but, instead of adding a raw beaten egg to the scrambled egg mixture, simply add one tablespoon mayonnaise. The cut top of each tomato can be replaced over the filling before baking, or omitted.

Imperial (Metric)	American
4 large tomatoes, each at least 4 oz (100g) in weight	**4 large tomatoes, each at least 4 ounces in weight**
2 oz (50g) butter and oil, mixed	**¼ cup butter and oil, mixed**
4 eggs	**4 eggs**
2 tablespoons double cream	**2 tablespoons heavy cream**
Sea salt and freshly ground black pepper	**Sea salt and freshly ground black pepper**
1 teaspoon chopped fresh parsley	**1 teaspoon chopped fresh parsley**
1 tablespoon chopped gherkins	**1 tablespoon chopped gherkins**
1 tablespoon chopped capers	**1 tablespoon chopped capers**
2 tablespoons wholemeal breadcrumbs *or* **Parmesan cheese**	**2 tablespoons wholewheat breadcrumbs** *or* **Parmesan cheese**

1 Wash the tomatoes and remove the eye from each. Cut approximately the top quarter off of each with a sharp knife. With a teaspoon, remove the seeds without damaging the flesh.

2 Heat the butter and oil in a saucepan. Meanwhile, beat three of the eggs in a bowl and add the cream. Pour this mixture into the bubbling butter and scramble gently with a wooden spoon until lightly cooked. Season with salt and pepper.

3 Remove from the heat and into this mixture mix the extra egg, beaten. Add the parsley, chopped gherkins and capers.

4 Stuff each tomato with some of this mixture. Place them in an earthenware baking dish and bake for 8 minutes at 400°F/200°C (Gas Mark 6), until the tomato flesh is soft. The raw egg will have cooked. On serving, sprinkle with a little Parmesan cheese or wholemeal breadcrumbs, to taste.

Tartelette de Carottes au Miel

Honeyed Carrots in a Little Wholemeal Tartlet

French cooks are renowned for their preparation of prime vegetables — the kind that are sold at the very start of their season. Baby carrots, like all dainty and flavoursome vegetables, have a particular appeal to gourmets. Neatly turned in a barrel shape, or left in their natural form, they are so easy to prepare that their use in *hors d'oeuvres*, such as my *Marinade de Légumes au Vin Blanc* (page 33), is most suitable. In this dish, honey imparts a touch of mellowness as well as bringing out the natural sweetness of the carrots, and fresh ginger adds piquancy.

Imperial (Metric)	American
For the pastry:	For the pastry:
1 oz (25g) cornflour	**2 tablespoons cornstarch**
½ lb (225g) wholemeal flour	**2 cups wholewheat flour**
5 oz (125g) butter	**⅔ cup butter**
1 egg	**1 egg**
4 tablespoons water *or* **milk**	**4 tablespoons water** *or* **milk**
Good pinch sea salt	**Good pinch sea salt**
For the filling:	For the filling:
½ lb (225g) baby carrots	**8 ounces baby carrots**
1 small slice freshly peeled ginger	**1 small slice freshly peeled ginger**
1 tablespoon honey	**1 tablespoon honey**
Juice and grated rind of 1 lemon	**Juice and grated rind of 1 lemon**
2 oz (50g) butter	**¼ cup butter**
Sea salt and freshly ground black pepper	**Sea salt and freshly ground black pepper**

1. To make the pastry: in a bowl, sift the cornflour and wholemeal flour together. Rub the butter into the flour.
2. Beat the egg and add it, with the water or milk and salt, to the flour and mix to form a soft dough. Roll into a ball and leave to rest for 20 minutes.
3. While the dough is resting, make the filling. Scrape the carrots very thinly, trying to retain their shape. Rinse and boil in a little water for 6 minutes. Reserve 3 tablespoons of the liquid.
4. Liquidize the ginger, honey, lemon juice and rind with the carrot water.
5. Reheat the carrots in this mixture, adding butter and seasoning when hot.
6. Roll out the pastry to ¼ inch (5mm) thick. Grease six little tartlet moulds. Cut out pastry circles to fit these moulds, press the pastry gently into the moulds and prick the bottoms with a fork. Bake for 20 minutes at 400°F/200°C (Gas Mark 6).
7. Arrange two spoonsful of cooked carrots and sauce onto each tartlet and serve hot.

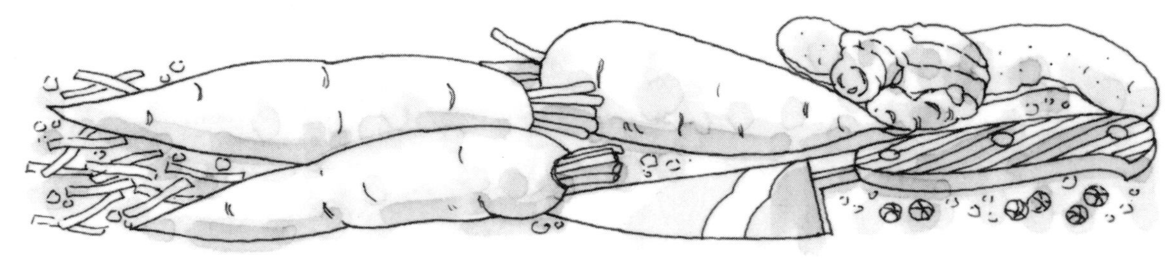

Opposite: *Le Pâté aux Champignons de Prairie* (page 16) and *Caviar d'Aubergines* (page 20).

macedonian
TAHINI

Marinade de Légumes au Vin Blanc

Marinade of Mixed Vegetables in a Lemon-Wine Dressing

This dish is not quite a pickle and yet it will keep for a week in refrigerated conditions. It is a delicious accompaniment to hard-boiled eggs or a hard cheese, but it is well worth savouring on its own, with just a hunk of crispy wholemeal French bread to mop up the sauce.

Imperial (Metric)	American
For the marinade:	For the marinade:
1 pint (600ml) half water, half dry white wine	**2½ cups half water, half dry white wine**
1 bay leaf	**1 bay leaf**
1 sprig thyme	**1 sprig thyme**
¼ pint (150ml) olive oil	**⅔ cup olive oil**
Juice and grated rind of 2 lemons	**Juice and grated rind of 2 lemons**
3 tablespoons white wine vinegar	**3 tablespoons white wine vinegar**
6 coriander seeds	**6 coriander seeds**
2 chilli peppers	**2 chili peppers**
4 black peppercorns, lightly crushed	**4 black peppercorns, lightly crushed**
½ oz (15g) peeled and chopped fresh ginger	**2 tablespoons peeled and chopped fresh ginger**
1 tablespoon sea salt	**1 tablespoon sea salt**
2 teaspoons turmeric	**2 teaspoons turmeric**
2 cloves garlic, chopped	**2 cloves garlic, chopped**
1 tablespoon raw cane sugar	**1 tablespoon raw cane sugar**
For the vegetables:	For the vegetables:
3 carrots	**3 carrots**
3 small turnips	**3 small turnips**
12 button mushrooms, whole or halved	**12 button mushrooms, whole or halved**
4 celery sticks	**4 celery stalks**
12 button onions, peeled	**12 button onions, peeled**
1 small cauliflower, divided into florets	**1 small cauliflower, divided into florets**

1 Boil together all the marinade ingredients for 5 minutes.

2 Wash and thinly peel the root vegetables and cut them into even-sized sticks, 2 inches (5cm) long by ¼ inch (5mm) thick, or into thin slices.

3 Trim the stalks of the mushrooms if necessary, wipe them clean and put them in a little cold water, acidulated with lemon juice to keep them white.

4 Boil the carrots and celery for 5 minutes and then add the turnips, onions and cauliflower. Cook for a further 4 minutes. Lastly, add the mushrooms and cook for 1 more minute. Cool in the marinade and then refrigerate all together for 24 hours. The vegetables will retain their crispness.

Note: Fennel, leeks, white radishes and artichoke bottoms can all be prepared in this way, for variety.

Opposite: *Artichaut, Sauce Gribiche* (page 30).

Terrine de Légumes Picardie

A Pancake (Crêpe)-lined Vegetable and Sour Cream Loaf

This was the dish I chose to demonstrate when, in 1978, I toured all the major cities in Britain promoting French cuisine. It is a dish which will appeal to the adventurous cook because of the several different stages involved in making up the whole, but the result is visually most attractive and the combination of flavours and textures will delight your guests at a special dinner party.

Imperial (Metric)	American
4 leeks	**4 leeks**
4 carrots	**4 carrots**
4 turnips	**4 turnips**
For the pancakes:	For the crêpes:
2 eggs	**2 eggs**
½ pint (300ml) milk	**1⅓ cups milk**
4 oz (100g) wholemeal flour	**1 cup wholewheat flour**
Pinch sea salt	**Pinch sea salt**
4 fl oz (120ml) vegetable oil	**½ cup vegetable oil**
For the loaf:	For the loaf:
3 oz (75g) polyunsaturated margarine *or* **butter**	**⅓ cup polyunsaturated margarine** *or* **butter**
2 oz (50g) grated cheese	**½ cup grated cheese**
4 fl oz (120ml) sour cream	**½ cup sour cream**
2 eggs, beaten	**2 eggs, beaten**
Sea salt and freshly ground black pepper	**Sea salt and freshly ground black pepper**
2 cloves garlic, chopped	**2 cloves garlic, chopped**
1 small onion, chopped	**1 small onion, chopped**
4 oz (100g) boiled new potatoes, diced	**4 ounces boiled new potatoes, diced**

1. Trim the leeks down to the white part only and boil until just cooked.
2. Wash the carrots and turnips and cut into matchsticks, 2 inches (5cm) long. Boil the turnips for 4 minutes and the carrots for 5 minutes. Set all these vegetables aside to cool.
3. To prepare the pancakes, beat the eggs and add them to the milk. Blend this mixture into the flour and salt, to make a smooth, lump-free batter.
4. Heat a little of the oil in a 6-inch (15cm) frying pan and pour in a quarter of the batter. Cook the pancake (crêpe)on both sides and reserve. Repeat until you have four neat, even-sized pancakes (crêpes).
5. Grease an oblong loaf tin well with the margarine or butter, then line it with three of the pancakes (crêpes). Trim the fourth so that it will neatly cover the top of the tin, but set it aside for the moment.
6. To make the filling, combine in a bowl the grated cheese, sour cream, beaten eggs, seasoning, garlic and onions. Stir the potatoes into this mixture.
7. In the bottom of the lined mould, place one of the leeks, flanked with a row of turnip sticks on one side and carrot sticks on the other. Cover with a layer of the sour cream and potato mixture. Repeat this procedure until all the ingredients are used. Top with the reserved pancake (crêpe), as a lid, and brush this with a little melted butter.
8. Bake the loaf at 400°F/200°C (Gas Mark 6) for 45 minutes. Cool, turn out onto a serving dish and

serve with a French dressing and a raw tomato salad, which could be arranged attractively around the loaf. When the loaf is sliced, a decorative pattern will be formed by the rows of different coloured vegetables in the pale creamy potato mixture.

Une Chinoiserie Magique

Stir-fried Vegetables in a Sweet and Sour Dressing

Serves 4

Nouvelle cuisine has been greatly influenced by the Oriental traditions of vegetable cookery, where vegetables are cooked very briefly to retain all their texture and flavour. This goes back partly to the days of the French Indo-Chinese Empire, but more recently it is due to the many Vietnamese emigrants who have made their home in France and whose style of cooking has become very fashionable.

The blender is an invaluable tool in preparing sauces, such as the one below, which give such a distinctive flavour to these quickly prepared dishes. It also means that fresh garlic and ginger can easily be used, rather than resorting to the powdered varieties which will not give the delicacy of flavour so essential to successful Oriental cuisine. Another important element is the use of the natural protein of the soya bean, in the form of pure soya sauce. Blended with the acid juices of fresh fruits it gives the sauce a body and mellowness which is quite delicious.

Imperial (Metric)	American
1 red pepper, seeded	**1 red pepper, seeded**
1 green pepper, seeded	**1 green pepper, seeded**
4 oz (100g) white mushrooms, sliced	**4 ounces white mushrooms, sliced**
4 oz (100g) celery	**4 ounces celery**
4 oz (100g) spring onions	**4 ounces scallions**
4 oz (100g) courgettes	**4 ounces zucchini**
4 fl oz (120ml) peanut oil	**½ cup peanut oil**
4 oz (100g) peanuts	**¾ cup peanuts**
4 oz (100g) cooked brown rice	**⅔ cup cooked brown rice**
For the sweet-sour dressing:	For the sweet-sour dressing:
2 cloves garlic, peeled	**2 cloves garlic, peeled**
½ oz (15g) fresh ginger, peeled	**1 tablespoon fresh ginger, peeled**
1 ring fresh pineapple	**1 ring fresh pineapple**
4 tablespoons soya sauce	**4 tablespoons soy sauce**
Juice and grated rind of 1 lemon	**Juice and grated rind of 1 lemon**
1 tablespoon wine vinegar	**1 tablespoon wine vinegar**
2 tablespoons clear honey	**2 tablespoons clear honey**
1 green chilli	**1 green chili**
Sea salt	**Sea salt**

1. Cut all the vegetables into fine strips of equal length and thickness — about 2 inches (5cm) long and ¼ inch (5mm) thick.
2. Heat the oil in a sauté pan and stir-fry the vegetables, nuts and rice for 5 minutes, but no more.
3. Liquidize all the dressing ingredients in a blender and pour them over the vegetables, tossing to mix thoroughly. Serve hot or cold.

La Tourte d'Asperge Béarnaise

Fresh Asparagus in a Pastry Case with a Tarragon Sauce

Serves 4

A true Béarnaise Sauce is an emulsion of butter, egg yolks and wine vinegar, flavoured with chopped shallots and tarragon, and is one of the classic sauces of French *haute cuisine*. It is delicious served with fresh asparagus.

For this recipe I have modified the sauce to suit its use in my little asparagus tartlets. Because they are baked in the oven, the sauce has to be stabilized with flour. A proper Béarnaise would break up and resemble scrambled eggs by the end of the baking process! I think you will find that my variation suits its purpose admirably and complements the asparagus just as well as the original.

Imperial (Metric)	American
16 stems asparagus (4 per person)	**16 stems asparagus (4 per person)**
For the sauce:	For the sauce:
1 oz (25g) butter	**2 tablespoons butter**
1 oz (25g) wholemeal flour	**¼ cup wholewheat flour**
½ pint (300ml) milk	**1⅓ cups milk**
Sea salt and freshly ground black pepper	**Sea salt and freshly ground black pepper**
Freshly grated nutmeg	**Freshly grated nutmeg**
2 egg yolks	**2 egg yolks**
2 beaten eggs	**2 beaten eggs**
2 oz (50g) grated Gruyère *or* Cheddar cheese	**½ cup grated Gruyère *or* Cheddar cheese**
1 tablespoon each freshly chopped parsley and tarragon	**1 tablespoon each freshly chopped parsley and tarragon**
Juice of 1 lemon	**Juice of 1 lemon**
For the pastry:	For the pastry:
½ lb (225g) wholemeal flour	**2 cups wholewheat flour**
4 oz (100g) butter	**½ cup butter**
1 egg	**1 egg**
3 tablespoons cold water	**3 tablespoons cold water**
Pinch sea salt	**Pinch sea salt**
1 oz (25g) melted butter	**2½ tablespoons melted butter**

1. Prepare the asparagus for cooking: scrape the stem of each, avoiding any damage to the tip. Wash well and cut off the woody end of the stem. Tie into two bundles with string.
2. Boil in salted water for 12 to 15 minutes. Lift carefully out of the water and refresh in a bowl of cold water until cold. Drain well.
3. Cut each asparagus spear in two, so that the stems and tips are separated.
4. In a saucepan, heat the butter and add the flour to make a roux. Cook without browning for 1 minute and then add cold milk, stirring it in gradually, to avoid lumps. Boil gently for 5 minutes. Season with salt and pepper and nutmeg.
5. Away from the heat, add the egg yolks and beaten egg, grated cheese and herbs. Cool the sauce completely and then add the lemon juice.
6. In a large bowl or on a pastry board, rub the butter into the flour to form a crumble consistency. Beat the egg, water and salt together and add slowly to the flour and butter, rubbing in and kneading

to form a dough. This should only take about 1 minute. Roll the dough into a ball and leave to rest for 20 minutes.

7 Lightly oil a flan ring 10 inches (25cm) in diameter and 2 inches (5cm) deep.
8 Dust a board with flour and roll out the pastry into a round 14 inches (35cm) in diameter. It should be an even ¼-inch (5mm) thick. Line the flan mould with the pastry. Trim the surplus, if any, and press gently round the edges to make the sides and border neat and even. Crimp the edges by pinching.
9 Brush the bottom of the pastry base with melted butter and arrange the well-drained asparagus stems and tips over it in a pattern, with the stems at the bottom and the tips on the top. Cover with the cold Béarnaise Sauce. Bake for 30 minutes at 400°F/200°C (Gas Mark 6) until the pastry is thoroughly cooked underneath and at the sides. Serve hot or cold.

La Papaya à la Gauguin

Stuffed Pawpaw in a Lime Juice Dressing

Serves 4
Illustrated opposite page 48.

Here is a dish created in honour of the famous French painter who loved this fruit so much.

The import of the pawpaw into non-tropical countries has increased so rapidly over the last few years that most people are now familiar, if only by sight, with this yellow, melon-shaped fruit. It is grown in all the tropical countries of the world, but the best comes from Africa, Tahiti, Jamaica and the Caribbean. The pawpaw is an excellent source of vitamin C and provides a fair amount of vitamin A as well. The milky juice is also the source of the enzyme papain, which breaks down protein and so is often used to tenderize meat. It also aids the digestion of protein in the body, and can alleviate certain skin infections when applied to the affected place.

When buying a pawpaw, look for a yellow colouring as a sign of ripeness; the flesh should also yield to gentle pressure. The pawpaw does not discolour when cut, and so can be prepared well in advance. As a starter, it makes a nice change from melon. It is delicious served, as here, with a lime juice dressing but, like melons, it can also be flavoured with a liqueur, spirit or port.

Imperial (Metric)	American
2 large pawpaws	**2 large pawpaws**
2 oz (50g) cooked brown rice	**¼ cup cooked brown rice**
2 oz (50g) cooked green peas	**⅓ cup cooked green peas**
1 small spring onion, chopped	**1 small scallion, chopped**
2 oz (50g) diced pineapple	**⅓ cup diced pineapple**
2 fl oz (60ml) natural yogurt	**¼ cup plain yogurt**
2 oz (50g) chopped walnuts	**⅓ cup chopped English walnuts**
1 tablespoon raisins, soaked in 2 tablespoons brandy	**1 tablespoonful raisins, soaked in 2 tablespoons brandy**
Juice of 1 lime	**Juice of 1 lime**
2 limes, for garnish	**2 limes, for garnish**

1 Halve the pawpaws and remove the seeds.
2 Combine all the rest of the ingredients, except the garnish, in a bowl.
3 Spoon some of the mixture into the cavity of each pawpaw. Serve decorated with slices of fresh lime.

Variation:
The same filling could be used for avocados or melon, especially Ogen, Cantaloupe or Charentais melon.

Galantine de Riz aux Champignons

Rice and Mushroom Loaf with Garlic Dressing

There are upwards of 1300 varieties of rice, most of which are consumed in the regions in which they are grown, in their natural, unpolished state. For commercial distribution, most rice is finely polished, the bran, embryo and skin being entirely removed. A diet which relied heavily or exclusively upon rice, especially the polished type, would almost certainly lead to malnutrition because, of all the cereals, rice is lowest in protein, fat, minerals and vitamins. Vitamin B_1, a deficiency of which causes beri-beri, is contained almost exclusively in the skin of the rice grain. On the other hand, what nutrients rice does contain are absorbed almost completely into the body.

Brown rice is obviously, therefore, to be recommended. It takes up to twice as long as white rice to cook, but is well worth the wait. In most dishes, rice is eaten with one or more types of protein, so can easily form part of a well-balanced meal, nutritionally. Most savoury rice dishes are served hot, but this is one of the exceptions. With a sharp dressing, a rice salad is a delicious part of an *hors d'oeuvre*, but here I have used that principle to create something a little more adventurous and attractive.

Imperial (Metric)	American
2 oz (50g) butter	**¼ cup butter**
2 tablespoons olive oil	**2 tablespoons olive oil**
1 medium onion, chopped	**1 medium onion, chopped**
4 oz (100g) short-grain brown rice	**½ cup short-grain brown rice**
4 oz (100g) white mushrooms, washed and sliced	**2 cups white mushrooms, washed and sliced**
2 oz (50g) peas, fresh or frozen	**⅓ cup peas, fresh or frozen**
3 oz (75g) baked beans in tomato sauce	**6 tablespoons baked beans in tomato sauce**
2 oz (50g) crushed peanuts	**4 tablespoons crushed peanuts**
¾ pint (450ml) water	**2 cups water**
1 clove garlic, chopped	**1 clove garlic, chopped**
1 teaspoon turmeric	**1 teaspoon turmeric**
1 teaspoon sea salt	**1 teaspoon sea salt**
Freshly ground black pepper	**Freshly ground black pepper**
1 bay leaf	**1 bay leaf**
1 sprig thyme	**1 sprig thyme**
3 eggs, beaten	**3 eggs, beaten**
2 fl oz (60ml) natural yogurt	**¼ cup plain yogurt**
Lettuce leaves for garnish	**Lettuce leaves for garnish**
1 orange, segmented, for garnish	**1 orange, segmented, for garnish**

For the garlic dressing:	For the garlic dressing:
4 tablespoons olive oil	**4 tablespoons olive oil**
1 tablespoon wine vinegar	**1 tablespoon wine vinegar**
1 clove garlic, chopped	**1 clove garlic, chopped**
Sea salt and freshly ground black pepper	**Sea salt and freshly ground black pepper**
½ tablespoon chopped parsley	**½ tablespoon chopped parsley**

1 Heat the butter and oil in a large pan. Stir-fry the onion for a few minutes without browning. Add the rice and stir-fry for 1 minute to impregnate the grains with the fat.

2 Add the sliced mushrooms, the peas, baked beans and peanuts. Mix well.

3 Stir in the water, garlic, turmeric and seasoning. Add the bay leaf and the sprig of thyme. Place the dish in the oven and bake at 400°F/200°C (Gas Mark 6) for 20 minutes or until the rice is cooked.

4 Cool the rice mixture and, when it is cold, blend in the beaten eggs and yogurt. Transfer this mixture to an oblong terrine dish and return to the oven for 25 minutes.
5 Leave the loaf to cool in the terrine. When cold, turn it out onto a flat serving dish. Garnish with the lettuce leaves and orange segments.
6 Mix all the dressing ingredients together in a screw-top jar.
7 Serve the loaf cut into thick slices, with a sauceboat of dressing on the side.

Champignons Farçie au Brie

Mushroom Caps Stuffed with Brie on Wholemeal Croûtons

Serves 4

The general tendency is to overcook mushrooms and thus lose much of their wonderful fresh flavour. In this dish they are cooked just long enough to bring out their best and to cook the delicious stuffing mixture. The best mushrooms for this dish are the large field mushrooms, particularly the French variety known as *cèpes*. This is an ideal hot starter, and one which my customers are delighted with whenever it appears on my menus.

Imperial (Metric)	American
4 large field mushrooms	**4 large field mushrooms**
1 clove garlic, chopped	**1 clove garlic, chopped**
1 small onion, chopped	**1 small onion, chopped**
2 oz (50g) walnuts, chopped finely	**⅓ cup finely chopped English walnuts**
2 oz (50g) soft French butter	**¼ cup soft French butter**
2 oz (50g) mature Brie cheese	**2 ounces mature Brie cheese**
Sea salt and freshly ground black pepper	**Sea salt and freshly ground black pepper**
Pinch mace	**Pinch mace**
1 tablespoon each fresh chopped parsley and tarragon	**1 tablespoon each fresh chopped parsley and tarragon**
1 egg, beaten	**1 egg, beaten**
2 oz (50g) wholemeal breadcrumbs	**1 cup wholewheat breadcrumbs**
4 slices wholemeal bread, cut into perfect squares slightly larger than mushrooms	**4 slices wholewheat bread, cut into perfect squares slightly larger than mushrooms**

1 Remove the stalks from the mushrooms. Wash the mushroom caps and stalks and dry thoroughly.
2 Chop the stalks finely and mix with the garlic, onion and walnuts.
3 Cream the butter and Brie together and blend into the mushroom mixture with the seasoning, mace and herbs. Gradually add the egg and breadcrumbs to form a manageable, smooth paste.
4 Lightly oil an ovenproof dish and arrange the mushroom caps on it. Divide the paste into four balls and place one on each upturned mushroom cap.
5 Bake in a hot oven, 400°F/200°C (Gas Mark 6), or place under a hot grill, for 10 minutes or until the filling is golden.
6 While the mushrooms are cooking, either fry or grill the *croûtons* of bread and serve the mushrooms on these.

Les Poires au Fromage Blanc Ravigote

Pears with a Lemon and Cream Cheese Stuffing and Ravigote Sauce

Serves 4

Pears ripen by an enzyme process which is affected by heat. So, if you buy unripe pears which you wish to ripen quickly, leave them on a bed of kitchen paper in a warm place in the kitchen until they are ripe. Many fruits, such as peaches, pineapples or large plums can be used as an *hors d'oeuvre* with cream or cottage cheese. The idea is not a new one, although it has only recently become fashionable in France. Nonetheless, it has for many years been common practice to eat fresh strawberries with *Petit-Suisse* fresh cream cheese.

If you find cream cheese too rich, you could lighten it with a couple of spoons of whipped cream, or a little lemon jelly could be blended into the cheese just before it sets. Either of these methods will also stretch the filling to provide enough for six people.

Imperial (Metric)	American
4 large, ripe pears, preferably *Doyenne du Comice*	**4 large, ripe pears, preferably *Doyenne du Comice***
4 oz (100g) cream cheese	**½ cup cream cheese**
2 egg yolks	**2 egg yolks**
Juice and grated rind of 1 lemon	**Juice and grated rind of 1 lemon**
Sea salt and freshly ground black pepper	**Sea salt and freshly ground black pepper**
Pinch ground ginger	**Pinch ground ginger**
4 lettuce leaves	**4 lettuce leaves**
1 grapefruit, peeled and segmented	**1 grapefruit, peeled and segmented**
1 oz (25g) toasted, flaked almonds	**¼ cup toasted, slivered almonds**

1 Peel, core and halve the pears.
2 In a bowl combine the cream cheese, egg yolks, lemon juice and grated rind. Season to taste and add ginger.
3 Arrange the lettuce leaves in a small oval serving dish and place the pear halves decoratively on the leaves. Fill the centre of each pear half with a spoonful of the cheese mixture.
4 Decorate the dish with segments of grapefruit and sprinkle with almonds.
5 Serve with a separate dish of Ravigote Sauce.

Imperial (Metric) For the Sauce Ravigote:	American For the Sauce Ravigote:
1 oz (25g) butter	**2 tablespoons butter**
½ oz (15g) wholemeal flour	**2 tablespoons wholewheat flour**
2½ fl oz (75ml) water *or* vegetable stock	**¼ cup water *or* vegetable stock**
2½ fl oz (75ml) single cream	**¼ cup light cream**
Sea salt and freshly ground black pepper	**Sea salt and freshly ground black pepper**
2 tablespoons white wine vinegar	**2 tablespoons white wine vinegar**
2 tablespoons white wine	**2 tablespoons white wine**
2 mushrooms, sliced	**2 mushrooms, sliced**
1 tablespoon chopped shallot *or* onion	**1 tablespoon chopped shallot *or* onion**
1 bay leaf	**1 bay leaf**
Cayenne *or* Tabasco (optional)	**Cayenne *or* Tabasco (optional)**

1 First, prepare a velouté sauce. Heat the butter in a pan and stir in the flour. Cook for 1 minute without

colouring. Gradually pour on the water or stock, boil for 4 minutes and then whisk in the cream. Simmer for 10 minutes. Season with salt and pepper.

2 While the sauce is simmering, put all the rest of the ingredients into another pan and boil fiercely until reduced by one third. Then whisk in the velouté sauce. Boil for 5 minutes and then strain. Check the seasoning and add a pinch of cayenne or Tabasco, or just extra black pepper if preferred.

Note: Chopped parsley or other herbs or chopped peppers could be added to the sauce for extra flavour.

3 Les Petites Entrées Chaudes

Hot Starters

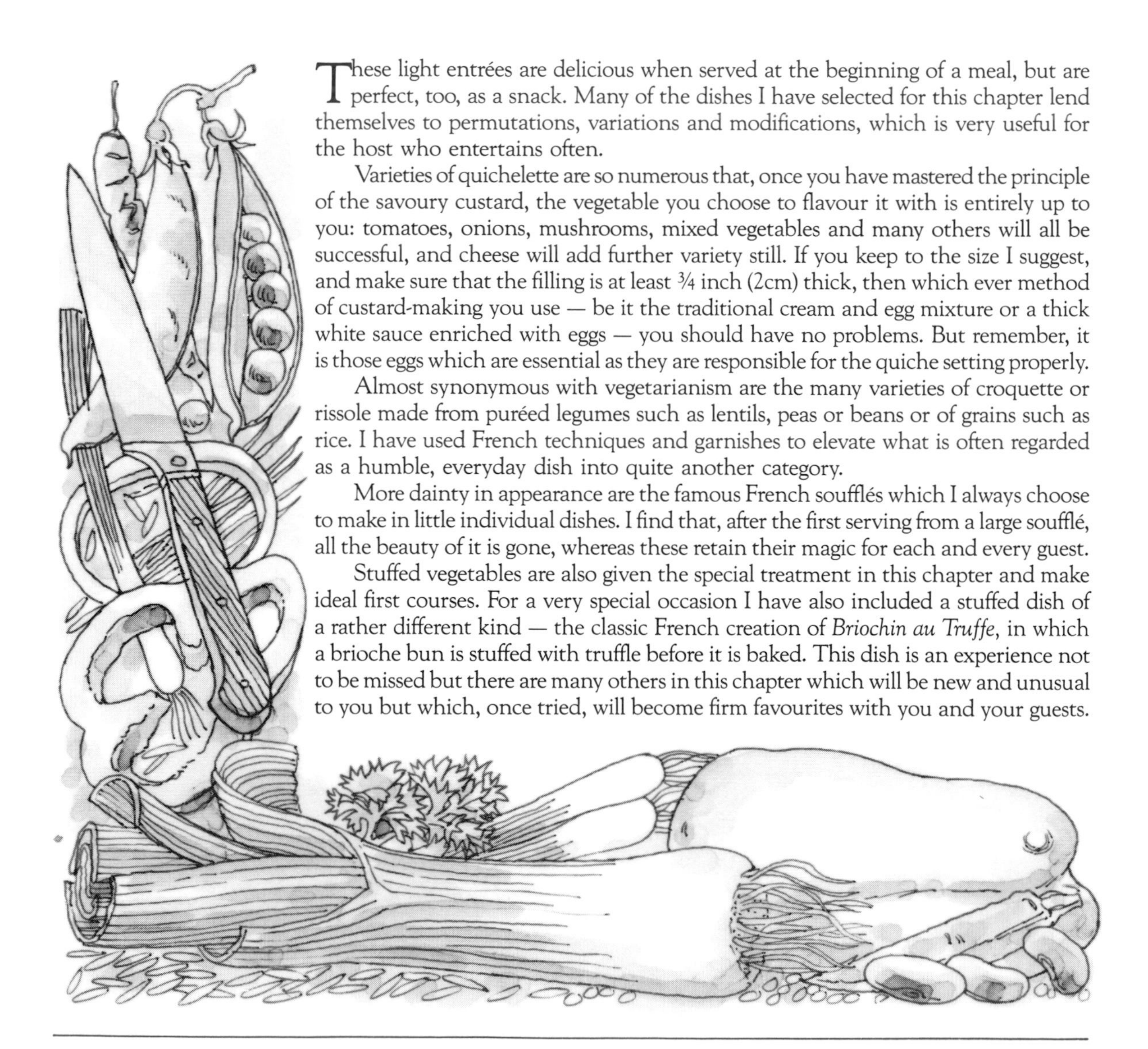

These light entrées are delicious when served at the beginning of a meal, but are perfect, too, as a snack. Many of the dishes I have selected for this chapter lend themselves to permutations, variations and modifications, which is very useful for the host who entertains often.

Varieties of quichelette are so numerous that, once you have mastered the principle of the savoury custard, the vegetable you choose to flavour it with is entirely up to you: tomatoes, onions, mushrooms, mixed vegetables and many others will all be successful, and cheese will add further variety still. If you keep to the size I suggest, and make sure that the filling is at least ¾ inch (2cm) thick, then which ever method of custard-making you use — be it the traditional cream and egg mixture or a thick white sauce enriched with eggs — you should have no problems. But remember, it is those eggs which are essential as they are responsible for the quiche setting properly.

Almost synonymous with vegetarianism are the many varieties of croquette or rissole made from puréed legumes such as lentils, peas or beans or of grains such as rice. I have used French techniques and garnishes to elevate what is often regarded as a humble, everyday dish into quite another category.

More dainty in appearance are the famous French soufflés which I always choose to make in little individual dishes. I find that, after the first serving from a large soufflé, all the beauty of it is gone, whereas these retain their magic for each and every guest.

Stuffed vegetables are also given the special treatment in this chapter and make ideal first courses. For a very special occasion I have also included a stuffed dish of a rather different kind — the classic French creation of *Briochin au Truffe*, in which a brioche bun is stuffed with truffle before it is baked. This dish is an experience not to be missed but there are many others in this chapter which will be new and unusual to you but which, once tried, will become firm favourites with you and your guests.

Poivron au Riz Saffrané

Pepper Stuffed with Saffron Rice

Serves 4

There are several types of capsicum. The one I have chosen for this recipe is the red, or paprika, pepper. It is easy to get confused by all the different names and types of pepper and the terms capsicum, chilli, cayenne and all the different colours of pepper, especially when some are interchangeable and others should never be so. In particular, the small chilli pepper and its powder are quite fiery and their use is very specialist. As to the colour of peppers, like tomatoes they change colour with their stages of ripeness, from green to yellow to red. Their flavour changes, too, becoming sweeter as the fruit matures. The soil and climate where the pepper is grown will affect its pungency, too. Peppers are rich in vitamin C when used raw in salad.

Many cooks recommend skinning peppers before use, by grilling until the skin blisters and can be peeled away. Personally, I prefer to leave it on.

Imperial (Metric)	American
4 fl oz (120ml) olive oil	**½ cup olive oil**
1 green pepper, seeded and cubed	**1 green pepper, seeded and cubed**
1 medium onion, chopped	**1 medium onion, chopped**
1 stalk fennel, chopped	**1 stalk fennel, chopped**
2 cloves garlic, chopped	**2 cloves garlic, chopped**
4 oz (100g) brown rice	**½ cup brown rice**
2 tablespoons tomato purée	**2 tablespoons tomato paste**
4 oz (100g) chopped fresh spinach *or* **sorrel leaves**	**1 cup chopped fresh spinach** *or* **sorrel leaves**
Large pinch saffron *or* **turmeric**	**Large pinch saffron** *or* **turmeric**
2 oz (50g) green peas	**⅓ cup green peas**
4 red peppers, equal-sized	**4 red peppers, equal-sized**
Sea salt and freshly ground black pepper	**Sea salt and freshly ground black pepper**

1. Heat the oil in a saucepan and stir-fry all the chopped vegetables for 4 minutes without browning.
2. Then add the rice and mix well. Stir in three times the volume of rice in water. Add the tomato purée (paste), spinach or sorrel, saffron and peas. Bring to the boil and cook for 30 to 40 minutes, covered, or until the rice is cooked but still firm and has absorbed all the water. Add more water during cooking if it is being absorbed too quickly. Season to taste.
3. Slice off the top of each pepper and remove the seeds and white membranes. Fill the peppers with the rice mixture.
4. Place the peppers, upright, in a shallow baking dish. Add water to about half-way up the peppers. Season the water and cover the dish.
5. Braise in the oven for about 35 minutes at 400°F/200°C (Gas Mark 6).
6. Flavour the cooking water, if necessary, with a little yeast extract to form a stock and serve the peppers hot or cold, with a little of the stock to moisten.

Variation:
A more substantial supper dish could be made by enriching the cooked rice mixture with diced hard-boiled eggs, nuts or cooked beans, grated cheese or diced mushrooms, to taste.

Quichelette Capucine

A Mushroom, Brandy and Cream Custard, Cooked in a Pastry Case

Serves 4-6
Illustrated opposite page 49.

Rather than make this type of quiche in a large flan ring as is conventional, I have devised an individual one, ¾ inch (2cm) deep and 2¼ inches (6cm) in diameter. An individual quiche looks more attractive and, since they can be frozen and then baked when required from the frozen state at normal baking temperature, they are ideal for an impromptu party, an unexpected extra guest or when you wish to concentrate on an elaborate and time-consuming main course.

There are many varieties of traditional French quiche: Quiche Lorraine will include Gruyère cheese (but the vegetarian gourmet will have to replace the other traditional ingredient of bacon); a Quiche Savoyarde will be filled with diced boiled potatoes and the creamy custard flavoured with garlic; Quiche Boulonnaise, from Boulogne where I spent my youth, is a simple custard flavoured with onions and cheese; Quiche Niçoise is filled with a custard mixed with beans, tomatoes, stoned black olives and onions.

If you wish, you can replace the cream in any quiche recipe with milk, but the result will be better if the quiche is made with cream.

Imperial (Metric)	American
For the pastry:	For the pastry:
½ lb (225g) wholemeal flour	**2 cups wholewheat flour**
4 oz (100g) vegetable margarine	**½ cup vegetable margarine**
1 egg, beaten	**1 egg, beaten**
2 tablespoons water	**2 tablespoons water**
Pinch sea salt	**Pinch sea salt**
Extra vegetable margarine, melted	**Extra vegetable margarine, melted**
For the filling:	For the filling:
2 tablespoons vegetable oil	**2 tablespoons vegetable oil**
5 oz (125g) white button mushrooms	**2¼ cups white button mushrooms**
1 tablespoon finely chopped onion	**1 tablespoon finely chopped onion**
2 tablespoons brandy	**2 tablespoons brandy**
4 fl oz (120ml) double cream	**½ cup heavy cream**
2 eggs, beaten	**2 eggs, beaten**
Freshly chopped basil, parsley and tarragon, to taste	**Freshly chopped basil, parsley and tarragon, to taste**
Sea salt and freshly ground black pepper	**Sea salt and freshly ground black pepper**

1. Rub the flour and margarine together in a bowl to form a breadcrumb consistency. Add the beaten egg, water and salt and mix to form a dough. Roll into a ball and leave to rest for 30 minutes.
2. Divide the pastry into four or six balls. Roll each one out to a thickness of about ¼ inch (5mm) and cut out circles about 2¼ inches (6cm) in diameter. Brush the quichelette tins with a little melted fat and line them with pastry, crimping the edges neatly. Brush the base of the pastry with a little more fat.
3. Heat the oil in a small sauté pan and stir-fry the mushrooms and onion for 5 minutes, then add the brandy and cream and boil for a further 4 minutes. Strain and collect the sauce in a small bowl. Leave to cool.

4 When the sauce is cool, add to it the beaten eggs, herbs and seasoning.
5 Fill the tartlets with the mushroom and onion mixture and top up with the cream sauce. Bake in a hot oven, 400°F/200°C (Gas Mark 6) for 25 minutes, until the custard is set. Serve hot or cold.

Crépinettes de Poireaux Mornay

Pancakes (Crêpes) Stuffed with Leeks and Coated with Cheese Sauce

Serves 4
Illustrated opposite page 49.

The leek is a member of the onion family. It is a biennial plant and its many varieties ensure that it is available all the year round. In modern cookery the small, young leek is preferred to the monsters which are often grown for show. Leeks are delicious in soups or stews, and a simple leek and potato pie with a cream sauce is hard to beat. You could serve the dish described here as a starter, snack or main course.

Leeks are low in calories, but are similarly low in nutritive value. They are, however, well known for their medicinal properties — my grandmother used to cure my colds with a concoction of leeks! In this recipe, their lack of nutrients is made up for by the wholemeal pancakes (crêpes) and cheese.

Imperial (Metric)	American
1 quantity pancake batter (page 34)	**1 quantity crêpe batter (page 34)**
Vegetable oil	**Vegetable oil**
8 small leeks	**8 small leeks**
1 oz (25g) butter	**2½ tablespoons butter**
1 oz (25g) wholemeal flour	**¼ cup wholewheat flour**
½ pint (300ml) milk	**1⅓ cups milk**
Sea salt and freshly ground black pepper	**Sea salt and freshly ground black pepper**
Freshly grated nutmeg	**Freshly grated nutmeg**
4 oz (100g) grated cheese	**1 cup grated cheese**
2 egg yolks	**2 egg yolks**

1 Prepare four pancakes (crêpes) as described in *Terrine de Légumes Picardie* (page 34).
2 Clean the leeks. Cut away most of the green part and wash the white part again very thoroughly to remove any grit. Boil in salted water for 20 minutes. Drain well, reserving ¼ pint (150ml/⅔ cup) liquid. Squeeze the leeks gently to remove as much liquid as possible.
3 Prepare the sauce. Melt the butter in a pan and add the flour, stirring all the time. Cook for 1 minute without colouring. Gradually add the milk and reserved leek stock, stirring to prevent lumps forming. Season and add half the grated cheese and the nutmeg. Remove from the heat and stir in the egg yolks.
4 Spread a pancake (crêpe) on a clean flat surface. Pour on a little sauce and then arrange two leeks with a little protruding over each end of the pancake (crêpe).
5 Roll the pancake (crêpe) up around the leeks and sauce and arrange in a shallow baking dish. Repeat with the rest of the ingredients.
6 Cover the pancakes (crêpes) with the remaining sauce and sprinkle with the rest of the cheese. Brown under the grill or bake in a hot oven for 8 minutes.

Champignons et Chou-Fleurs Frits

Mushroom and Cauliflower Fritters

The new style of cooking makes much use of mushrooms. Some chefs excel in producing delicate combinations of three types of wild mushrooms. You will find my own variation on this theme in Chapter 6.

Little vegetable fritters make ideal accompaniments to drinks for a cocktail party. They could also be used to fill the centre of a *bouquetière* as we have shown in the picture opposite page 112. I have found the most popular to be the two which you will find here, mushrooms and cauliflower. Some chefs like to blanch the cauliflower florets prior to frying. I find it much more satisfactory to simply marinate them in an oil and lemon mixture before coating them ready for cooking. That way, the crunchiness is retained, which is the appeal of the dish. The same applies to the mushrooms, a simple marinade is sufficient. Any pre-cooking will spoil their texture and flavour.

Cauliflower Fritters

Imperial (Metric)	American
For the marinade:	For the marinade:
4 fl oz (120ml) salad oil	**½ cup salad oil**
Juice and grated rind of 1 lemon	**Juice and grated rind of 1 lemon**
1 clove garlic, crushed	**1 clove garlic, crushed**
For the batter:	For the batter:
2 eggs, beaten	**2 eggs, beaten**
½ pint (300ml) flat beer	**1⅓ cups flat beer**
4 oz (100g) wholemeal flour	**1 cup wholewheat flour**
Sea salt	**Sea salt**
1 medium cauliflower	**1 medium cauliflower**
4 oz (100g) wholemeal flour	**1 cup wholewheat flour**
Vegetable oil for deep frying	**Vegetable oil for deep frying**

1. Prepare the marinade by shaking all the ingredients together well in a screw-top jar. Set aside.
2. Prepare the batter by beating the eggs and beer into the flour and salt to form a smooth batter mix.
3. Clean the cauliflower and soak in cold water for 30 minutes. Divide it into florets. Soak these in the marinade for 30 minutes.
4. Toss the florets in flour and then dip into the batter.
5. Heat the oil to 360°F/190°C and deep fry the cauliflower florets for a maximum of 4 minutes.

Mushroom Fritters

Imperial (Metric)	American
½ lb (225g) even-sized white or field mushrooms	**4 cups even-sized white or field mushrooms**
For the marinade:	For the marinade:
4 fl oz (120ml) salad oil	**½ cup salad oil**
Juice of 1 lemon	**Juice of 1 lemon**
1 teaspoon finely grated onion	**1 teaspoon finely grated onion**
Sea salt	**Sea salt**
For the panure:	For the panure:
4 oz (100g) seasoned wholemeal flour	**1 cup seasoned wholewheat flour**
2 eggs, beaten	**2 eggs, beaten**
4 fl oz (120ml) water	**½ cup water**
4 oz (100g) mixed wholemeal breadcrumbs and crushed flaked almonds *or* **peanuts**	**1 cup mixed wholewheat breadcrumbs and crushed slivered almonds** *or* **peanuts**

1. Clean the mushrooms and trim off the ends of the stalks neatly.
2. Marinate for 15 minutes in the mixed marinade ingredients.
3. Drain, coat in flour, then in the egg and water mixture, then in the crumb and nut mixture.
4. Fry as for the cauliflower, but for 1 minute only, by which time they should be golden-brown.
5. Drain and arrange decoratively on a serving plate with the cauliflower fritters, with cocktail sticks and a bowl of Tartare Sauce below.

Tartare Sauce

Imperial (Metric)	American
½ pint (300ml) basic mayonnaise (page 29)	**1⅓ cups basic mayonnaise (page 29)**
2 tablespoons chopped capers	**2 tablespoons chopped capers**
4 tablespoons chopped gherkins	**4 tablespoons chopped gherkins**
1 tablespoon chopped parsley	**1 tablespoon chopped parsley**
1 tablespoon chopped tarragon	**1 tablespoon chopped tarragon**

1. Stir all the ingredients together to make a well-blended, even-flavoured sauce.
2. Store, covered, in the refrigerator until required.

Cromesquis de Lentilles

Sautéd Lentil Croquettes

Serves 4

There is, in fact, a distinction between a cromesqui and a croquette of which most people are unaware, partly because the former is untranslatable and the two terms are used interchangeably. Strictly speaking, a cromesqui is usually coated in batter and shallow-fried, a croquette is rolled in breadcrumbs and deep-fried. In this recipe I have created a delicious blend of green lentils, minced vegetables and hard-boiled eggs, which is shaped into a cylinder, rolled in flour and beaten eggs to form a light batter and sautéd in olive oil. Other pulses could be substituted for the lentils.

Since lentils are such a good source of protein, this dish need not be reserved for dinner or cocktail parties but makes a delicious snack and is handy to pack into a school lunch box, too.

Imperial (Metric)	American
½ lb (225g) green lentils	**1 cup green lentils**
2 pints (1.15 litres) water	**5 cups water**
4 oz (100g) potatoes, sliced	**4 ounces potatoes, sliced**
4 oz (100g) carrots, peeled and chopped	**4 ounces carrots, peeled and chopped**
4 oz (100g) onions, chopped	**4 ounces onions, chopped**
1 clove garlic, chopped	**1 clove garlic, chopped**
1 sprig thyme	**1 sprig thyme**
2 hard-boiled eggs, shelled and chopped	**2 hard-boiled eggs, shelled and chopped**
2 raw eggs, beaten	**2 raw eggs, beaten**
Sea salt and freshly ground black pepper	**Sea salt and freshly ground black pepper**
2 oz (50g) butter	**¼ cup butter**
Wholemeal flour	**Wholewheat flour**
2 extra beaten eggs, for batter	**2 extra beaten eggs, for batter**
Vegetable oil, preferably olive	**Vegetable oil, preferably olive**

1. Pick over the lentils for impurities, wash, soak for 3-6 hours and drain.
2. Boil the lentils in the fresh water, with the vegetables and thyme, for 45 minutes. Drain, remove the thyme and mince the lentils and vegetables to a purée.
3. Blend the purée with the hard-boiled and the fresh eggs. Season lightly and blend in the butter.
4. Divide the mixture into 16 equal pieces. Roll in flour and then shape into cylinders. Coat them in beaten egg to batter them.
5. Heat the oil in a large pan and shallow-fry the cromesquis for 3 minutes, until golden-brown all over. Drain and serve with a tomato salad or as a snack.

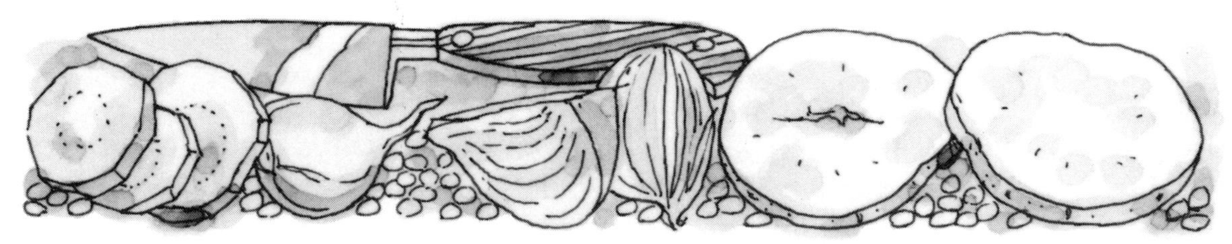

Opposite: *La Papaya à la Gauguin* (page 37).

Pojarskis de Fèves à la Crème

Broad (Windsor) Bean Cutlet with Sour Cream Sauce

Serves 4

Pojarski is a Russian name which is used in French cuisine to denote a mixture of meat, poultry or vegetables shaped into a flat cutlet shape and shallow-fried in a pan. For this recipe I have used broad (Windsor) beans, but fresh butter (Lima) beans make a very good purée too, so use either for this dish. Broad beans are rich in protein and make a very succulent dish when served with a sour cream or buttermilk sauce.

Imperial (Metric)	American
2 lb (900g) broad beans, in their pods	**2 pounds Windsor beans, in their pods**
8 fl oz (200ml) vegetable oil	**1 cup vegetable oil**
1 medium onion, chopped	**1 medium onion, chopped**
1 hard-boiled egg, peeled and chopped	**1 hard-boiled egg, peeled and chopped**
2 eggs, beaten	**2 eggs, beaten**
6 oz (150g) wholemeal breadcrumbs	**3 cups wholewheat breadcrumbs**
Sea salt and freshly ground black pepper	**Sea salt and freshly ground black pepper**
Pinch rosemary *or* **basil**	**Pinch rosemary** *or* **basil**
3 oz (75g) wholemeal flour	**¾ cup wholewheat flour**
4 fl oz (120ml) sour cream	**½ cup sour cream**
1 teaspoon arrowroot	**1 teaspoon arrowroot**

1. Shell the broad (Windsor) beans — they should yield about half their unshelled weight.
2. Boil the beans in salted water for 25 minutes. If any of the skins are tough, peel to reveal the inner, tender bean. Mince the beans to a coarse purée.
3. Heat one third of the oil in a pan and stir-fry half the chopped onion until translucent. Add the bean purée and the hard-boiled egg. Stir until well mixed. Blend in half the beaten egg and half the breadcrumbs to make a thick paste. Season to taste, and add the herbs. Remove from the heat and allow to cool.
4. When cold, divide into four balls. Roll in the flour to make handling easier. Form the balls into flat, pear-shaped cakes. Pass each one through the remaining beaten egg and the remaining breadcrumbs.
5. Heat most of the remaining oil and sauté the cakes until golden; about 2 minutes on each side.
6. For the sauce, heat the last of the oil and stir-fry the remaining onion until soft. Add the sour cream. Boil for 3 minutes and thicken with a mixture of the arrowroot and water. When thick, season to taste and serve separately, alongside the pojarskis.

Opposite: *Quichelettes Capucine* (page 44) and *Crêpinettes de Poireaux Mornay* (page 45).

Petits Soufflés de Carotte et Broccoli

Individual Carrot and Broccoli Soufflés

The successful appearance of this light, mousse-like mixture which, when straight out of the oven, should be well raised above the rim of its dish and should stay up without collapsing instantly, has defeated many cooks. Success depends upon the addition of an extra egg white, beaten stiffly as if for a meringue, and the way in which this is added to the custard-like purée base. Here is the opportunity to attempt a soufflé with every chance of success, even if you have never dared to before!

Imperial (Metric)	American
2 oz (50g) softened butter	**¼ cup softened butter**
2 oz (50g) crushed salted peanuts	**½ cup crushed salted peanuts**

For the soufflé:	For the soufflé:
1 oz (25g) butter	**2½ tablespoons butter**
1 oz (25g) chopped onion	**2 tablespoons chopped onion**
3 oz (75g) wholemeal breadcrumbs	**1½ cups wholewheat breadcrumbs**
3 oz (75g) cooked and puréed carrot	**3 ounces cooked and puréed carrot**
3 oz (75g) cooked and puréed broccoli	**3 ounces cooked and puréed broccoli**
3 oz (75g) cream cheese	**3 ounces cream cheese**
1 whole egg, beaten	**1 whole egg, beaten**
3 egg yolks	**3 egg yolks**
Sea salt and freshly ground black pepper	**Sea salt and freshly ground black pepper**
Pinch each freshly grated nutmeg and ground ginger	**Pinch each freshly grated nutmeg and ground ginger**
5 egg whites	**5 egg whites**

1 Thickly coat the sides of 6 individual soufflé dishes with butter and then sprinkle in the crushed peanuts so that they stick to the sides of the dishes.

2 In a saucepan, melt the butter and add the onion. Stir-fry for 1 minute then add the breadcrumbs, the two purées (make sure there is no excess liquid with these) and the cream cheese. Beat the mixture well to make sure it is thoroughly blended.

3 Stir in the beaten whole egg and the three egg yolks. Heat gently and thoroughly, but do not allow to bubble. Remove from the heat and cool for 10 minutes. Season the mixture with salt, pepper, nutmeg and ginger and transfer to a bowl.

4 In another bowl which is completely free from grease or dust, beat the egg whites stiffly with a pinch of salt. Blend half the egg white into the vegetable mixture and mix well. Then stir the rest in very gently and lightly. It does not matter that there will be streaks of egg white in the mixture.

5 Fill each mould with the mixture, right up to the brim. Then, with the back of a teaspoon or your thumb, make a channel around the top of the mixture to separate the soufflé mix from the edge of the dish by at least ¼ inch (5mm), and to the same depth. With a fork, mark the top of the soufflé in a criss-cross pattern, levelling the mixture at the same time.

6 Place the soufflé dishes on a baking tray in the centre of the oven and cook for 16 to 20 minutes at 400°F/200°C (Gas Mark 6). Do not open the oven door during this time.

7 Serve immediately, in their dishes.

Oignon Farçi aux Épinards

Onion Stuffed with Spinach, Walnuts and Cream Cheese

Serves 4

Spanish onions, or those from Brittany, are most suited to this recipe. This method of preparing onions turns them from a ubiquitous flavouring in their chopped form into the central ingredient of the dish and gives the diner a chance to really appreciate the delicate, sweet flavour of the onion itself.

It is for their flavouring capacities that onions are best known, but they have always been acknowledged as having certain medicinal properties. When eaten raw they are supposed to be mildly antiseptic and diuretic. Onion juice is also used in syrup form as a cure for coughs and colds, although I personally prefer leeks for this remedy.

Imperial (Metric)	American
4 large onions (about 5 oz/150g each)	**4 large onions (about 5 ounces each)**
5 oz (150g) dry spinach purée	**5 ounces dry spinach purée**
2 oz (50g) chopped walnuts	**½ cup chopped English walnuts**
Juice and grated rind of ½ lemon	**Juice and grated rind of ½ lemon**
5 oz (125g) wholemeal breadcrumbs	**2½ cups wholewheat breadcrumbs**
1 hard-boiled egg, shelled and chopped	**1 hard-boiled egg, shelled and chopped**
1 raw egg, beaten	**1 raw egg, beaten**
2 oz (50g) cream cheese	**¼ cup cream cheese**
Sea salt and freshly ground black pepper	**Sea salt and freshly ground black pepper**
Pinch ground mace	**Pinch ground mace**
4 fl oz (120ml) vegetable oil	**½ cup vegetable oil**
2 oz (50g) grated cheese	**½ cup grated cheese**

1. Peel the onions and cut a slice off the top of each one, about ⅓ inch (1cm) from the top. Boil the onions in salted water for 15 minutes.
2. Drain and, when cooled, squeeze each one gently to push out most of the inner layers, leaving 2 or 3 of the outside ones as a shell.
3. Chop the inner layers of onion and blend with the spinach, nuts and lemon.
4. Combine this mixture with the breadcrumbs, eggs, cream cheese and seasonings. Fill the empty onion shells with this mixture.
5. Lift the onions into a shallow baking dish and drizzle oil over them. Sprinkle with the grated cheese. Bake for 30 minutes at 400°F/200°C (Gas Mark 6), basting occasionally with the oil, or extra butter if preferred. Serve hot.

Variations:
A favourite variation of mine is to cool the cooked onions and then wrap in puff pastry and reheat at the same temperature until the pastry is cooked and golden.

Another delicious alternative is to prepare a rich tomato sauce, by stir-frying 1 pound (450g) peeled, seeded and chopped tomatoes with a little onion and garlic in olive oil, thickening the sauce with 1 teaspoon arrowroot blended in 4 tablespoons water, and then spooning this sauce into individual serving dishes, with the cooked onion placed on top, and a sprinkling of grated cheese on top of that. Brown quickly under the grill and serve.

Briochin au Truffe

Brioche Roll Stuffed with Truffle

Serves 4

Truffles are sometimes called, in France, the 'diamonds of the kitchen' — not surprisingly, as they are as expensive as finest caviar. Those from the southern part of France are the most highly prized, especially the black winter truffles of Périgueux. There, the local people flavour their pâtés with truffles as though they were cheap nuts. In appearance, the truffle is about the size of a plum. It has a gnarled skin which should be thoroughly washed. Some chefs never peel truffles, other more extravagant ones always do. I confess that, if I peel a truffle for a special dish, I always save peelings to flavour sauces. Even a little sliver makes all the difference to a dish — a chef appreciates the aroma of a truffle as a perfumier would a fine perfume, and even an uninitiated diner will detect that there is something very special about the dish being tasted.

It is an accepted gastronomical law that one should try to sample every special food or dish at least once. Well, this dish is one in a million. In my youth, I worked at the celebrated *Rôtisserie Périgourdine* restaurant in the Latin Quarter of Paris as a commis cook. There, truffles wrapped in pastry were cooked in the ashes of a wood fire. Although I worked in some of the most exclusive and finest restaurants of Paris after that, learning a dish or a secret in each one, that is the dish which stays dearest in my memory.

Imperial (Metric)	American
2 medium-sized, fresh truffles, halved	**2 medium-sized, fresh truffles, halved**
2 oz (50g) seasoned wholemeal flour	**½ cup seasoned wholewheat flour**
2 eggs, beaten	**2 eggs, beaten**
2 oz (50g) wholemeal breadcrumbs *or* **finely chopped nuts** *or* **a mixture of both**	**½ cup wholewheat breadcrumbs** *or* **finely chopped nuts** *or* **a mixture of both**
Olive oil	**Olive oil**
1 lb (450g) brioche dough (page 178)	**1 pound brioche dough (page 178)**
1 extra beaten egg, for egg wash	**1 extra beaten egg, for egg wash**
4 teaspoons port *or* **brandy**	**4 teaspoons port** *or* **brandy**

1. Boil the truffles, peeled if possible, in salted water for 15 minutes.
2. Remove the truffles and coat in flour, then dip in beaten egg, then roll in breadcrumbs or nuts.
3. Heat some oil in a small pan and shallow fry the truffles briefly to brown the coating. Remove and cool.
4. Divide the brioche dough into four even-sized rounds. Break off a little knob of dough from each one and form into neat rounds too. Insert a truffle into each of the large balls of dough and close the dough around it. Place the smaller rounds onto the brioche buns as a 'head', like a cottage loaf. Brush with egg wash and allow to rest for 15 minutes.
5. Bake at 400°F/200°C (Gas Mark 6) for 16 to 20 minutes.
6. Remove from the oven and, just before serving, remove the head of each brioche and carefully pour in a teaspoon of port or brandy. Replace the head and serve warm.

Note: If preferred, the truffle can be inserted into the dough without pre-frying. Tinned truffles may be used but their flavour will be milder.

Pain de Chou-Fleur à la Reine Antoinette

Baked Cauliflower Loaf

Serves 4

I can see no reason why the leaves and core of the cauliflower are so seldom used in cooking and in this dish I have made a point of incorporating every part of the vegetable, to demonstrate that it is not only possible but very good indeed. So many people have been put off cauliflower by tasting it only when overcooked to the point where all flavour and texture are lost and then smothered in a heavy, floury cheese sauce. Delight your dinner guests by introducing them to this new way of using a much-maligned yet delicious vegetable.

To prepare this dish successfully you should look for a fresh, firm cauliflower with a compact head which shows no tinges of green or yellow and which, of course, has not been stripped of its leaves. Early cauliflowers from France or the Channel Islands are good; the best come from Brittany.

Imperial (Metric)	American
1 medium cauliflower (approx. 2 lb/900g)	**1 medium cauliflower (approx. 2 pounds)**
1 teaspoon wine or cider vinegar	**1 teaspoon wine or cider vinegar**
¼ pint (140ml) vegetable oil	**⅔ cup vegetable oil**
1 small onion, chopped	**1 small onion, chopped**
1 red pepper, seeded and chopped	**1 red pepper, seeded and chopped**
1 green pepper, seeded and chopped	**1 green pepper, seeded and chopped**
¼ teaspoon each turmeric, paprika, coriander and basil	**¼ teaspoon each turmeric, paprika, coriander and basil**
2 cloves garlic, chopped	**2 cloves garlic, chopped**
2 oz (50g) tomato purée	**¼ cup tomato paste**
½-¾ pint (300-450ml) water	**1⅓-2 cups water**
6 oz (150g) wholemeal breadcrumbs	**3 cups wholewheat breadcrumbs**
4 eggs, beaten	**4 eggs, beaten**
Sea salt to taste	**Sea salt to taste**
2 oz (50g) butter	**¼ cup butter**

1. Remove the stem and leaves from the cauliflower and separate the head into florets. Discard any wilted leaves. Dice the core and shred the leaves. Soak the vegetable pieces in water with the vinegar added. Drain.
2. Heat the oil in a large sauté pan and stir-fry the onion for 5 minutes. Then add the peppers and the stem, leaves and florets of the cauliflower. Cook for 5 more minutes, stirring in all the spices and the garlic after 1 minute. Add the tomato purée and cover level with water.
3. Cover the pan with a lid and cook for 30 minutes. At this stage the liquid will be reduced by about half. Thicken it with the breadcrumbs, blending them in well.
4. Mince all the ingredients to a purée. Blend in the eggs and season with salt.
5. Use the butter to thoroughly coat a loaf tin or a shallow baking dish. Fill it with the mixture and bake at 400°F/200°C (Gas Mark 6) for 35 minutes. Serve from the dish or turn out onto a flat dish.

Note: When the mixture has been puréed it can be used in several different ways. It could be used to stuff marrow (squash) before being baked, or as a filling for a flan, or could be blended with one quarter its weight in mashed potatoes and then baked, for a more substantial supper dish.

The loaf looks very attractive when garnished on top with freshly cooked mushrooms, toasted almonds and a sprinkling of freshly chopped parsley.

Timbales d'Épinard Viroflay

Little Individual Baked Spinach Moulds

Serves 4

Spinach was first cultivated in Europe in the monastic gardens of the fourteenth century, although it had been eaten in the East for much longer. A famous French physician calls it the *balai de l'éstomac* — the broom of the stomach — because of its mild laxative effect which cleanses and purifies the system.

Its uses are many and varied, but most are favourites with gourmets. In fashion at the moment is the use of raw spinach leaves in salads, but it is also good in soups, the famous Jamaican Hot-Pot Soup made with spinach, potatoes and chillies being especially delicious. It was the Italians who first made the best use of spinach, so much so that any dish with the word Florentine in its name is sure to have spinach in it or as a garnish.

This dish is named after the town of Viroflay in the French region of *Ile-de-France* which was once famous for its spinach.

Imperial (Metric)	American
2 lb (900g) fresh spinach	**2 pounds fresh spinach**
4 oz (100g) butter	**½ cup butter**
2 oz (50g) wholemeal breadcrumbs	**1 cup wholewheat breadcrumbs**
½ pint (300ml) single cream	**1⅓ cups light cream**
3 eggs, beaten	**3 eggs, beaten**
Sea salt and freshly ground black pepper	**Sea salt and freshly ground black pepper**
Freshly grated nutmeg	**Freshly grated nutmeg**
4 tomatoes, skinned and sliced, for decoration	**4 tomatoes, skinned and sliced, for decoration**

For the lemon sauce:	For the lemon sauce:
4 fl oz (120ml) natural yogurt	**½ cup plain yogurt**
Juice and grated rind of ¼ lemon	**Juice and grated rind of ¼ lemon**
1 clove garlic	**1 clove garlic**
Sea salt and freshly ground black pepper	**Sea salt and freshly ground black pepper**
1 teaspoon honey	**1 teaspoon honey**

1. Remove any coarse stems from the spinach and wash in plenty of cold water. Select 16 large, undamaged leaves and boil these for 2 minutes. Refresh in cold water and drain on kitchen paper.
2. Use half the butter to lavishly coat the insides of four dariole moulds and then line them with the cooked spinach leaves.
3. Boil the rest of the spinach for 6 minutes. Drain, refresh in cold water and drain again. Squeeze dry and then chop finely.
4. Heat a sauté pan with the remainder of the butter and reheat the chopped spinach until all the butter has been absorbed. Add the breadcrumbs and the cream. Remove from the heat and blend in the beaten eggs. Season with salt, pepper and nutmeg.
5. Fill the lined moulds with this mixture and cover with buttered foil. Place the moulds in a shallow tray and pour in the hot water to come half-way up their sides. Bake at 350°F/180°C (Gas Mark 4) for 45 to 50 minutes or until the mixture is set and firm.
6. Remove the moulds from the *bain marie*. Cool for 12 minutes and then turn out onto a serving dish. Decorate with slices of tomato, with one slice on the top of each mould.
7. While the spinach moulds are cooking, liquidize all the sauce ingredients in a blender. Serve separately.

Variations:
A hot béchamel sauce, flavoured with a little lemon, goes well with this dish, as does a simple tomato sauce, or a cheese sauce. The moulds can be garnished with *croûtons* of fried bread. Lettuce or chard leaves can be used as a substitute for spinach.

Aubergine au Gruyère

Aubergine (Eggplant) Topped with Gruyère Cheese

Serves 4

This is a favourite hot starter. Any cheese with good melting qualities will do if you have no Gruyère, such as Cheddar, Gouda, Double Gloucester, Port Salut or Cantal. You can experiment to see which one you like best.

For reasons of health one is inclined to use soya or sunflower oils in fried dishes, but this dish really benefits from the special flavour of olive oil, the favourite of the French. If it is the correct temperature before you start to fry, the aubergines (eggplants) will cook before they have a chance to absorb too much oil, anyway, so make sure your oil is heated to 360°F/190°C. If you have no thermometer, drop a cube of bread into the oil and if it is golden brown within ten seconds the oil is hot enough. Try not to let it get too hot, though, to smoking point, as this affects the flavour and the aubergines (eggplants) may burn. Never overfill your *friture* (frying pot), keep it just half full, and do not fry too many items at a time. It is better to cook in small batches and keep the rest hot, otherwise the temperature of the oil will drop and the food will be oily and unpleasant. Allow the oil to reheat between batches, too.

Imperial (Metric)	American
2 large aubergines	**2 large eggplants**
Sea salt	**Sea salt**
4 oz (100g) wholemeal flour, seasoned with sea salt and freshly ground black pepper	**1 cup wholewheat flour, seasoned with sea salt and freshly ground black pepper**
1 clove garlic, crushed	**1 clove garlic, crushed**
2 pints (1.15 litres) olive oil	**5 cups olive oil**
½ lb (225g) Gruyère cheese, thinly sliced	**1 cup Gruyère cheese, thinly sliced**

1. Cut the aubergines (eggplants) into slices ¼-inch (5mm) thick along the length of the vegetable. Sprinkle each slice with salt and leave to exude its bitter juices for 25 minutes. Wash, drain and dry thoroughly.
2. Mix the seasoned flour with the finely crushed clove of garlic and coat each aubergine (eggplant) slice in this mixture, shaking off any excess.
3. Heat the oil as instructed above and deep fry the slices for 1 minute. Drain on kitchen paper.
4. Lay the aubergine (eggplant) slices out in a single layer on a flat tray and place a slice of cheese on each one. Grill until the cheese is golden and serve at once.

Variations:
Each slice could be placed on toasted bread as a snack meal.

Italian Mozzarella is an excellent cheese to use in this dish, especially when sandwiched with the aubergine (eggplant) between two pieces of hot toast in a variation on the famous French *Croque-Monsieur.*

Rissoles de Pois Vert à l'Ail

Green Pea Rissoles with Garlic and Mint

The name rissole is derived from the French verb *rissoler* meaning to fry until brown. Unlike British rissoles, the true French rissole is always wrapped in pastry and then deep-fried.

I have devised a low-fat pastry for this dish which is similar to a noodle paste. It can be made with strong wholemeal flour or with wholemeal semolina which, like pasta, is made from durum wheat. Both are high in gluten and protein.

You can vary these rissoles endlessly by substituting different purées in place of the peas.

Imperial (Metric)	American
For the pastry:	For the pastry:
½ lb (225g) strong wholemeal flour *or* **fine wholemeal semolina**	**2 cups strong wholewheat flour** *or* **fine wholewheat semolina**
Pinch sea salt	**Pinch sea salt**
1 egg, beaten	**1 egg, beaten**
¼ pint (150ml) water	**⅔ cup water**
1 tablespoon vegetable oil	**1 tablespoon vegetable oil**
For the filling:	For the filling:
5 oz (125g) cooked and puréed peas, as dry as possible	**¾ cup cooked and puréed peas, as dry as possible**
1 hard-boiled egg, shelled and chopped	**1 hard-boiled egg, shelled and chopped**
1 oz (25g) cream cheese	**2½ tablespoons cream cheese**
1 egg, beaten	**1 egg, beaten**
1 clove garlic, finely chopped	**1 clove garlic, finely chopped**
2 oz (50g) wholemeal breadcrumbs	**1 cup wholewheat breadcrumbs**
Vegetable oil for deep-frying	**Vegetable oil for deep-frying**

1. Prepare the pastry by combining the flour or semolina and salt in a bowl with the beaten egg, water and oil. Knead the dough, form into a ball and leave to rest for 30 minutes.
2. Dust the pastry with a little extra flour for easy handling and, on a floured board, divide the dough into 6 balls. Roll them out into very thin circles about 5 inches (12cm) in diameter.
3. Combine all the filling ingredients, except the frying oil, to make a smooth, stiff paste, and divide into 6 balls. Place a ball of filling on each pastry circle.
4. Brush the edges of the pastry with cold water and fold in half over the filling into half-moon shapes.
5. Half fill a large pan with the oil and heat to 360°F/180°C. Deep-fry the rissoles for about 2 minutes until golden. Serve hot or cold.

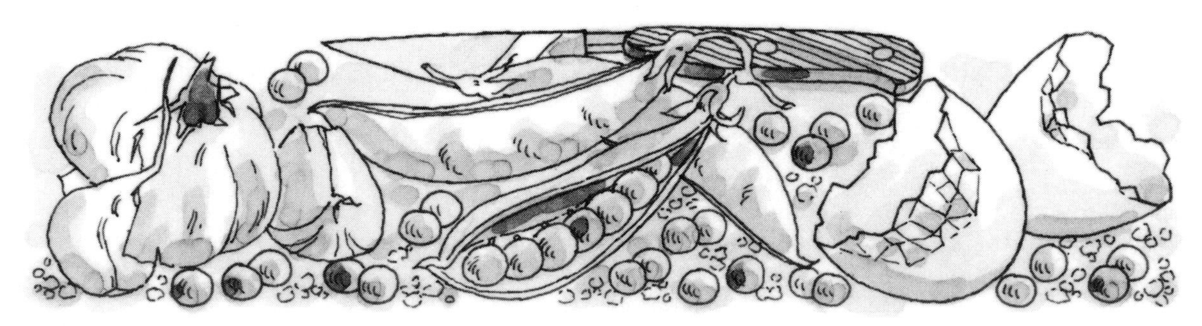

La Tartine aux Fruits Secs

Dried Fruit and Nut Toasts

Serves 8

Nuts and dried fruits keep well and so are easy to keep on hand as a vitamin- and protein-rich snack instead of sweets. Nuts are high in fibre and in Vitamin B_6 as well, and the fat they contain is polyunsaturated, so they are a healthy treat for all ages. This dish takes their use as a snack one stage further and they become a delicious starter, cocktail party nibble, or even a children's teatime meal. It is also an interesting extension of the modern fashion for using fruits in savoury dishes.

Imperial (Metric)	American
4 oz (100g) chopped dried dates	**⅔ cup chopped dried dates**
4 oz (100g) chopped dried figs	**⅔ cup chopped dried figs**
4 oz (100g) seedless raisins	**⅔ cup seedless raisins**
½ lb (225g) coarsely chopped mixed hazelnuts and peanuts	**1⅔ cups coarsely chopped mixed hazelnuts and peanuts**
1 egg, beaten	**1 egg, beaten**
2 oz (50g) wholemeal breadcrumbs	**1 cup wholewheat breadcrumbs**
2 oz (50g) curd cheese	**¼ cup curd cheese**
Juice and grated rind of ½ lemon	**Juice and grated rind of ½ lemon**
1 tablespoon honey	**1 tablespoon honey**
4 tablespoons vegetable oil *or* **butter**	**4 tablespoons vegetable oil** *or* **butter**
Thin slices wholemeal bread	**Thin slices wholewheat bread**

1 Mince all the ingredients except the wholemeal bread to form a well-mixed paste.

2 Toast the bread. Spread the paste on the toasts quite thickly. Cut into fingers or triangles.

Note: There should be sufficient paste for 18 slices of bread. If you do not require all the paste at once, the remainder can be stored, covered, in the fridge for 10 days, or frozen for 3 months.

Almonds, Brazil nuts, cashews or pecans can be substituted for some or all of the nuts in the recipe. Seeds such as sesame, sunflower and pumpkin can also be used. Serving the nuts or seeds with a grain, in the form of wholemeal bread, makes a balanced protein, just as useful to the body as that obtained from meat.

Galette de Maïs, Sauce Rougeole

Sweetcorn Porridge Sautéd in Butter with Spicy Sauce

Corn or maize is grown all over France, but once it was primarily food for cattle and chickens. What little was eaten went to make traditional peasant dishes, and variations of this recipe can be found in most Third World countries as well as in more familiar forms like the famous Italian *polenta*. Today, with the growing recognition of the healthiness of simple country foods, as well as a better understanding of our food resources, corn is enjoyed in France, as in the rest of the world, by humans as well as livestock. Corn on the cob was probably the first, and most familiar, starter using this produce, but corn fritters and popcorn have been introduced to Europe from America, cornflakes are now a standard breakfast for millions of people and corn oil is well known for its good culinary properties. For a complete protein corn must be eaten with a pulse (such as peas, beans or lentils) or a seed (either nuts or seeds come into this group). In this recipe, cheese and eggs provide extra protein, but the dish could be served with a green salad sprinkled with seeds or chopped nuts to complement the grains.

Imperial (Metric)	American
2 pints (1.15 litres) water	**5 cups water**
½ lb (225g) cornmeal, coarse	**1⅓ cups cornmeal, coarse**
2 oz (50g) butter	**¼ cup butter**
Sea salt and freshly ground black pepper	**Sea salt and freshly ground black pepper**
3 eggs, beaten	**3 eggs, beaten**
Wholemeal flour	**Wholewheat flour**
Butter for frying	**Butter for frying**
4 oz (100g) hard cheese, grated	**1 cup grated hard cheese**

1. Boil the water and sprinkle on the cornmeal. Stir with a wooden spoon and cook gently for 25 to 35 minutes. Add butter and seasoning. Remove the mixture from the heat and stir in the eggs.
2. Reheat the mixture, stirring, for 4 minutes. Pour into a greased Swiss-roll tin to a depth of ¾ inch (2cm). Leave to cool.
3. When the mixture is cold and set, cut into small rounds about 2 inches (5cm) in diameter. Coat the cornmeal rounds in flour and sauté in butter until golden on both sides, about 4 minutes. Keep warm on a serving dish and serve with Rougeole Sauce.

Imperial (Metric) For the Rougeole Sauce:	American For the Rougeole Sauce:
4 fl oz (120ml) vegetable oil	**½ cup vegetable oil**
1 clove garlic, chopped	**1 clove garlic, chopped**
1 red pepper, seeded and chopped	**1 red pepper, seeded and chopped**
1 lb (450g) tomatoes, peeled, seeded and diced	**1 pound tomatoes, peeled, seeded and diced**
2 tablespoons tomato purée	**2 tablespoons tomato paste**
Sea salt to taste	**Sea salt to taste**
Freshly grated nutmeg to taste	**Freshly grated nutmeg to taste**
Large pinch cayenne pepper *or* 1 fresh chilli, chopped	**Large pinch cayenne pepper *or* 1 fresh chili, chopped**

1. Heat the oil and stir-fry the garlic and peppers for 4 minutes.
2. Add the chopped tomatoes and cook for a further 3 minutes, then add the tomato purée (paste), salt, nutmeg and cayenne.

3 Pour this sauce over the fried cornmeal galettes.
4 Serve with the grated cheese passed around separately, or sprinkled over the galettes and browned lightly under the grill.

Petits Gateaux de Semoule aux Pistaches Vertes

Semolina Tartlets with Pistachio Nuts

The pistachio is a luxury nut because of its price. It is used mostly in nougats, ice-creams and, by the French, in pâtés. In Europe, pistachio ice-cream is the favourite with most children. Gourmets are often rather like children, thrilled with a delicate tit-bit but, unlike children, they usually prefer a savoury delicacy and it was for this reason that I created these little quichelettes.

Imperial (Metric)	American
1 quantity wholemeal pastry (page 44)	**1 quantity wholewheat pastry (page 44)**
½ pint (300ml) water and milk, mixed	**1⅓ cups water and milk, mixed**
2 oz (50g) wholemeal semolina	**½ cup wholewheat semolina**
4 tablespoons pistachio nuts, skinned and coarsely chopped*	**4 tablespoons pistachio nuts, skinned and coarsely chopped***
1 oz (25g) grated Gruyère cheese	**¼ cup grated Gruyère cheese**
1 tablespoon Kirsch *or* anisette	**1 tablespoon Kirsch *or* anisette**
1 oz (25g) butter	**2½ tablespoons butter**
1 egg, beaten	**1 egg, beaten**
Pinch each sea salt and raw cane sugar	**Pinch each sea salt and raw cane sugar**
Extra grated cheese	**Extra grated cheese**

1 Make pastry as described in *Quichelette Capucine* (page 44).
2 While the pastry is resting, boil the milk and water and sprinkle the semolina onto it. Cook for 10 minutes at simmering point.
3 Remove from the heat, add the pistachios, cheese, liqueur, butter, egg and seasoning.
4 On a floured board, roll the pastry to a thickness of ¼ inch (5mm). Cut rounds 2 inches (5cm) across and place in greased tartlet moulds.
5 Fill the cases three quarters full of semolina mixture. Bake at 400°F/200°C (Gas Mark 6) for 15 to 20 minutes until golden-brown.
6 Sprinkle the quichelettes with a little grated cheese and brown under the grill before serving.

* To skin the pistachios, scald them in boiling water for 2 minutes, then refresh in cold water. The skin should slip off easily.

Variations:
I have created this as a savoury dish but it could be sweetened with honey and garnished with raisins or other dried fruit, with the cheese omitted. As a savoury tartlet, it could be garnished with asparagus tips or lightly sautéd mushrooms. Since pistachios are so costly, you could prepare this dish more economically with almonds, peanuts or shelled young broad (Windsor) beans.

Épigrammes de Riz Elysée

Exotic Pancake (Crêpe) Rolls

Rice on its own is not a complete protein and must be eaten with pulses or seeds, or both, to supply the body with proper nourishment. This dish provides further protein in the form of eggs, too.

I find that American rice, from Carolina in particular, is the best for the pilaff-style cooking which this recipe requires, but any patna rice with long slender grains will do.

Imperial (Metric)	American
2 oz (50g) green peas	**⅓ cup green peas**
2 oz (50g) sweetcorn kernels	**⅓ cup sweetcorn kernels**
4 fl oz (120ml) peanut oil	**½ cup peanut oil**
1 medium onion, chopped	**1 medium onion, chopped**
1 red pepper, seeded and chopped	**1 red pepper, seeded and chopped**
1 clove garlic, chopped	**1 clove garlic, chopped**
4 oz (100g) brown rice	**½ cup brown rice**
1 teaspoon turmeric	**1 teaspoon turmeric**
Sea salt and freshly ground black pepper	**Sea salt and freshly ground black pepper**
2 eggs, beaten	**2 eggs, beaten**
2 oz (50g) diced dried figs	**⅓ cup diced dried figs**
6 pancakes, 8 inches (20cm) in diameter (page 34)	**6 crêpes, 8 inches in diameter (page 34)**
Wholemeal flour	**Wholewheat flour**
Vegetable oil	**Vegetable oil**

1 Boil the sweetcorn and peas, if raw, for 5 minutes and set aside to cool.

2 Heat the peanut oil in a large saucepan and stir-fry the onion until transparent. Then add the pepper and garlic and cook for a further 2 minutes.

3 Stir in the rice, making sure it becomes well impregnated with oil. Then add ¾ pint (425ml/2 cups) water and the turmeric and stir well. Transfer to a shallow earthenware dish and bake at 400°F/200°C (Gas Mark 6) for 45 minutes, adding the sweetcorn and peas 5 minutes before the end of cooking time. Season to taste.

4 Remove the dish from the oven and stir in the beaten eggs to bind to a semi-solid paste. Blend in the diced figs and adjust seasoning if necessary. Leave the mixture to cool.

5 When the mixture is cold, lay the pancakes (crêpes) out flat and drop spoonsful of the mixture onto each one, taking care to put an equal amount on each and not overfill any. Then fold the pancake (crêpe) around the mixture like an envelope, to form neat, oblong rolls. Make sure the filling is securely wrapped.

6 Roll the pancakes (crêpes) in the flour. Heat the oil in a shallow pan and sauté the rolls until golden all over. Serve with a salad of beansprouts tossed in a Vinaigrette sauce.

4 Les Potages Chauds et Froids

Hot and Cold Soups

Under the broad heading of 'Soups' the professional chef will list many different types, classified according to their style, texture, flavour, basic foundation and other factors. Yet, despite all these variations, the principle is always much the same, and has its basis in frugal country cooking, when poorer ingredients, old vegetables, off-cuts, left-overs, all went into the stock pot with filling ingredients such as pulses to make cheap and nourishing meals. Long before the French revolution, when only the wealthy landowners could afford meat, the peasants and country people were often kept from starvation by these types of soup. During the Second World War they experienced a revival through necessity, but now they are being given a new lease of life by nutritionists because of their healthy qualities. These days, of course, we do not have to use poor quality ingredients to make our soups, though a stock pot will still provide you with a better stock on which to base your soup than any bouillon cube will. All the soups in this chapter, and the stock as well, freeze well, so large quantities can be made at once, saving time and labour.

Soup-making need not be a lengthy process, though. As far back as 1951, when I was writing my weekly column for the *Sunday Times*, which I was to continue for seven years, I was advocating the use of the blender in soup-making. Even then I was able to list dozens of soups which could be prepared in fifteen minutes — soups which retained their own fresh flavour, rather than it being dissipated by the long simmering of traditional soups.

The Fifties, too, saw the rebirth of the cold soup, which has existed in parts of Europe for centuries but which was given a new lease of life under the hot sun of California. Modern cookery has adapted these icy cold soups as a perfect Summer starter: cold, jellied consommé; cool Vichyssoise; and spicy, refreshing Gazpacho (but try my special Basquaise version of this, which is far superior!).

Every province of France has its own specialities. Many have a base of meat stock, and the fishing ports have their Cotriade or Bouillabaisse, but the vegetarian has a wealth still to choose from, for the reasons we have talked about earlier. I have included some of our traditional recipes in this chapter — the Pumpkin Soup of my childhood is as delicious today as it has always been, and the Onion Soup, made as during the days of my apprenticeship in Paris, is unchanged. Others I have found to benefit from the light touch a vegetable, rather than meat, base brings, whereby the subtle flavours of the ingredients can be savoured individually and in unison. From a simple peasant broth to a gourmet's delight, French cuisine holds soups for every occasion and for every palate.

Crème d'Oseille

Cream of Sorrel Soup

Sorrel (*Rumex Scutatus*) has juicy, fleshy leaves which are acid-tasting due to their high oxalic acid content. Oxalic acid combines with calcium and magnesium in the body to form an insoluble salt which renders these minerals unusable, and the calcium oxalate crystals must be passed out of the body in the urine. Foods containing oxalic acid are, as well as sorrel, beetroot, rhubarb, spinach and green tomatoes, so if you eat these foods in any quantity it is advisable to drink plenty of liquids with them to avoid any chance of the build-up of kidney stones.

In France, sorrel is often used like spinach in salads. Like spinach it is high in iron and vitamin A, and French sorrel is lower in oxalic acid than common wild sorrel. One variation of this soup is to use half spinach and half sorrel. Perhaps the most popular use of sorrel in France, though, is as a garnish for omelettes and stews.

Imperial (Metric)	American
4 oz (100g) leek, white part only	**4 ounces leek, white part only**
½ lb (225g) sorrel leaves	**8 ounces sorrel leaves**
2 oz (50g) butter	**¼ cup butter**
2 fl oz (60ml) vegetable oil	**¼ cup vegetable oil**
4 oz (100g) sliced potatoes	**4 ounces sliced potatoes**
2¾ pints (1.5 litres) water	**7 cups water**
4 egg yolks	**4 egg yolks**
½ oz (15g) arrowroot	**1 tablespoon arrowroot**
4 fl oz (120ml) cream	**½ cup cream**
Sea salt and freshly ground black pepper	**Sea salt and freshly ground black pepper**
Freshly grated nutmeg	**Freshly grated nutmeg**
1 teaspoon raw cane sugar	**1 teaspoon raw cane sugar**

1. Wash the leeks and the sorrel and drain. Cut both into shreds 2 inches (5cm) long.
2. Heat the butter and oil in a large saucepan and add the sorrel leaves, leeks and potatoes and cook gently for 5 minutes. Add the water, reserving ¼ pint (120ml/⅔ cup), and boil for 20 minutes.
3. In a bowl, blend the egg yolks, arrowroot and cream with the remaining water and stir this mixture into the soup to thicken it. Cook the soup for a further 4 minutes at just boiling point until it is perfectly smooth in texture. Season to taste and sprinkle on the sugar to counteract the acidity of the soup. Serve with sippets of fried wholemeal bread.

La Vichyssoise

Chilled Leek and Potato Soup

So much fuss is made about this simple composition that one would think it was some sort of culinary masterpiece. I even know one chef who claims to have invented it! Yet this soup has been a favourite for as long as the leek has been used in soups. My grandmother was making it over fifty years ago. I remember we had it hot and freshly-made one day, and then drank the rest of it cold the next day — a perfect dish for that fine Summer's evening. Today, when made correctly with not too much potato, this soup is as popular as ever.

Imperial (Metric)	American
½ lb (225g) leeks, white part only, cleaned and sliced	**8 ounces leeks, white part only, cleaned and sliced**
4 oz (100g) potatoes, peeled and thinly sliced	**4 ounces potatoes, peeled and thinly sliced**
4 oz (100g) butter	**½ cup butter**
1 pint (600ml) water *or* vegetable stock	**2½ cups water *or* vegetable stock**
1 pint (600ml) milk	**2½ cups milk**
Sea salt and freshly ground black pepper	**Sea salt and freshly ground black pepper**
1 teaspoon raw cane sugar	**1 teaspoon raw canc sugar**
4 fl oz (120ml) double *or* sour cream	**½ cup heavy *or* sour cream**
2 tablespoons chopped chives	**2 tablespoons chopped chives**

1. Sauté the vegetables in the butter, without browning, for 4 minutes. Then add the water and boil for 20 minutes.
2. When the vegetables are tender, add the milk and reheat for 5 minutes.
3. Liquidize the vegetables and liquid to a thin purée. Reheat for 5 minutes. Season with salt, pepper and sugar.
4. At this stage the soup could be served hot if desired, with or without cream swirled in. If you wish to serve it cold, as is usual with a Vichyssoise, chill the soup to below 40°F/5°C and then add the cream and sprinkle with chives before serving.

Note: The sugar enhances the flavour of the leek. The same can be achieved, as many cooks do, with monosodium glutamate. This is a nature-identical substance which, while being tasteless on its own, brings out the flavour of foods just as salt and sugar do. Many stock cubes contain monosodium glutamate. However, many people have an allergic reaction to this substance, so you may prefer, for the sake of your guests, to avoid its use. Stock cubes or yeast extract will enhance the flavour of a soup if necessary (but read the labels carefully), but I prefer of all these to add just a pinch of sugar as above. That way the vegetables retain their natural good flavour.

La Pomme d'Amour

Tomato and Red Pepper Soup

Serves 12

To make a really good tomato soup you need the large, ribbed, sweet variety of tomato. Plum Italian tomatoes are very good indeed. At certain times of year shop-bought tomatoes are inclined to be flavourless and will need supplementing with concentrated tomato purée. I created this soup using red pepper because I feel it gives even poor tomatoes a zesty flavour which is very pleasing. Although garlic is almost always used in a tomato sauce it is rare to find it in a tomato soup, unless the soup is of Mediterranean origin, like my *Bouillabaisse de Légumes Riviera* on page 76. I have used garlic here, too, because it complements the spiciness of the pepper and paprika.

Imperial (Metric)	American
4 oz (100g) onions	**4 ounces onions**
4 oz (100g) carrots	**4 ounces carrots**
1 red pepper	**1 red pepper**
4 oz (100g) celery	**4 ounces celery**
4 oz (100g) potatoes	**4 ounces potatoes**
4 fl oz (120ml) vegetable oil	**½ cup vegetable oil**
1 small clove garlic, crushed	**1 small clove garlic, crushed**
¼ teaspoon Hungarian paprika	**¼ teaspoon Hungarian paprika**
Freshly ground black pepper	**Freshly ground black pepper**
Pinch ground ginger	**Pinch ground ginger**
Pinch dried thyme	**Pinch dried thyme**
4 pints (2.25 litres) water	**10 cups water**
4 oz (100g) tomato purée	**½ cup tomato paste**
1 tablespoon sea salt	**1 tablespoon sea salt**
1 tablespoon raw cane sugar	**1 tablespoon raw cane sugar**
4 fl oz (120ml) single cream	**½ cup light cream**
1 oz (25g) cornflour	**¼ cup cornstarch**
1 oz (25g) wholemeal flour	**¼ cup wholewheat flour**
4 very large tomatoes, skinned, seeded and cut into small cubes	**4 very large tomatoes, skinned, seeded and cut into small cubes**
1 tablespoon freshly chopped parsley	**1 tablespoon freshly chopped parsley**

1 Clean and prepare the vegetables and cut them into uniform thin slices.
2 Heat the oil in a large saucepan. Sauté all the vegetables and the garlic for 8 minutes and then add the paprika, pepper, ginger and thyme, and the water. Bring to the boil and cook for 15 minutes. Then add the tomato purée, salt and sugar.
3 After another 15 minutes, by which time all the vegetables should be tender, strain the soup and liquidize the vegetables with a little of the cooking liquid, and then stir the vegetable purée back into the rest of the liquid and reheat.
4 In a bowl blend the cream with the flours and gradually add it to the hot soup, stirring all the time as the soup thickens. Cook for 4 minutes. Check the seasoning, add the tomato and parsley and simmer for 3 more minutes. Serve with *croûtons* or crackers.

Note: This soup freezes well, so it is worth making this double quantity and freezing half for another occasion.

Le Dragon Rouge

Beetroot (Beet) Soup with Red Wine

Illustrated opposite page 80.

Most people are familiar with beetroot (beet) in a salad, but few have ever tried a true Bortsch, as made by the Russian peasants of pre-revolutionary days. My family is descended from a small branch of the French aristocracy who, since pre-Napoleonic times, had lived on their own lands in northern France. The French revolution took many heads and all our lands, but my family's recipes were a closely guarded secret, and now they will live on for ever because, over the years, I have published the whole repertoire in one form or another. This soup, an amalgam of French and Russian cuisine, is named after the 'red dragon' of the Russian revolution, but is reminiscent of the past splendour of earlier days.

Imperial (Metric)	American
2 lb (900g) beetroot	**2 pounds beets**
½ pint (300ml) red wine	**1⅓ cups red wine**
Large pinch aniseeds	**Large pinch aniseeds**
4 oz (100g) mixed butter and oil	**½ cup mixed butter and oil**
1 medium onion, chopped	**1 medium onion, chopped**
2 sticks celery, chopped	**2 stalks celery, chopped**
2 sticks fennel, chopped	**2 stalks fennel, chopped**
2 carrots, peeled and sliced	**2 carrots, peeled and sliced**
4 oz (100g) cabbage, sliced	**4 ounces cabbage, sliced**
1 *bouquet garni* (sprig each of thyme and parsley and 1 bayleaf)	**1 *bouquet garni* (sprig each of thyme and parsley and 1 bayleaf)**
Sea salt and freshly ground black pepper	**Sea salt and freshly ground black pepper**
Pinch raw cane sugar	**Pinch raw cane sugar**
¼ pint (150ml) sour cream	**⅔ cup sour cream**
***Croûtons* or slices of wholemeal bread**	***Croûtons* or slices of wholewheat bread**

1. Wash the beetroot (beets) and boil half of them in salted water for 30 minutes or until tender. Then peel them and cut into thin shreds or strips. Place them in a bowl with the red wine and aniseeds for 1 hour to marinate.
2. Peel and slice the rest of the beetroot (beets).
3. Heat the butter and oil in a large pan and sauté the raw beetroot (beet) and the rest of the raw vegetables and the *bouquet garni* for 8 minutes, then add 2 pints (1.15 litres/5 cups) water and boil for 30 minutes. When the vegetables are tender, remove the *bouquet garni*, strain the soup and purée the vegetables in a blender with just a little liquid.
4. Reheat the purée, add the marinated beetroot (beet) and the wine, season to taste with salt, pepper and sugar and lastly stir in the sour cream, diluted with a little water if very thick. Serve with *croûtons* or bread. This soup is also quite delicious served cold.

Note: Beetroot (beet) are best marinated in wine rather than vinegar. The acid gives the soup its characteristic red colour. Red beetroot without this acid will colour the broth a golden-yellow.

Le Potage aux Petits Pois Mange-Tout

Mangetout (Snow) Pea Soup

Thirty years ago, in my bestselling book *Haute Cuisine*, I listed thirty variations on a simple pea soup. I included many which we all know well, such as St Germain, Lamballe, Fontagne and Clamart, all rich soups enriched even further with vermicelli, tapioca or other garnishes, but one soup which was not mentioned was a soup made from mangetout (snow) peas, as it might have been considered a crime to use such a luxury item to make a soup. Now we tend to forego the rich and heavy tastes and garnishes of classical cuisine for the simpler and more delicate flavours of the vegetables themselves. And without the more fancy flourishes, a soup using mangetout (snow) peas becomes an affordable treat.

Imperial (Metric)	American
1 lb (450g) mangetout peas	**1 pound snow peas**
5 fresh mint leaves	**5 fresh mint leaves**
1 teaspoon raw cane sugar	**1 teaspoon raw cane sugar**
4 oz (100g) butter	**½ cup butter**
4 oz (100g) spring onions *or* **shallots**	**4 ounces scallions** *or* **shallots**
4 oz (100g) leek, white part only, cleaned and sliced	**4 ounces leek, white part only, cleaned and sliced**
4 oz (100g) potatoes, peeled and sliced	**4 ounces potatoes, peeled and sliced**
Sea salt and freshly ground black pepper	**Sea salt and freshly ground black pepper**
1 tablespoon cornflour	**1 tablespoon cornstarch**
4 fl oz (120ml) sour cream	**½ cup sour cream**

1 Top and tail the peas. Wash and drain them, reserve 12 even-sized and unblemished pods and shred the rest coarsely.

2 Boil the whole pods in salted water for 4 minutes and refresh in cold water and drain. They should be a vivid green.

3 Blanch the rest of the peas in 2 pints (1.15 litres/5 cups) lightly salted water (this water will form the main liquid for the soup, so do not over-salt). Boil the peas for 4 minutes, strain and reserve the liquid.

4 Liquidize the peas with the mint and sugar and a little of the water. Combine the purée with half the liquid.

5 Heat the butter in a large pan and sauté the onion and leek for 4 minutes until transparent. Then add the sliced potatoes and cook for a further 3 minutes. Add the reserved water and cook for 15 minutes, or until the potatoes are tender.

6 Liquidize the potatoes and leeks and onions with their cooking liquid and blend this purée into the pea purée. Season to taste.

7 In a bowl, blend the cornflour (cornstarch) with the sour cream and gradually add 1 cup of soup. Pour this into the main soup and cook for 5 minutes. Serve with 2 whole pods floating on each bowl of soup.

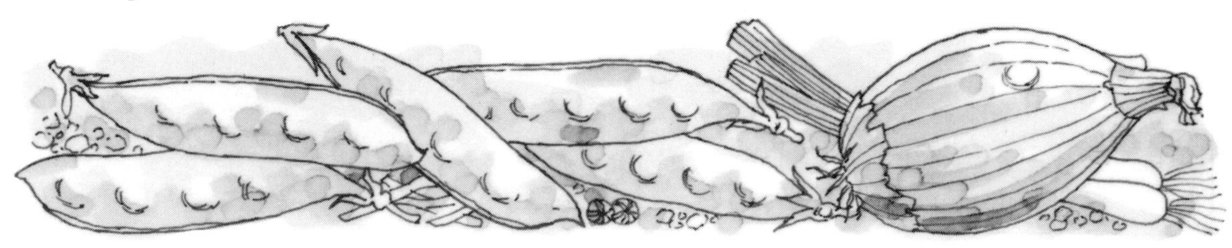

Potage aux Noix

Walnut Soup with Yogurt

Yogurt is made by adding a culture of special bacteria (*Cremolis Bulgaricus*) to boiled milk which is then kept warm for several hours. The bacteria multiply and convert the milk sugar (lactose) into lactic acid, which suppresses the growth of harmful bacteria as well as partly curdling the milk. This explains why yogurt developed, and is most used, in hot countries where fresh milk cannot be kept for any length of time. In France, as in most countries, yogurt is now being used in cooking more than ever before. Yogurt is as good for you as milk, and is less fattening as the sugar is converted to lactic acid.

Imperial (Metric)	American
4 fl oz (120ml) vegetable oil	**½ cup vegetable oil**
1 clove garlic, crushed	**1 clove garlic, crushed**
5 oz (150g) shelled walnuts, pounded to a paste	**1 cup English walnuts, pounded to a paste**
¾ pint (400ml) water	**2 cups water**
1 oz (25g) cornflour	**2 tablespoons cornstarch**
2 pints (1.15 litres) yogurt	**5 cups yogurt**
Sea salt and freshly ground black pepper	**Sea salt and freshly ground black pepper**
1 small cucumber, peeled and cut into small cubes	**1 small cucumber, peeled and cut into small cubes**
Chopped dill and parsley	**Chopped dill and parsley**

1. Heat the oil in a large pan and sauté the garlic and walnut paste for 4 minutes and then add two-thirds of the water and boil for 5 minutes.
2. Dilute the cornflour with the rest of the water, and add to the soup to thicken. Boil for 4 minutes until very thick. Remove from the heat and stir in the yogurt, whisking the mixture to obtain a smooth, creamy soup.
3. Chill the soup and season with salt and pepper to taste only when very cold. Serve sprinkled with chopped cucumber and herbs.

Variations:

This soup also makes a delicious sauce for vegetables such as leeks, asparagus or turnips.

Almonds may be substituted for the walnuts and are especially tasty if lightly toasted before use.

La Soupe au Potiron

Pumpkin Soup

Pumpkin is becoming increasingly popular around the world, but some people still do not know quite what to do with this attractive-looking vegetable. There are, of course, many uses for it, in soups, stews, and desserts such as the famous American Pumpkin Pie. Provençal dishes combine it with herbs and garlic, rice or pasta to make delicious and filling meals, and home brewers may be interested to know that an excellent cordial can be made from the pumpkin. In this soup, the pumpkin's bright orange flesh gives it an attractive appearance, particularly appealing to children, and the flavour will be appreciated by everyone, even gourmets. It was my favourite soup as a child, and this recipe of my grandmother Mathilda's is still the best I have found.

Imperial (Metric)	American
4 oz (100g) butter	**½ cup butter**
1 large onion, thinly sliced	**1 large onion, thinly sliced**
1 lb (450g) pumpkin flesh, thinly sliced	**1 pound pumpkin flesh, thinly sliced**
½ lb (225g) potatoes, thinly sliced	**8 ounces potatoes, thinly sliced**
2 pints (1.15 litres) water	**5 cups water**
8 fl oz (240ml) sour cream	**1 cup sour cream**
Sea salt and freshly ground black pepper	**Sea salt and freshly ground black pepper**
Pinch ground ginger	**Pinch ground ginger**
Fried wholemeal bread *or* crackers	**Fried wholewheat bread *or* crackers**

1. Heat the butter in a large pan and sauté the onion until transparent — about 4 minutes.
2. Add the pumpkin and potatoes and cook gently for a further 4 minutes.
3. Stir in the water and boil for 30 minutes, until the vegetables are soft. Pass the soup through a *mouli-légumes* or sieve.
4. Reheat, stir in the cream and season with salt, pepper and ginger. Serve with sippets of fried bread or crackers.

La Basquaise

Chilled Pepper, Cucumber, Tomato and Onion Soup

Serves 20
Illustrated opposite page 80.

It was during the reign of Louis XIV that cookery in France began to flourish. The previous period of Italian influence under the Medicis was replaced by that of Spain, since Louis' queen was a Spanish princess. The court employed Spanish chefs and thus were introduced to France many dishes and styles which have long since been absorbed into classic French cuisine, such as Mayonnaise and all kinds of tomato-based soups and sauces. This recipe has been in the family cookbook which we have treasured for centuries. It is rare soup in that it requires no cooking.

Imperial (Metric)	American
½ lb (225g) red peppers	**8 ounces red peppers**
½ lb (225g) green peppers	**8 ounces green peppers**
1 lb (450g) cucumber	**1 pound cucumber**
1 lb (450g) tomatoes	**1 pound tomatoes**
4 oz (100g) tomato purée	**½ cup tomato paste**
½ pint (300ml) olive oil	**1⅓ cups olive oil**
½ pint (300ml) wine vinegar	**1⅓ cups wine vinegar**
1 medium onion, chopped	**1 medium onion, chopped**
2 cloves garlic, crushed	**2 cloves garlic, crushed**
2 pints (1.15 litres) water	**5 cups water**
1 tablespoon sea salt	**1 tablespoon sea salt**
1 tablespoon raw cane sugar	**1 tablespoon raw cane sugar**
2 teaspoons paprika	**2 teaspoons paprika**
½ teaspoon freshly ground black pepper	**½ teaspoon freshly ground black pepper**
½ lb (225g) dry French bread	**8 ounces dry French bread**
2 oz (50g) stuffed olives	**½ cup stuffed olives**

For the garnish:	For the garnish:
1 red and 1 green pepper, seeded and neatly diced into tiny cubes	**1 red and 1 green pepper, seeded and neatly diced into tiny cubes**
½ cucumber, skinned and neatly diced into tiny cubes	**½ cucumber, skinned and neatly diced into tiny cubes**
4 oz (100g) wholemeal croûtons	**4 ounces wholewheat croûtons**

1 Seed and coarsely chop the peppers. Peel and slice the cucumber. Slice the tomatoes but do not skin or seed.
2 Place all the ingredients except those for the garnish into a very large container and leave to marinate overnight in the refrigerator. During this time the flavours will mingle and develop.
3 Next day, mince or blend the mixture to a coarse purée. Serve in individual bowls with a tray of the garnishes for your guests to help themselves.

Note: This soup freezes well, or will keep for weeks in the fridge, so it is well worth making in quantity in the Summer when vegetables are cheap and plentiful, and when this soup is most refreshing.

Le Potage des Paysans du Poitou

A Country Soup from Poitou

Serves 12-16

I was born in the Vendée, near the province of Poitou, raised in Boulogne and trained in Paris. My travels meant that I came to know many of the provincial soups of France at first hand, and I was able to observe the ways in which they varied and developed throughout France, changing character according to local produce and temperament, as well as observing their basic similarities. All peasant soups are similar in the simplicity of their preparation and ingredients. All are very substantial and are often eaten as a meal in themselves. My wife and I make a batch of this soup each week. It provides several tasty and nutritious meals — ideal for we members of the 'older generation'! I expect a family of energetic youngsters will get through the lot in one sitting.

Imperial (Metric)	American
1 onion	**1 onion**
2 carrots	**2 carrots**
2 turnips	**2 turnips**
1 leek	**1 leek**
2 sticks celery	**2 stalks celery**
4 oz (100g) potatoes	**4 ounces potatoes**
4 oz (100g) cabbage	**4 ounces cabbage**
4 oz (100g) green beans	**4 ounces green beans**
4 oz (100g) butter	**½ cup butter**
4 oz (100g) cooked haricot beans	**4 ounces cooked navy beans**
4 oz (100g) shelled peas	**⅔ cup shelled peas**
6 pints (3.5 litres) water	**15 cups water**
1 *bouquet garni* (see page 65)	**1 *bouquet garni* (see page 65)**
2 oz (50g) tomato purée	**¼ cup tomato paste**
1 oz (25g) yeast extract	**2 tablespoons yeast extract**
Sea salt and freshly ground black pepper	**Sea salt and freshly ground black pepper**
Wholemeal bread — 1 slice per serving	**Wholewheat bread — 1 slice per serving**
4 oz (100g) grated cheese	**1 cup grated cheese**
Chopped basil, parsley and chervil *or* coriander (about 4 tablespoons in total)	**Chopped basil, parsley and chervil *or* cilantro (about 4 tablespoons in total)**

1. Clean and peel and thinly slice the onion, carrots, turnips, leek, celery and potatoes all of an equal size. This, in culinary terms, is called *paysanne*.
2. Thinly shred the cabbage and slice the green beans into diamond shapes.
3. In a large pan (a proper stock pot if possible) melt the butter and sauté all the vegetables except the potatoes, haricot (navy) beans and peas.
4. After 5 minutes, add the water and the *bouquet garni* and the potatoes. Boil for 30 minutes and then add the cooked beans and the peas. Cook for 10 more minutes.
5. Add the tomato purée (paste), yeast extract and seasoning and boil for 8 more minutes, stirring well.
6. Place a small slice of bread into each soup bowl and fill the bowls with soup. Onto each sprinkle some cheese and a pinch of fresh herbs and serve immediately.

Variation:
You can make a most impressive dinner party dish of this simple country soup by baking it in individual tureens

with a pastry case over the top. To do this, cool your soup once cooked and then pour it into *ovenproof* soup bowls. Roll out a batch of puff pastry (see page 144) and cut circles to fit over the rim of each dish. Moisten the rim with water and press the pastry over the bowls to form a sealed lid. Trim any excess pastry. Then bake your bowls of soup at 400°F/200°C (Gas Mark 6) for about 20 minutes. The pastry will puff up and the soup will be reheated. Serve immediately, and your guests can gently break open the crust of their soups, and be greeted by a wonderful cloud of aroma which has been sealed in by the pastry lid.

La Soupe aux Choux d'Amiens

Cabbage Soup, Amiens-Style

Serves 8

My sister, Marie-Thérèse, lives with her family in the village of Thézy-Glimont, a few kilometres from Amiens. She grows her own cabbages, as well as most of her other vegetables. Their house is always full of hungry children, so the soup pot is very handy and this dish is one of the favourites. (She also makes a delicious vegetable stew, my version of which can be found on page 88.) Our grandmother used to say 'God bless the cabbage, for all good children come from it.' We innocent children used to believe every word!

The high sugar content of the cabbage encourages fermentation, so this soup should be eaten on the day it is made.

Imperial (Metric)	American
1 small green cabbage, about 1 lb (450g)	**1 small green cabbage, about 1 pound**
1 onion	**1 onion**
½ lb (225g) potatoes	**8 ounces potatoes**
½ lb (225g) carrots	**8 ounces carrots**
2 celery sticks	**2 celery stalks**
4 oz (100g) butter	**½ cup butter**
2 tablespoons yeast extract	**2 tablespoons yeast extract**
1 *bouquet garni* (see page 65)	**1 *bouquet garni* (see page 65)**
4 pints (2.3 litres) water	**10 cups water**
Sea salt and freshly ground black pepper	**Sea salt and freshly ground black pepper**

1. Wash, peel where necessary, rinse and drain the vegetables and cut into thin shreds.
2. Heat the butter in a large saucepan and sauté the vegetables for 8 minutes.
3. Add the yeast extract, *bouquet garni* and water and boil for 45 minutes. Season to taste, remove the *bouquet garni* and serve from a large tureen with crusty wholemeal bread for dunking.

Variations:

This soup can also be liquidized in a blender and served with a little cream stirred in for a more sophisticated starter.

The carrots could be replaced with turnips or swedes (rutabaga) for a change.

White cabbage could be used instead of green, if you prefer, but I find the green variety has a more agreeable texture and flavour for this particular dish.

La Soupe aux Aubergines et Saffran

Aubergine (Eggplant) Soup with Saffron

Serves 8

There was a time, not so long ago, when aubergines (eggplants) were a rare sight in the greengrocer's shop. Now, with the advent of the Common Market and the vast international food trade, as well as the movement of people from one country to another, they are becoming more and more well known. Some people may, of course, be in doubt as to how best to use them, but they are a wonderfully versatile vegetable, and I have included them in many recipes in this book because of this versatility. Here is another illustration of the use of the extraordinary aubergine (eggplant).

Imperial (Metric)	American
½ lb (225g) aubergines	**8 ounces eggplants**
Sea salt	**Sea salt**
4 fl oz (120ml) olive oil	**½ cup olive oil**
1 onion, sliced	**1 onion, sliced**
1 stick celery	**1 stalk celery**
4 oz (100g) potatoes, sliced	**4 ounces potatoes, sliced**
1 clove garlic, crushed	**1 clove garlic, crushed**
2 oz (50g) tomato purée	**4 tablespoons tomato paste**
3 pints (1.75 litres) water	**7½ cups water**
1 *bouquet garni* (see page 65)	**1 *bouquet garni* (see page 65)**
Freshly ground black pepper	**Freshly ground black pepper**
Pinch saffron powder	**Pinch saffron powder**
4 oz (100g) cooked brown rice	**1 cup cooked brown rice**

1. Wash the aubergines and cut into thick slices. Sprinkle with salt and allow to exude their bitter juices for 30 minutes. Wash and drain again. Clean, wash and slice the other vegetables thinly.
2. Heat the oil in a large pan and sauté the garlic and the vegetables until soft, about 8 minutes.
3. Add the tomato purée (paste) and water with the *bouquet garni* and boil for 35 minutes.
4. Remove the *bouquet garni* and put the rest of the ingredients into a blender with a little of the cooking liquid. Blend to a purée.
5. Combine all the ingredients together in the pan and reheat. Season to taste with black pepper and more sea salt and serve with a garnish of rice — about 2 tablespoons per portion.

Variations:
This soup could be made hot with the addition of a finely chopped chilli pepper, or milder by the addition of ¼ pint (150ml/⅔ cup) cream. A good pinch of curry powder will give an 'Oriental' flavour. Marrow (squash), courgettes (zucchini) or red peppers could be used to enrich this soup.

La Soupe au Fromage

Soup with Cheese

Serves 8

Cheese is important in the diet of most vegetarians. Most cheeses are excellent sources of protein, minerals and vitamins. Calcium, for example, is abundant — about 2 ounces (50g) of Cheddar or Parmesan will supply the recommended daily intake of calcium for an adult. Cheese is, however, high in fat, which means it is high in calories, and that fat is saturated which means high cholesterol. A light soup such as this, of course, can counterbalance this excess and the result is a delicious, satisfying and wholesome dish.

Imperial (Metric)	American
4 oz (100g) butter	**½ cup butter**
1 onion, sliced	**1 onion, sliced**
2 carrots, peeled and sliced	**2 carrots, peeled and sliced**
½ lb (225g) potatoes, peeled and sliced	**8 ounces potatoes, peeled and sliced**
2 pints (1.15 litres) water	**5 cups water**
1 pint (600ml) milk	**2½ cups milk**
Sea salt	**Sea salt**
Freshly ground black pepper	**Freshly ground black pepper**
Freshly ground nutmeg	**Freshly ground nutmeg**
4 slices wholemeal bread	**4 slices wholewheat bread**
4 slices Cheddar or Gruyère cheese	**4 slices Cheddar or Gruyère cheese**

1. Heat the butter in a large pan and sauté the vegetables for 6 minutes without browning. Add the water and boil for 20 minutes.
2. Place the vegetables in a blender with a little of the liquid and purée. Stir back into the rest of the cooking liquid to form a thin purée.
3. Reheat with the milk and season to taste with salt, pepper and nutmeg.
4. Toast the bread and put a slice of cheese onto each one. Toast again to melt the cheese. Place a slice of bread in each bowl and pour the soup over it, allowing the bread to absorb a little of the soup as it is served.

Note: The character of this soup is modified according to the cheese used. The best English cheese other than Cheddar is Double Gloucester, the best French are Cantal and Port Salut. Dutch Gouda and Edam have the necessary melting qualities, and Edam is low in fat, too.

Le Bouillon de Légumes

Vegetable Soup and Vegetable Purée

Serves 20

This dish is just what its English name says — with a little simple preparation you will have a flavoursome clear vegetable broth which can be eaten as a soup in its own right but which will also be invaluable to you in those recipes which call for vegetable stock (since it is far superior to even the best vegetable stock cube), *and* a delicious savoury purée which can be served as a side dish, used to stuff vegetables, or thinned with cream, milk or stock to make a warming thick vegetable soup.

Imperial (Metric)	American
4 oz (100g) chopped onions	**2/3 cup chopped onions**
4 oz (100g) carrots, peeled and sliced	**4 ounces carrots, peeled and sliced**
4 oz (100g) cabbage, shredded	**4 ounces cabbage, shredded**
4 oz (100g) celery, chopped	**2/3 cup chopped celery**
4 oz (100g) turnips *or* swedes, sliced	**4 ounces turnips *or* rutabaga, sliced**
4 oz (100g) parsnips, sliced	**4 ounces parsnips, sliced**
4 oz (100g) green peas, shelled	**2/3 cup shelled green peas**
4 oz (100g) green beans	**4 ounces green beans**
4 oz (100g) leeks, sliced	**4 ounces leeks, sliced**
4 oz (100g) peeled beetroot	**4 ounces peeled beet**
4 fl oz (120ml) vegetable oil	**1/2 cup vegetable oil**
4 oz (100g) toasted peanuts, crushed	**2/3 cup toasted peanuts, crushed**
8 pints (4.6 litres) water	**20 cups water**
4 teaspoons yeast extract (optional)	**4 teaspoons yeast extract (optional)**
1 good pinch each thyme and turmeric	**1 good pinch each thyme and turmeric**
1 teaspoon celery seeds	**1 teaspoon celery seeds**
Sea salt and freshly ground black pepper	**Sea salt and freshly ground black pepper**
1 level teaspoon raw cane sugar	**1 level teaspoon raw cane sugar**

1. Rinse all the prepared vegetables and allow to drain thoroughly.
2. Heat the oil in a large saucepan and sauté the onions and nuts for 4 minutes, then add the rest of the vegetables.
3. Add the water, yeast extract, herbs and spices. Boil gently for 35 to 40 minutes.
4. Strain the stock off of the vegetables and season.
5. Purée the vegetables and season to taste.

Note: The stock and the purée can be used as suggested above. If serving the stock as a soup on its own, add some cooked wholemeal vermicelli or cooked brown rice to each portion before serving. Some of the vegetables could be retained whole to serve in the broth, too. Both broth and purée can be frozen for use another time.

La Crème d'Asperge aux Oeufs de Cailles

Asparagus Soup with Quails' Eggs

The asparagus spear has been held in the highest esteem by gourmets since ancient Greek and Roman times. It is raised from seed and grows best in very rich soil. The best French varieties are Lauris and Argenteuil, but there are many different varieties, and variations in colour and size. In Britain, asparagus is usually of the green variety, while we French prefer the white shoots. The thinnest spears are known as 'grass'. Soups are usually made from the stalks of the plant, the tips being used for decoration or served on their own with Hollandaise Sauce or melted butter.

Imperial (Metric)	American
1 lb (450g) green asparagus	**1 pound green asparagus**
2 oz (50g) butter	**¼ cup butter**
1 small onion, sliced	**1 small onion, sliced**
1 stick celery, chopped	**1 stalk celery, chopped**
2 pints (1.15 litres) water	**5 cups water**
3 egg yolks	**3 egg yolks**
8 fl oz (240ml) single *or* **sour cream**	**1 cup light** *or* **sour cream**
1 oz (25g) cornflour	**2 tablespoons cornstarch**
Sea salt and freshly ground black pepper	**Sea salt and freshly ground black pepper**
Freshly grated nutmeg	**Freshly grated nutmeg**
12 fresh quails' eggs	**12 fresh quails' eggs**
Juice and rind of 1 lemon (optional)	**Juice and rind of 1 lemon (optional)**

1. Scrape the stems of the asparagus gently with a potato peeler, taking care not to damage the tips. Reserve 12 tips for garnish. Cut the rest of the asparagus into small pieces.
2. Heat the butter and sauté the onion, celery and the chopped asparagus spears for 4 minutes. Add the water and bring to the boil. Boil for 15 minutes.
3. Strain the liquor and put the onion and asparagus into a blender with a little of the liquid. Blend to a purée. Transfer the purée back into the pan with the reserved liquor and reheat for 5 minutes. Season to taste.
4. In a bowl blend the egg yolks, cream and cornflour (cornstarch) to a smooth mixture. Add to this 1 cup of the soup, stir well and then return this mixture to the pan of soup. Reheat to boiling point and adjust seasoning.
5. Boil the asparagus tips for 6 minutes in lightly salted water. Drain.
6. Boil the quails' eggs for 6 minutes and then shell them.
7. Just before serving, stir the lemon juice and rind into the soup, if extra piquancy is desired. Serve the soup in individual bowls with 2 asparagus spears floating in each bowl, and with 2 quails' eggs either served separately by each bowl, or in the soup also.

Note: The quails' eggs may be poached instead, and served in the soup.

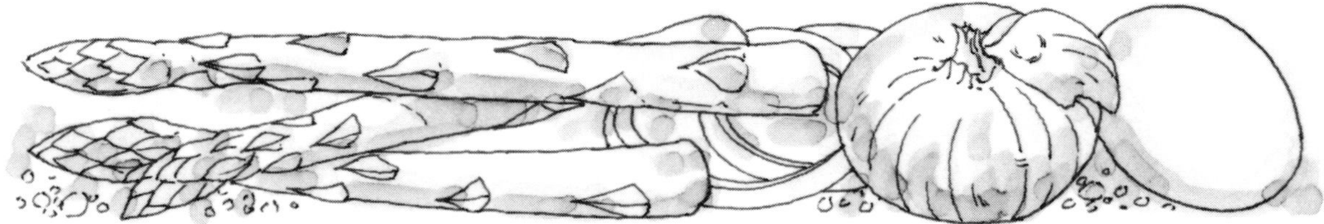

La Bouillabaisse de Légumes Riviera

Riviera Soup with Garlic, Saffron and Basil

Serves 12

Although a fish-eater will tell you that a bouillabaisse without fish is a contradiction in terms, Bouillabaisse Borgne — literally, 'one-eyed Bouillabaisse' — is a traditional French vegetable soup, made along the same lines as the better-known version. After all, the rich combination of herbs, garlic and vegetables which plays such an important part in a standard bouillabaisse is more than worthy of being savoured alone. I have tried many variations to find just the right balance of ingredients to convey the evocative flavours and aromas of southern France, and my attempts have resulted in a soup which is always in demand by my customers at the Arts Club since I began to feature it on the menu at special functions. I have been asked for the recipe many times and this seems the ideal opportunity to present it.

Imperial (Metric)	American
4 oz (100g) onions, slivered	**4 ounces onions, slivered**
4 oz (100g) leek, white part only, sliced	**4 ounces leek, white part only, sliced**
1 lb (450g) tomatoes, skinned, seeded and chopped	**1 pound tomatoes, skinned, seeded and chopped**
1 lb (450g) potatoes, diced	**1 pound potatoes, diced**
4 cloves garlic, chopped	**4 cloves garlic, chopped**
4 fl oz (120ml) olive oil	**½ cup olive oil**
2 oz (50g) tomato purée	**4 tablespoons tomato paste**
Pinch each of thyme, celery seeds and saffron powder	**Pinch each of thyme, celery seeds and saffron powder**
1 bay leaf	**1 bay leaf**
1 teaspoon freshly chopped basil	**1 teaspoon freshly chopped basil**
Juice and finely grated rind of 1 orange	**Juice and finely grated rind of 1 orange**
3 pints (1.75 litres) water	**7½ cups water**
2 tablespoons yeast extract	**2 tablespoons yeast extract**
Sea salt and freshly ground black pepper	**Sea salt and freshly ground black pepper**
For the liaison:	For the liaison:
3 egg yolks	**3 egg yolks**
1 clove garlic, crushed	**1 clove garlic, crushed**
2 tablespoons olive oil	**2 tablespoons olive oil**
1½ oz (40g) cornflour	**3 tablespoons cornstarch**
4 fl oz (120ml) water	**½ cup water**
1 teaspoon turmeric	**1 teaspoon turmeric**
Pinch chilli powder (optional)	**Pinch chili powder (optional)**
For the garnish:	For the garnish:
4 slices toasted wholemeal French bread, rubbed with a cut clove of garlic	**4 slices toasted wholewheat French bread, rubbed with a cut clove of garlic**
2 tablespoons chopped fresh parsley	**2 tablespoons chopped fresh parsley**

1 Sauté all the vegetables in the oil in a large pan until soft, about 8 minutes.

2 Add the tomato purée (paste), the herbs and spices and the orange rind and juice. Stir in the water and the yeast extract and cook for 30 minutes.

3 Strain the soup and remove the bay leaf. Purée the vegetables in a blender with a little of the stock, then return the purée and the liquid to the pan and reheat.
4 In a bowl, combine all the ingredients for the liaison. Add this mixture very slowly to the soup, stirring all the time, and boil for 5 more minutes.
5 Cut the garlic bread into small pieces or sippets. Serve the soup in individual bowls with a sprinkling of bread and parsley on each one.

La Soupe à l'Oignon Ducastaing

Onion Soup with Madeira Wine

Serves 12

In 1932 my father, Octave, bought a fashionable brasserie-restaurant in Paris. This is how I had the opportunity to train as a chef, not only in our own restaurant but in many others whose owners were friends of our family. Escoffier himself was one of those who patronized our restaurant. One of the great features of the Ducastaing, as it was called, was our onion soup. This was always cooked to order — never in advance. My father used to say that onion soup was ideal for hangovers. At the Ducastaing most of our patrons gave themselves frequent opportunities to try this out!

Imperial (Metric)	American
4 oz (100g) butter *or* oil	**½ cup butter *or* oil**
1 lb (450g) onions, thinly sliced	**1 pound onions, thinly sliced**
2 oz (50g) wholemeal flour	**½ cup wholewheat flour**
4 fl oz (120ml) dry Madeira	**½ cup dry Madeira**
4 pints (2.3 litres) water *or* vegetable stock	**10 cups water *or* vegetable stock**
4 oz (100g) grated Gruyère cheese	**1 cup grated Gruyère cheese**
1 tablespoon sea salt	**1 tablespoon sea salt**
Freshly ground black pepper	**Freshly ground black pepper**
Large pinch dried thyme	**Large pinch dried thyme**
Large pinch ground mace	**Large pinch ground mace**
1 tablespoon yeast extract	**1 tablespoon yeast extract**
For the garnish:	For the garnish:
4 oz (100g) grated Gruyère cheese	**1 cup grated Gruyère cheese**
1 egg yolk	**1 egg yolk**
1 oz (25g) butter	**2½ tablespoons butter**
12 slices toasted French bread, wholemeal	**12 slices toasted French bread, wholewheat**

1 Heat the butter in a large saucepan and sauté the onions until translucent (about 6 minutes) and then allow them to turn slightly golden.
2 Sprinkle on the flour and stir in well, and then add the Madeira and the water. Boil for 20 minutes. Then add the grated cheese, seasonings, herbs and yeast extract.
3 Simmer for a further 5 minutes, and during this time prepare the garnish. Blend the cheese, egg yolk and butter to a paste. Spread a little of the paste on each slice of toast and brown under the grill.
4 Serve the soup in individual tureens with one slice of cheesy toast per bowl, floating on the soup.

Note: If you have no Madeira, dry or medium sherry or white port will do, or even a dry white wine.

La Citronelle

Lemony Vegetable Soup with Cream

Serves 12-16

The richest lemon flavour is in the oil which is obtained from the skin — hence the need to use finely grated lemon rind in many dishes to obtain a true lemon flavour. There is a herb with a subtle lemony flavour which is very pleasant. In France we call it citronelle (*Andropogon schoenanthus*) and we use it frequently in dishes. It is not widely available in some areas but can easily be grown and is worth it for the delicacy of flavour which it imparts to a dish. Use it in a salad and you will be delighted with the piquant flavour it brings to the meal. It is also very fragrant — which is why it is often used in soap-making to impart a lemon scent. This soup uses lemon and citronelle — though the latter can be replaced by the more common lemon mint, or even ordinary mint, if necessary. It is a light and refreshing soup which is just as good served hot or cold.

Imperial (Metric)	American
4 fl oz (120ml) vegetable oil	**½ cup vegetable oil**
4 oz (100g) chopped onion	**⅔ cup chopped onion**
4 oz (100g) diced potatoes	**⅔ cup diced potatoes**
4 oz (100g) chopped leeks	**⅔ cup chopped leeks**
4 oz (100g) chopped celery	**⅔ cup chopped celery**
4 oz (100g) chopped fennel	**⅔ cup chopped fennel**
4 oz (100g) diced turnips	**⅔ cup diced turnips**
4 oz (100g) shelled green peas	**⅔ cup shelled green peas**
4 oz (100g) diced swede	**⅔ cup diced rutabaga**
4 oz (100g) chopped spinach	**⅔ cup chopped spinach**
5 pints (3 litres) water	**12½ cups water**
Sea salt and freshly ground black pepper	**Sea salt and freshly ground black pepper**
1 teaspoon raw cane sugar	**1 teaspoon raw cane sugar**
1 teaspoon turmeric	**1 teaspoon turmeric**
4 leaves citronelle *or* **fresh mint, chopped**	**4 leaves citronelle** *or* **fresh mint, chopped**
Grated rind and juice of 1 lemon	**Grated rind and juice of 1 lemon**
4 egg yolks	**4 egg yolks**
4 fl oz (120ml) single cream	**½ cup light cream**
1 oz (25g) cornflour	**2 tablespoons cornstarch**
4 fl oz (120ml) water	**½ cup water**

1. Heat the oil in a large pan. Sauté the vegetables for 8 minutes, covered with a lid. Then add the water and boil for 30 minutes.
2. Place the vegetables in a blender with a little of the liquid, and blend to a thin purée, adding more liquid if necessary.
3. Reheat the soup, adding seasoning, sugar, turmeric and herbs, and the grated lemon rind.
4. Blend the egg yolks, cream, cornflour (cornstarch) and water in a bowl with a little of the soup. Pour this mixture into the soup pan. Boil for 4 minutes to thicken and, lastly, stir in the lemon juice.
5. If served hot the soup could be garnished with 2 tablespoons cooked brown rice per portion; if served cold, stir ½ pint (300ml/1⅓ cups) double (heavy) cream into the pan and chill before serving.

Velouté aux Champignons

Mushroom Soup with Eggs and Cream

Serves 12

The problem when cooking mushrooms for soups and sauces is to keep them white. Cultured button mushrooms can be used, but they tend to be flavourless, and even then to retain their whiteness they must be blanched in lemon juice. Field mushrooms give the soup or sauce a wonderful flavour, but turn black when cooked and discolour the dish. Nevertheless, you may find it worth the poorer colour to get a richer-flavoured soup — it is certainly worth a try this way. For this soup I have used white mushrooms, since this is an elegant dish whose appearance might be important to you, and also to show that their flavour can be enhanced by the addition of other vegetables and herbs without being swamped.

Imperial (Metric)	American
1 lb (450g) mushrooms, cultivated variety	**1 pound mushrooms, cultivated variety**
1 medium onion, chopped	**1 medium onion, chopped**
1 small leek, cleaned and sliced	**1 small leek, cleaned and sliced**
3 celery sticks, sliced	**3 celery stalks, sliced**
4 oz (100g) potatoes, peeled and sliced	**4 ounces potatoes, peeled and sliced**
2 oz (50g) butter	**¼ cup butter**
2 fl oz (60ml) vegetable oil	**¼ cup vegetable oil**
2 pints (1.15 litres) water	**5 cups water**
2 pints (1.15 litres) milk	**5 cups milk**
2 egg yolks	**2 egg yolks**
4 fl oz (120ml) double cream	**½ cup heavy cream**
1 oz (25g) cornflour	**2 tablespoons cornstarch**
Sea salt and freshly ground black pepper	**Sea salt and freshly ground black pepper**
Pinch ground mace	**Pinch ground mace**
Pinch ground turmeric	**Pinch ground turmeric**
Pinch celery seeds	**Pinch celery seeds**
1 clove garlic, crushed	**1 clove garlic, crushed**
Juice and finely grated rind of 1 lemon	**Juice and finely grated rind of 1 lemon**

1. Trim the ends off the mushroom stalks and wash and dry the mushrooms carefully. Rinse and dry well all the other vegetables.
2. Heat the butter and oil together in a large pan and sauté all the vegetables for 8 minutes, covered with a lid but stirring now and then. Add the water and boil for 25 minutes.
3. Strain the stock and return to the pan. Liquidize the vegetables in a blender with a little of the stock and then return to the pan. Add the milk.
4. Mix together the egg yolks, cream and cornflour in a bowl and then add to the soup. Reheat and allow to boil for 5 minutes. Season to taste and add the spices and garlic. Lastly add the lemon juice and rind and serve.

Le Potage d'Ésaü

Lentil Soup with Red Wine

Serves 10

Lentils by themselves are rather bland and must be supplemented in flavour by other vegetables, tomato purée, herbs or perhaps a little yogurt. Red lentils are in fact green or brown continental lentils which have been split and stripped of their outer coating. They take only 30 minutes to cook and become mushier when cooked than their whole counterparts. They are ideal for soup-making and other dishes which do not require the firmness and separate grains of whole lentils. Most French lentil soups involve boiling the lentils with some type of bacon offcut. My soup uses spices and red wine to create a delicious full flavour which everyone can enjoy.

Imperial (Metric)	American
½ lb (225g) red lentils	**1 cup red lentils**
3 fl oz (90ml) vegetable oil	**⅓ cup vegetable oil**
1 large onion, chopped	**1 large onion, chopped**
2 carrots, peeled and sliced	**2 carrots, peeled and sliced**
1 clove garlic, crushed	**1 clove garlic, crushed**
A large pinch of each of the following: cumin, coriander, turmeric, paprika, thyme, basil and celery seed	**A large pinch of each of the following: cumin, coriander, turmeric, paprika, thyme, basil and celery seed**
Sea salt to taste	**Sea salt to taste**
2 oz (50g) tomato purée	**4 tablespoons tomato paste**
4 fl oz (120ml) red wine	**½ cup red wine**
3 pints (1.75 litres) water	**7½ cups water**
3 large field mushrooms, cleaned and chopped	**3 large field mushrooms, cleaned and chopped**
1 teaspoon yeast extract	**1 teaspoon yeast extract**
1 teaspoon raw cane sugar	**1 teaspoon raw cane sugar**

1. Soak the lentils for 1 hour in plenty of water. Drain and rinse.
2. Heat the oil and sauté the onion, carrot and garlic for 5 minutes without browning. Sprinkle the spices into the pan and cook gently for a few seconds to develop their flavour.
3. Stir in the tomato purée (paste) and the red wine. Boil for 4 minutes and then add the water, lentils, mushrooms and yeast extract. Boil for 40 minutes.
4. Liquidize the soup to a thin purée, check the seasoning and adjust the acidity if necessary with a little sugar. Serve with *croûtons* of fried wholemeal bread.

Variation:
To give the soup an 'Eastern' flavour, stir in a pinch of saffron or curry powder and 5 tablespoons yogurt before serving.

Opposite: *Le Dragon Rouge* (page 65) and *La Basquaise* (page 69).

COUS
UPA
NA CEREAL
MOYEN

Le Potage Breton

Brittany Bean Soup

Serves 8-10

Baked beans on toast seem to have achieved universal popularity with children, but it is a rare child who has even heard of bean soup — let alone tasted or enjoyed one. Yet a delicious teatime soup for children can be made simply liquidizing a tin of baked beans and thinning it with a little milk. The idea of puréeing beans is common in French cooking — I have already given one such recipe, beans blended with spices, as a dip in Chapter One (page 15). The familiar dish of beans baked in a rich tomato sauce originated in Brittany, but it was the Americans who exploited this colonist's dish to best advantage with the advent of an efficient canning process. So what has made this simple meal so popular? The fact that it is convenient. Cooking beans is a long and tiresome process for many people, especially if they live in a hard water area such as London, where I live. The soaking process, followed by a long, slow cooking is replaced in an instant by the tin opener! However, as a casserole or, as in this recipe, as a soup, true baked beans are deliciously different from their canned copies and are well worth the time. After all, little effort is needed in the preparation and cooking of them — you just need to plan ahead a bit.

Imperial (Metric)	American
½ lb (225g) haricot beans	**1 cup navy beans**
3 fl oz (90ml) vegetable oil	**⅓ cup vegetable oil**
1 large onion, chopped	**1 large onion, chopped**
2 carrots, peeled and sliced	**2 carrots, peeled and sliced**
4 oz (100g) cabbage, chopped	**4 ounces cabbage, chopped**
2 sticks celery, sliced	**2 stalks celery, sliced**
2 cloves garlic, crushed	**2 cloves garlic, crushed**
2 oz (50g) tomato purée	**4 tablespoons tomato paste**
1 *bouquet garni* (see page 65)	**1 *bouquet garni* (see page 65)**
2 pints (1.15 litres) water	**5 cups water**
Sea salt and freshly ground black pepper	**Sea salt and freshly ground black pepper**
1 tablespoon yeast extract	**1 tablespoon yeast extract**
Pinch freshly chopped oregano *or* mint	**Pinch freshly chopped oregano *or* mint**

1 Soak the beans, preferably in distilled water. Do not use bicarbonate of soda, as is sometimes recommended, as it destroys vitamin B.

2 Heat the oil in a large pan and stir-fry the vegetables and garlic for 5 minutes until just golden-brown. Add the tomato purée (paste), *bouquet garni* and water. Add the beans and boil all together for 10 minutes.

3 Transfer the mixture to a casserole with a tight-fitting lid. Bake in the oven at 350°F/180°C (Gas Mark 4) for 2 hours.

4 Remove from the oven and blend the mixture, in a liquidizer, to a thick purée. Season to taste and stir in the yeast extract and herbs, and serve. The soup can be thinned with a little milk or water if desired, and reheated when needed.

Variations:

You can vary the soup by using different types of beans — butter (Lima) beans, flageolet or red kidney beans in particular could be used. To save time, canned beans could be used, this saves the soaking time, and also much of the cooking time. Simply cook the vegetables and liquid on top of the stove and stir in the beans towards the end of cooking, and then purée.

Opposite: *Le Couscous aux Raisins et Amandes* (page 85).

5 *Les Plats du Jour Légumiers*

Main Dishes

People who take cooking seriously, and especially vegetarians, should spend more time searching out, and trying out, unusual vegetables. The healthfood and wholefood shops, which have blossomed all over Europe, have taken on and fulfilled the task of providing their customers with an enormous variety of pulses, grains and other sources of protein and vitamins, as well as spices and herbs which, until recently, could not be found in ordinary supermarkets. Now, with modern, speedy transportation, vegetables which were previously unknown have found their way into greengrocers and markets, and a whole world of flavour is available to us all the year round.

No longer can sceptics paint a picture of a healthy diet with masochism and abstinence standing well to the fore, and no longer need nutritionists prepare diet sheets in which the 'don'ts' outnumber the 'dos' by ten to one. It is now so obvious that, with common sense and imagination, you need not miss out on a single pleasure of eating just because you choose not to eat meat. The permutations of vegetable flavours far outweigh the handful of animal ones. Why, from eleven basic ingredients, a combination or selection can result in 124 different-tasting tomato soups!

Some chefs of the 'old school' have tended to treat the changes in attitudes to cooking and eating with contempt, associating them with the old-fashioned view of the dietitian as a medical witch, or a scientist who should keep out of the kitchen. Thank God, we have a new generation of well-educated chefs who are trained not only in the art of cooking but also in the equally important fields of biology and nutrition. They, and their customers, have welcomed and encouraged the new style of cooking with excitement and enthusiasm, and the rigidly old-fashioned chefs have, I feel, lost out on something, even when they try to win back favour by attempting a *nouvelle* dish or two.

In this chapter I have included a wide range of dishes guaranteed to bring flavour and variety to your table. The variations are endless, and I hope you will learn to adapt a dish to suit your own tastes once you have tried and mastered it. I have made a point of including dishes in which the cooking of another country has influenced French cuisine over the years, whether because they are neighbours of ours, or because they once were colonies, or because their peoples have settled in France for some reason. North Africa and the Middle East have given us cracked wheat and couscous, both tastier than rice and more nourishing; Italy has brought us its pasta and cornmeal porridge, not to mention its pizza — transformed by the natives of southern France to their own *pissaladière*; Russia has contributed a dish to our classic cuisine, the Coulibiac, from which I have developed my own very special version, which I have

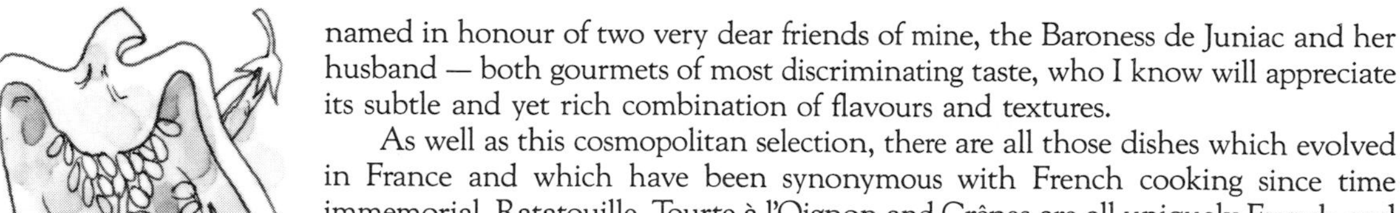

named in honour of two very dear friends of mine, the Baroness de Juniac and her husband — both gourmets of most discriminating taste, who I know will appreciate its subtle and yet rich combination of flavours and textures.

As well as this cosmopolitan selection, there are all those dishes which evolved in France and which have been synonymous with French cooking since time immemorial. Ratatouille, Tourte à l'Oignon and Crêpes are all uniquely French and are full of evocative flavours and aromas, whether you spent your youth amongst them, as I did, or have just visited and sampled these dishes, or even if you have never actually been to France at all — one mouthful will transport you to Brittany, the Riviera, Burgundy . . . wherever your palate and imagination choose.

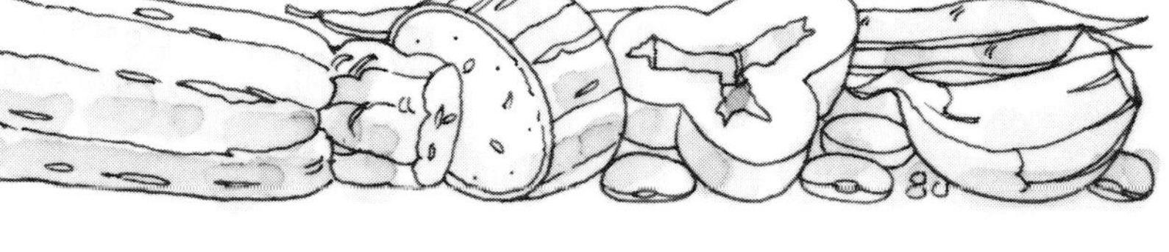

La Tourte à l'Oignon

Onion Tart

The warmer the climate, the sweeter the onion. This is why Spanish onions are still imported into France, despite the protests of our farmers. From a chef's point of view they certainly are the best, but Brittany onions are very good, too. Bretons often eat them as we would an apple — raw, with just a hunk of bread to accompany them. The health-giving antiseptic properties of the onion are well-known, so perhaps this will 'keep the doctor away' — but the effect on the breath might keep everyone else away, too!

Onions are used to enhance almost every savoury dish, it seems, and as a vegetable in their own right, and as a main course too, when stuffed with a suitable filling, or used to fill a quiche, as in this recipe.

Imperial (Metric)	American
1 quantity pastry (page 44)	**1 quantity pastry (page 44)**
4 oz (100g) mixed butter and oil	**½ cup mixed butter and oil**
½ lb (225g) onions, sliced	**8 ounces onions, sliced**
4 oz (100g) grated Gruyère cheese	**1 cupful grated Gruyère cheese**
3 eggs, beaten	**3 eggs, beaten**
4 fl oz (120ml) double cream	**½ cup heavy cream**
Sea salt	**Sea salt**
Freshly ground black pepper	**Freshly ground black pepper**
Freshly grated nutmeg	**Freshly grated nutmeg**
6 black olives, stoned	**6 black olives, stoned**

1. Roll out the pastry, after it has rested, to ¼-inch (5mm) thick, and use it to line a well-greased 8-inch (20cm) flan tin. The pastry will come slightly above the rim of the tin — crimp this edge into a fluted pattern with your thumb and forefinger.
2. Heat the butter and oil in a pan and gently sauté the onions for 8 minutes without browning. Remove from the heat.
3. Mix together in a bowl the grated cheese, eggs, cream, salt, pepper and nutmeg.
4. Off the heat, stir this mixture into the onions. Pour the onions and cream into the pastry case and bake for 30 minutes at 400°F/200°C (Gas Mark 6).
5. Decorate the flan with the olives and serve hot or cold.

Couronne de Maïs à la Française

Cornmeal 'Crown' Filled with Mixed Vegetables

Serves 4
Illustrated opposite page 96.

Time and time again throughout this book you will find that I use the term 'stir-fry' in the cooking of fresh vegetables. This is a technique which has entered modern French cookery from Oriental cuisine, in which vegetables are cooked quickly in a little oil, just to the point where they are no longer raw but still retain their crispy texture, all their flavour and all their vitamins. It is a quick and easy technique to perfect — the important thing is to keep stirring to ensure that the vegetables are cooked evenly, and to slice vegetables evenly and finely and put them in the pan in order according to the length of time they normally take to cook. (For example, you would put carrots in before mushrooms.)

Corn has an affinity with peppers just as mint has with peas. In this dish, red and green peppers are amongst the vegetables used, and I have incorporated both cornmeal and corn kernels into the dish — the former in the 'crown' and the latter in the mixed vegetable filling.

Imperial (Metric)	American
1 pint (600ml) mixed milk and water	**2½ cups mixed milk and water**
4 oz (100g) cornmeal	**¾ cup cornmeal**
4 oz (100g) butter	**½ cup butter**
Sea salt and freshly ground black pepper	**Sea salt and freshly ground black pepper**
Pinch ground mace	**Pinch ground mace**
1 clove garlic, crushed	**1 clove garlic, crushed**
2 eggs, beaten	**2 eggs, beaten**
3 fl oz (90ml) vegetable oil	**⅓ cup vegetable oil**
1 onion, sliced into strips	**1 onion, sliced into strips**
1 green pepper, seeded and cut into strips	**1 green pepper, seeded and cut into strips**
1 red pepper, seeded and cut into strips	**1 red pepper, seeded and cut into strips**
4 oz (100g) white mushrooms, sliced	**2 cups white mushrooms, sliced**
3 oz (75g) cooked green peas	**½ cup cooked green peas**
1 fresh chilli, sliced thinly	**1 fresh chili, sliced thinly**
3 oz (75g) cooked sweetcorn kernels	**½ cup cooked sweetcorn kernels**
3 oz (75g) baked beans in tomato sauce	**½ cup baked beans in tomato sauce**
1 teaspoon freshly chopped rosemary, marjoram *or* parsley	**1 teaspoon freshly chopped rosemary, marjoram *or* parsley**

1. Boil the milk and water. Rub 1 ounce (2 tablespoons) butter into the cornmeal, then add to the boiled milk and water. Stir well. Simmer for 7 to 8 minutes until thick and tender, like porridge. Season to taste with salt, pepper and mace, and add the garlic.
2. Remove from the heat and add the beaten egg and half the remaining butter.
3. With the rest of the butter, liberally grease a ring mould, preferably crown-shaped, and pour the mixture in. Smooth the top of the mixture and leave to set for a few minutes.
4. When the cornmeal seems firm enough, turn it out onto a flat dish and place in the oven at 350°F/180°C (Gas Mark 4) for 10 minutes to keep warm while you prepare the vegetables.
5. Heat the oil in a sauté pan and stir-fry the onion and peppers for 4 minutes. Add the mushrooms and cook for a further 2 minutes.

6 Lastly, blend in the peas, chilli, sweetcorn and beans and allow all the vegetables to heat together for 4 minutes. Taste and season if necessary.
7 Remove the cornmeal crown from the oven, fill the centre and decorate the edges with the vegetable mixture. Sprinkle with the herbs just before serving.

Le Couscous aux Raisins et Amandes

Couscous with Raisins and Almonds

Serves 4
Illustrated opposite page 81.

Some years ago I spent a holiday in Albi, where my uncle was Bishop at the time. There I was introduced by his housekeeper to the traditional Moroccan dish of Couscous. By then the French occupation was experiencing great difficulties and it is the opinion of some people that couscous is about the best thing France ever got from her North African colonies!

The semolina which is used in couscous is made from durum wheat, the same hard type of wheat from which pasta is made. It is higher in protein and altogether far more nourishing than rice and can be used in its stead for puddings, pilaffs and as a thickening in soups and stews.

Imperial (Metric)	American
2 fl oz (60ml) olive oil	**¼ cup olive oil**
1 small onion, chopped	**1 small onion, chopped**
4 oz (100g) shelled green peas	**⅔ cup shelled green peas**
1 red pepper, seeded and chopped	**1 red pepper, seeded and chopped**
Sea salt and freshly ground black pepper	**Sea salt and freshly ground black pepper**
Large pinch ground cumin	**Large pinch ground cumin**
½ lb (225g) couscous semolina	**2 cups couscous semolina**
2 oz (50g) mixed oil and butter	**5 tablespoons mixed oil and butter**
½ pint (300ml) water	**1⅓ cups water**
Sea salt	**Sea salt**
2 oz (50g) seedless raisins, soaked in ¼ pint (150ml) hot water	**⅓ cup seedless raisins, soaked in ⅔ cup hot water**
2 oz (50g) flaked almonds, lightly toasted	**½ cup slivered almonds, lightly toasted**

1 Heat the olive oil in a pan and sauté the onion for 5 minutes without colouring. Stir in the peas, pepper and seasoning. Cook for 3 minutes and then set this mixture aside while the couscous is prepared.
2 Rub the semolina, by hand, with the oil and butter to coat all the grains.
3 In a large pan, bring the water to the boil, add salt and the semolina. Simmer for 8 minutes, stirring constantly with a fork to separate the grains.
4 Stir the onion mixture into the couscous and pile into an earthenware dish. Sprinkle with a little extra ground cumin, if wished, and with the raisins and almonds. Reheat for a couple of minutes in a hot oven and serve piping hot, accompanied with a selection of salads with a Middle Eastern flavour. Cucumber with a yogurt dressing is good, or a plain green salad with a curd cheese dressing, or a simple tomato vinaigrette.

La Ratatouille Niçoise

A Classic French Vegetable Stew

Serves 8

The French chef of a very famous London hotel once sacked one of his young cooks because he could not prepare a ratatouille properly. It caused a kitchen strike at the time. But all of us older chefs felt the blame lay with the chef for not being able to teach a dish which is simplicity itself.

Aubergines (eggplants) are the chief ingredient of a ratatouille and we have discussed already the importance of preparing this vegetable fruit correctly. In this recipe there is no need to salt the chunks of aubergine (eggplant) so long as they are soaked in cold water before cooking. Aubergines (eggplants) do not usually need to be skinned — in fact, the best flavour is in the skin, and its rich purple colour is most pleasing in a dish. Aubergines (eggplants) are wonderfully versatile. Slices can be floured and seasoned and grilled or fried, it can be baked and then liquidized with tahini to make a pâté, and it can be casseroled, as in this recipe.

Ratatouille can be served in the same earthenware dish in which it is cooked, or in little individual dishes. You can sprinkle grated cheese over it to add extra flavour and nourishment. In Nice, ratatouille is served hot or cold, quite simply, with black olives as its only embellishment.

Imperial (Metric)	American
1 lb (450g) aubergines	**1 pound eggplants**
1 lb (450g) tomatoes	**1 pound tomatoes**
1 lb (450g) courgettes	**1 pound zucchini**
1 red pepper	**1 red pepper**
1 green pepper	**1 green pepper**
½ lb (225g) onions	**8 ounces onions**
3 cloves garlic	**3 cloves garlic**
4 fl oz (120ml) olive oil	**½ cup olive oil**
2 oz (50g) tomato purée	**4 tablespoons tomato paste**
Sea salt and freshly ground black pepper	**Sea salt and freshly ground black pepper**
2 tablespoons freshly chopped parsley	**2 tablespoons freshly chopped parsley**
Pinch freshly chopped basil *or* **oregano**	**Pinch freshly chopped basil** *or* **oregano**
12 black olives for decoration	**12 black olives for decoration**

1. Cut the aubergines (eggplants) into 1 inch (2.5cm) cubes and soak in cold water for 20 minutes. Drain and pat dry.
2. Scald the tomatoes so that their skins slip off easily. Halve them and gently squeeze out their seeds. Chop into rough pieces.
3. Slice the courgettes (zucchini). Halve the peppers, remove their seeds and cut into regular 1 inch (2.5cm) squares.
4. Chop the onions and garlic.
5. Heat the oil in a large pan and stir-fry the onion and garlic for 4 minutes.
6. Add all the other vegetables and stir-fry for 4 minutes. Stir in ½ pint (300ml/1⅓ cups) water and the tomato purée (paste). Season to taste.
7. Transfer to an earthenware casserole dish and bake at 350°F/180°C (Gas Mark 4) for 40 minutes.
8. Remove from the oven, sprinkle with herbs and decorate with black olives before serving.

Variations:
As mentioned above, a little grated cheese, sprinkled onto the dish and browned lightly under the grill is very

good. To make more of a meal of the dish, quartered hard-boiled eggs can be stirred in carefully just before serving and go very well with the rich flavours of the ratatouille.

Gratin Dauphinois aux Poireaux

Layered Leeks and Potatoes Baked with Cheese and Cream

The Dauphiné province of France is noted for its walnuts and chestnuts, and for its dairy produce. It has many regional specialities, the most luxurious of which is probably the *Omelette aux Truffes de Grignan* while the most famous must be the more economical, but no less delicious, *Gratin Dauphinois*. This is a simple dish, but one which many people spoil by not paying attention to one important detail. Raw potatoes contain an acid which curdles raw milk when the two are cooked together. If using raw potatoes the milk must be boiled before it is added to the dish. My method avoids this curdling by scalding the potatoes first, thus neutralizing the acid.

Imperial (Metric)	American
2 lb (900g) potatoes	**2 pounds potatoes**
2 cloves garlic	**2 cloves garlic**
2 oz (50g) butter	**¼ cup butter**
2 eggs, beaten	**2 eggs, beaten**
½ pint (300ml) double cream	**1⅓ cups heavy cream**
Sea salt	**Sea salt**
Freshly ground black pepper	**Freshly ground black pepper**
Freshly grated nutmeg	**Freshly grated nutmeg**
6 small leeks	**6 small leeks**
5 oz (150g) grated Gruyère cheese	**⅔ cup grated Gruyère cheese**

1. Wash, peel and rewash the potatoes. Cut into thin slices, ¼-inch (5mm) thick. Place in a pan with ½ pint (300ml/1⅓ cups) water and scald for 4 minutes, then drain well.
2. Rub a shallow earthenware baking dish with a cut clove of garlic or with both cloves, crushed. Butter the dish thickly.
3. In a bowl beat together the eggs and cream. Season with salt, pepper and nutmeg, and add the rest of the crushed garlic, if not already used.
4. Clean the leeks by trimming off most of the green part, splitting any remaining green and running plenty of cold water over them to remove any grit. Boil for 8 minutes, drain and gently squeeze out excess moisture without crushing the leeks.
5. Arrange half the potato slices in an overlapping pattern in the bottom of the dish. Pour half the egg and cream mixture over them, then sprinkle with half the cheese. Arrange the leeks, folded if necessary, over this. Then layer the rest of the potatoes neatly as before over the leeks and cover with the rest of the egg and cream mixture and the rest of the cheese.
6. Bake for 1 hour at 375°F/190°C (Gas Mark 5) and serve in its dish.

Variations:

Almost any other vegetable may be substituted for the leeks, such as celery, fennel, mushrooms, cauliflower, broccoli or onions.

Ragoût de Pomme de Terre Thézy-Glimont

Country-Style Potato Stew

The Battle of the Somme was fought just half a kilometre from Thézy-Glimont, where my French family live. The once battle-scarred soil of this rich, marshy plain yields a harvest of the finest vegetables to be sold in the markets of Paris, and the only trenches to be seen are those dug for the potato crop — just as I used to dig them when a young man. If I had a pound for every potato I dug in those days . . . We really knew how to exploit the full value of this vegetable. A favourite supper after a hard day's work was potatoes baked on a bonfire, served with a lump of creamy butter and a bowl of home-made cider. Incidentally, my grandmother — a home wine-maker of some ingenuity — used to make a liqueur of potatoes, which she called 'Spirit of Jesus'! This ragoût of potatoes was a daily ritual at her house, and she would add to it whatever other vegetables were plentiful according to the season. My sister in Thézy-Glimont continues this tradition.

Imperial (Metric)	American
2 fl oz (60ml) olive oil	**¼ cup olive oil**
2 oz (50g) butter	**¼ cup butter**
1 large onion, chopped	**1 large onion, chopped**
1 clove garlic, crushed	**1 clove garlic, crushed**
4 oz (100g) celery	**4 ounces celery**
4 oz (100g) carrots	**4 ounces carrots**
4 oz (100g) turnips	**4 ounces turnips**
4 oz (100g) swedes	**4 ounces rutabaga**
4 oz (100g) cabbage	**4 ounces cabbage**
1 lb (450g) new potatoes, quartered	**1 pound new potatoes, quartered**
2 oz (50g) tomato purée	**4 tablespoons tomato paste**
2 pints (1.15 litres) water	**5 cups water**
Pinch freshly chopped thyme	**Pinch freshly chopped thyme**
1 bay leaf	**1 bay leaf**
4 oz (100g) shelled green peas	**4 ounces shelled green peas**
4 oz (100g) shredded runner beans *or* **mangetout peas, whole**	**4 ounces shredded green beans** *or* **snow peas, whole**
Sea salt and freshly ground black pepper	**Sea salt and freshly ground black pepper**
Pinch each freshly chopped chervil, parsley, marjoram and mint	**Pinch each freshly chopped chervil, parsley, marjoram and mint**

1. In a large casserole dish, heat the oil and butter and stir-fry the onion and garlic for 4 minutes.
2. Wash, peel where necessary, and cut into equal pieces the celery, carrots, turnip and swede (rutabaga) and shred the cabbage. Add to the pan, put on the lid to prevent steam escaping and cook for 5 minutes. Stir well.
3. Add the potatoes, tomato purée (paste), water, thyme and bay leaf. Cook, covered, for 20 minutes.
4. Add the peas and beans and cook for 10 minutes more. Season to taste.
5. Serve the stew in large soup bowls, with the rest of the herbs sprinkled on top and pass round plenty of fresh wholemeal bread with which to mop up all the delicious juices.

Les Nouilles à la Julienne de Légumes St Jérome

Oriental-Style Vegetables with Noodles

This is another dish featuring the technique of stir-frying. It is an appetizing and attractive dish which is always very popular with our younger guests when featured on the menu at Arts Club functions. Home-made noodles are easily prepared and taste quite delicious, but shop-bought wholemeal noodles can be used instead if time is short.

Imperial (Metric)	American
For the noodles:	For the noodles:
½ lb (225g) wholemeal semolina	**2 cups wholewheat semolina**
2 eggs, beaten	**2 eggs, beaten**
2 tablespoons vegetable oil	**2 tablespoons vegetable oil**
2 tablespoons water	**2 tablespoons water**
Pinch sea salt	**Pinch sea salt**
For the vegetables:	For the vegetables:
4 oz (100g) carrots	**4 ounces carrots**
4 oz (100g) turnips	**4 ounces turnips**
4 oz (100g) potatoes	**4 ounces potatoes**
4 oz (100g) celery	**4 ounces celery**
4 oz (100g) red and green peppers	**4 ounces red and green peppers**
4 oz (100g) French beans	**4 ounces string beans**
4 oz (100g) beansprouts	**4 ounces beansprouts**
4 oz (100g) white mushrooms	**4 ounces white mushrooms**
3 fl oz (90ml) pineapple juice	**⅓ cup pineapple juice**
Small piece fresh ginger, peeled and sliced	**Small piece fresh ginger, peeled and sliced**
2 tablespoons soya sauce	**2 tablespoons soy sauce**
Sea salt and freshly ground black pepper	**Sea salt and freshly ground black pepper**
2 oz (50g) mixed oil and butter	**¼ cup mixed oil and butter**

1. In a bowl combine the ingredients for the noodles to form a pliable dough. Rest this for 20 minutes and then roll out on a board dusted with semolina. You should aim to produce an oblong 10×5 inches (25×12cm), ⅛-¼ inch (3-5mm) thick.
2. Dust the surface of the dough with semolina and then roll carefully lengthways. Cut at ¼ inch (5mm) intervals. Place the 'rolls' onto a tray lined with greaseproof paper and dusted with semolina and leave to dry out for a while. Cook in plenty of boiling salted water for 4 minutes only. Refresh in cold water, drain well and chop into short lengths.
3. Clean and prepare the vegetables. Cut the carrots, turnips, potatoes, celery and peppers into 2-inch (5cm) long, ¼-inch (5mm) strips. Cut the beans into 2-inch (5cm) lengths. Blanch all these in boiling water for 4 minutes and refresh in cold water, then drain. Rinse and drain the beansprouts and slice the mushrooms.
4. Blend the pineapple juice with the ginger, soya sauce and seasoning. Set aside.
5. Heat the oil and butter in a large pan and stir-fry the cooked noodles and all the vegetables except the mushrooms and beansprouts.
6. Remove from the heat and stir in most of the mushrooms and beansprouts. Serve on a large platter with the rest of the mushrooms and beansprouts sprinkled over the top.

Coulibiac de Riz aux Champignons Baronne de Juniac

Rice and Mushroom Pastry Roll

Illustrated opposite page 96.

During my travels in Russia before and during the Second World War I encountered many versions of the traditional Coulibiac. This dish had been introduced into French cuisine many years before by French chefs who worked for the nobility in Russia before the revolution, but it was primarily the salmon version which was adopted into *haute cuisine.* A variation on a well-known theme is always permitted to a composer who knows his art, and therefore I proudly present my vegetarian version of this classic dish. I am so delighted with its outcome that I have dedicated it to my esteemed patrons the Baron and Baroness de Juniac, whose palates I trust most amongst all my clientele.

Imperial (Metric)	American
6 green cabbage leaves	**6 green cabbage leaves**
2 oz (50g) butter	**¼ cup butter**
2 fl oz (60ml) olive oil	**¼ cup olive oil**
4 oz (100g) onion, chopped	**⅔ cup chopped onion**
2 cloves garlic, chopped	**2 cloves garlic, chopped**
5 oz (125g) long grain brown rice	**⅔ cup long grain brown rice**
1 pint (300ml) water	**2½ cups water**
3 eggs, beaten	**3 eggs, beaten**
Sea salt and freshly ground black pepper	**Sea salt and freshly ground black pepper**
1 tablespoon each freshly chopped tarragon and parsley	**1 tablespoon each freshly chopped tarragon and parsley**
2 oz (50g) toasted flaked almonds	**½ cup toasted slivered almonds**
1½ lb (675g) puff pastry (page 144) *or* **brioche dough (page 178)**	**1½ pounds puff pastry (page 144)** *or* **brioche dough (page 178)**
4 oz (100g) white mushrooms, sliced	**1½ cups white mushrooms, sliced**
4 tomatoes, skinned, seeded and quartered	**4 tomatoes, skinned, seeded and quartered**
4 hard-boiled eggs	**4 hard-boiled eggs**
4 oz (100g) sliced Gruyère cheese	**4 ounces sliced Gruyère cheese**

1. Scald the cabbage leaves in boiling water for 3 minutes, then refresh in cold water and drain.
2. In a large saucepan, heat the butter and oil and stir-fry the onion and garlic for 2 minutes. Add the rice and stir to allow it to absorb the fat, then add the water and boil gently, covered tightly with a lid, for 40 to 45 minutes, or until the water has been absorbed and the rice is tender.
3. When the rice is cooked, remove it from the heat, blend in two-thirds of the beaten egg and season the mixture. Allow to cool and then stir in the herbs and almonds.
4. Lightly flour a large pastry board and roll out the pastry into an oblong about 12×18 inches (30×46cm). Lay 3 cabbage leaves out on this.
5. Cover the central 6×12 inches (15×30cm) of pastry with a layer of the rice mixture, using half the rice, then sprinkle with half the mushrooms and tomatoes. Cover with the rest of the rice, and then the rest of the mushrooms and tomatoes.
6. Top with the quartered hard-boiled eggs and the cheese and cover with the remaining cabbage leaves. Bring the two sides of the pastry up over the filling. Blend the remaining egg with 4 tablespoons of water and use a little of this to seal the edges. Bring the ends up over the top and seal them to the pastry roll.

7 Very carefully, turn the roll over, placing on a greased baking sheet so that the seams are underneath. Brush the top with the rest of the egg wash and use a fork to make a decorative criss-cross pattern on the top of the roll.
8 Bake at 400°F/200°C (Gas Mark 6) for 30 minutes — it should puff up and turn a delicious golden-brown. Serve hot with a tomato salad or a green endive (chicory) salad with lemon dressing.

Note: If you are unsure about the filling and rolling of the coulibiac, try this technique the first time you prepare the dish.

When the dough is rolled out, mark it lightly with a knife about 3 inches (8cm) in from each edge. Now cut out the squares made at each corner by your markings. Put the filling just into the centre oblong made by the marks and then fold up the sides and ends as instructed. If you like, you could re-roll the trimming and cut into thin strips. These can then be stuck with egg wash into a criss-cross or other decorative pattern on the coulibiac.

Instead of cabbage leaves, thin pancakes could be used. This will produce a more substantial dish.

Omelette Vendéenne

A Country Vegetable Omelette

Serves 4

The province of Vendée was the last bastion of the Monarchy during the French revolution, which says much about the character of the people of the region. The gastronomy of the area is very distinctive, too, and thrives in such towns as La Rochelle, Sables d'Olonnes and Fontenay-le-Comte, where I was born during the First World War. The rosé wine of the area is the finest in France and makes a perfect accompaniment to this dish.

There are over a hundred different types of omelette in France, all stemming from simple country cooking. This one is a flat, pancake-like omelette.

Imperial (Metric)	American
4 oz (100g) butter	**½ cup butter**
4 fl oz (120ml) olive oil	**½ cup olive oil**
2 oz (50g) onion, chopped	**2 ounces onion, chopped**
2 oz (50g) spinach, washed and shredded	**2 ounces spinach, washed and shredded**
2 oz (50g) cooked, diced potato	**2 ounces cooked, diced potato**
2 oz (50g) cooked, diced Jerusalem artichokes	**2 ounces cooked, diced Jerusalem artichokes**
2 oz (50g) cooked beans	**⅓ cup cooked beans**
Sea salt and freshly ground black pepper	**Sea salt and freshly ground black pepper**
12 eggs, beaten and seasoned with sea salt and freshly ground black pepper	**12 eggs, beaten and seasoned with sea salt and freshly ground black pepper**
Grated cheese (optional)	**Grated cheese (optional)**
Freshly chopped parsley	**Freshly chopped parsley**

1 In a sauté pan heat half the butter and half the oil. Stir-fry the onion and spinach for 4 minutes.
2 Add the potatoes, artichokes and beans and cook all together for a further 4 minutes. Remove from the heat and season. Place in a bowl.
3 In an omelette pan, heat 1 oz (25g) butter and 1 tablespoon oil. Reheat a quarter of the filling mixture in this and, when sizzling, immediately add a quarter of the beaten eggs. Stir the mixture, allowing it to cook on one side, then either toss it or brown it under the grill. Grated cheese could be sprinkled on before browning, if wished.
4 Repeat to make three more omelettes. Sprinkle with parsley and serve.

Aubergines à la Biarritz

Baked Aubergines (Eggplants) with Goat's Cheese, Garlic and Lemon

Serves 4

Goat's cheese gives this dish a flavour redolent of southern France, but it is an acquired taste and some people may prefer to substitute curd or cream cheese. Light, soft cheeses, be they made from cow's, ewe's or goat's milk, are often used in modern French cuisine. They blend well in sauces and make a good base for a stuffing. Garlic and lemon will enhance the tang of the goat cheese or brighten up a blander curd or cream-based soft cheese.

Imperial (Metric)	American
4 large aubergines (½ lb/225g each)	**4 large eggplants (8 ounces each)**
½ lb (225g) goat's *or* curd cheese	**1 cup goat's *or* curd cheese**
Juice and grated rind of 1 lemon	**Juice and grated rind of 1 lemon**
1 clove garlic, chopped	**1 clove garlic, chopped**
2 oz (50g) grated hard cheese	**½ cup grated hard cheese**
2 tablespoons chopped fresh parsley *or* mint	**2 tablespoons chopped fresh parsley *or* mint**
1 oz (25g) wholemeal flour	**¼ cup wholewheat flour**
2 eggs, beaten	**2 eggs, beaten**
Sea salt and freshly ground black pepper	**Sea salt and freshly ground black pepper**
¼ pint (150ml) olive oil for frying (optional)	**⅔ cup olive oil for frying (optional)**

1. Wash and dry the aubergines (eggplants). Cut them in two lengthwise. Make criss-cross incisions in their flesh without damaging the skin.
2. Sprinkle the cut sides with sea salt to draw out the bitter juices. Leave for 30 minutes, then rinse and dry.
3. Scoop out most of the flesh from the aubergines (eggplants), leaving some still attached to the skin to form a shell.
4. In a bowl, blend the goat's cheese, lemon juice and rind, garlic, grated cheese, parsley and the flour. When this is well mixed, stir in the beaten eggs, aubergine (eggplant) pulp and seasoning.
5. Place the shells in a roasting tin with a little olive oil. Fill each shell with some of the filling mixture. Bake at 400°F/200°C (Gas Mark 6) for 15 to 20 minutes, until the top of the filling is golden-brown.
6. Alternatively, shallow-fry the aubergines in olive oil for 3 minutes on each side. This method is quicker, but the baking method is more healthy as the aubergines (eggplants) do not soak up so much oil.
7. Serve on individual platters, on slices of toasted wholemeal bread if liked.

Les Feuilles de Vignes Adam et Ève

Vine Leaves Stuffed with Lentils, Rice and Nuts, in a Lemon and Grape Sauce

Serves 4

France is one of the largest wine-producers in the world, over half its agricultural land being covered in vines. The grapes, of course, are used to the full, but the vine leaves are usually left to rot, yet when young they are as tender as cabbage leaves and far more delicious.

Imperial (Metric)	American
16 vine leaves, fresh or tinned	**16 vine leaves, fresh or canned**
For the sauce:	For the sauce:
2 fl oz (60ml) vegetable oil	**¼ cup vegetable oil**
1 small onion, chopped	**1 small onion, chopped**
1 pint (300ml) water	**2½ cups water**
1 clove garlic, chopped	**1 clove garlic, chopped**
1 tablespoon yeast extract	**1 tablespoon yeast extract**
4 fl oz (120ml) cream	**½ cup cream**
4 egg yolks	**4 egg yolks**
1 tablespoon cornflour	**1 tablespoon cornstarch**
Juice and grated rind of 1 lemon	**Juice and grated rind of 1 lemon**
Sea salt and freshly ground black pepper	**Sea salt and freshly ground black pepper**
Seedless green grapes, for garnish	**Seedless green grapes, for garnish**
For the filling:	For the filling:
5 oz (125g) cooked brown rice	**1 scant cup cooked brown rice**
1 oz (25g) sultanas	**2 tablespoons golden seedless raisins**
2 oz (50g) cooked lentils	**⅓ cup cooked lentils**
2 oz (50g) chopped walnuts	**½ cup chopped English walnuts**
Sea salt and freshly ground black pepper	**Sea salt and freshly ground black pepper**
Pinch allspice *or* chilli powder	**Pinch allspice *or* chili powder**
1 egg, beaten	**1 egg, beaten**

1. If using fresh vine leaves, blanch them for 4 minutes in boiling salted water. Drain and set aside.
2. For the sauce, heat the oil in a saucepan and sauté the onion for 3 minutes without browning. Add the water and garlic and boil for 5 minutes. Stir in the yeast extract.
3. In a bowl, mix the cream, egg yolks and cornflour. Add to this a cup of the onion stock, stirring well. Pour this back into the rest of the onion liquor to thicken it. Boil for 4 minutes, then add the lemon juice and rind and seasoning. Taste and add a little more yeast extract if the flavour is too mild.
4. In a basin, combine all the filling ingredients, adding the egg last to bind the mixture together. You should have a stiff mixture which can be formed into neat little balls about the size of a walnut — one for each vine leaf.
5. Place a ball in the centre of each leaf, rolling the leaf up around it like an envelope.
6. Place these 'parcels', packed quite close together, in a lidded ovenproof dish and cover with sauce. Bake at 400°F/200°C (Gas Mark 6) for 20 minutes, covered with a lid. Serve in the dish, with green grapes pushed lightly into the sauce just before serving, and garnished with lemon slices if liked.

Les Crêpes Dentelles aux Noix

'Lace' Pancakes (Crêpes) with Nuts

Serves 4-8

You will find pancakes (crêpes) like this all over Brittany, made so thin that they are almost transparent, hence their name *dentelle* — lace.

During my time in the French navy I spent some time in Brest, cooking for the officers on a destroyer. I often featured these pancakes (crêpes) on my menu and they were especially popular as a breakfast dish or snack with a fried egg slipped onto each one. Better still, I liked to use them to wrap up a tasty surprise for the diners. Perhaps the most popular of these was this soufflé filling with walnuts and cheese.

Imperial (Metric)	American
For the pancakes:	For the crêpes:
4 oz (100g) wholemeal flour	**1 cup wholewheat flour**
Sea salt	**Sea salt**
2 eggs, beaten	**2 eggs, beaten**
½ pint (300ml) mixed milk and water	**1⅓ cups mixed milk and water**
1 teaspoon fresh yeast	**1 teaspoon fresh yeast**
1 teaspoon raw cane sugar	**1 teaspoon raw cane sugar**
Vegetable oil for cooking pancakes	**Vegetable oil for cooking pancakes**
For the filling:	For the filling:
1 tablespoon melted butter	**1 tablespoon melted butter**
1 tablespoon wholemeal flour	**1 tablespoon wholewheat flour**
¼ pint (150ml) mixed water and milk	**⅔ cup mixed water and milk**
1 whole egg plus 3 egg yolks, beaten	**1 whole egg plus 3 egg yolks, beaten**
Sea salt and freshly ground black pepper	**Sea salt and freshly ground black pepper**
2 oz (50g) grated cheese	**½ cup grated cheese**
2 oz (50g) chopped walnuts	**½ cup chopped English walnuts**
4 egg whites	**4 egg whites**
Sea salt	**Sea salt**
2 oz (50g) butter for dish	**¼ cup butter for dish**

1. In a bowl combine the flour and salt. Add the beaten eggs and the milk and water mixture, stirring to obtain a smooth batter.
2. In a cup, combine the yeast and sugar with 4 fl oz (120ml/½ cup) water heated to 81°F/27°C. Leave to foam for 15 minutes, then stir well and add to the batter. Leave the batter to ferment for 30 minutes.
3. Heat a 6 inch (15cm) pancake pan and add 1 tablespoon oil. When it is hot, pour in just enough batter to thinly coat the bottom of the pan. Cook on both sides and then transfer to kitchen paper to drain and cool. Repeat with the rest of the batter. You should make 8 pancakes (crêpes) in all.
4. To prepare the soufflé filling, heat the butter and flour together in a pan, cooking without colouring for 3 minutes. Gradually blend in the water and milk, stirring to avoid lumps.
5. Cool the mixture a little and then add the whole egg and the yolks. Beat well and add seasoning and half the grated cheese. Turn into a bowl and stir in the walnuts.
6. In a very clean, dry bowl beat the egg whites with a pinch of salt until stiff.
7. Add half the egg whites to the egg yolk mixture and mix well. Add the rest of the egg whites with a cutting motion. Do not attempt to mix thoroughly or the air bubbles will all be lost.

8 Place 2 tablespoons of this mixture down the centre of each pancake (crêpe) and roll them up carefully. Place them in a well-buttered, ovenproof, shallow baking dish and sprinkle with the remaining cheese. Bake on the middle shelf of the oven at 400°F/200°C (Gas Mark 6) for 15 to 20 minutes. Serve immediately.

Les Pommes aux Choux-Fleurs Oriental

Potatoes and Cauliflower in a Spicy Sauce

The French have never cared as much as the British for curries, perhaps because our connections with India were so long ago, but we do love spices which do not swamp the true taste of the food. The port of Marseilles has been the landing point, over the centuries, for immigrants from the East, and with them has come a wealth of strongly aromatic dishes, full of the odours of herbs, garlic and exotic spices such as saffron. This dish combines those exciting and evocative ingredients with two more humble, everyday ingredients, cauliflower and potatoes. Try them this way and you will never think of them as boring again!

Imperial (Metric)	American
¼ pint (150ml) olive oil	**⅔ cup olive oil**
4 oz (100g) chopped onion	**⅔ cup chopped onion**
½ teaspoon each of turmeric, paprika, cumin and mustard powder	**½ teaspoon each of turmeric, paprika cumin and mustard powder**
Pinch powdered saffron	**Pinch powdered saffron**
2 oz (50g) tomato purée	**4 tablespoons tomato paste**
2 cloves garlic, crushed	**2 cloves garlic, crushed**
1½ lb (675g) potatoes, cut into 1-inch (2.5cm) cubes	**1½ pounds potatoes, cut into 1-inch cubes**
1 large cauliflower, divided into florets	**1 large cauliflower, divided into florets**
1 pint (600ml) water	**2½ cups water**
Sea salt and freshly ground black pepper	**Sea salt and freshly ground black pepper**
Small piece fresh ginger, peeled and chopped	**Small piece fresh ginger, peeled and chopped**
4 fl oz (120ml) natural yogurt	**½ cup plain yogurt**
1 teaspoon chopped fresh coriander and mint	**1 teaspoon chopped cilantro and mint**

1 In a saucepan, heat the oil and sauté the onion until soft but not brown.

2 Add the spices and stir well. Stir in the tomato purée (paste) and garlic.

3 Add the potatoes and cauliflower, stirring well so that the flavours really penetrate the vegetables. Pour on the water, add seasoning and ginger. Boil for 15 to 20 minutes, until all the vegetables are cooked.

4 Strain off a little of the liquid into a bowl. Blend the yogurt into it and then stir this mixture into the vegetables. Mix well and serve with a generous sprinkling of herbs. This is good served over, or stirred in with, pasta shells, macaroni, or brown rice. Hard-boiled eggs can be added, too, cut in half with the sauce poured over them.

Note: If fresh coriander (cilantro) is unavailable, fresh chervil or parsley can be used.

La Tagine des Haricots Gombo

Bean and Okra Stew

This is a variation on the traditional Breton dish which we discussed in Chapter 4 as the basis for a soup (page 81). This time, the influence of Creole cooking is the important feature, though, with the use of okra. These little pod-like vegetables complement the flavour of tomatoes very well and also have the unusual property of acting as a thickening agent when cooked, thus producing a sauce for the bean stew which is richly flavoured and thick. I first came across okra (or ladies' fingers, or gombo, as it is sometimes called) during my travels in Latin America. At that time it was rarely found in Europe, but now is more readily obtainable in specialist shops, either fresh or tinned.

Imperial (Metric)	American
1 lb (450g) okra	**1 pound okra**
4 fl oz (120ml) olive oil	**½ cup olive oil**
1 medium onion, chopped	**1 medium onion, chopped**
3 cloves garlic, chopped	**3 cloves garlic, chopped**
1 green pepper, seeded and chopped	**1 green pepper, seeded and chopped**
1 green chilli, sliced	**1 green chili, sliced**
4 large tomatoes, skinned, seeded and chopped	**4 large tomatoes, skinned, seeded and chopped**
2 oz (50g) tomato purée	**4 tablespoons tomato paste**
Sea salt and freshly ground black pepper	**Sea salt and freshly ground black pepper**
2 tablespoons mixed fresh chopped herbs	**2 tablespoons mixed fresh chopped herbs**
1 teaspoon raw cane sugar	**1 teaspoon raw cane sugar**
1 teaspoon red wine vinegar	**1 teaspoon red wine vinegar**
5 oz (150g) haricot beans, soaked overnight	**1 cup navy beans, soaked overnight**

1. Wash and dry the okra. Cut off the stems without damaging or breaking open the pods.
2. Heat the oil in a sauté pan and stir-fry the okra and onion for 5 minutes.
3. Add the garlic, pepper, chilli, tomatoes, tomato purée (paste), seasoning and herbs. Stir in ½ pint (300ml/1⅓ cups) water and boil for 15 minutes. Lastly stir in the sugar and vinegar. Set aside.
4. Place the soaked beans in a large pot of water. Bring to the boil and boil for 2 hours, or bake at 350°F/180°C (Gas Mark 4) for the same length of time.
5. Drain the beans and place in a large earthenware dish. Cover with the okra sauce and place in the oven to reheat as necessary.

Note: As explained before, it is best if you can use distilled or boiling hot water to soak your beans, especially if you live in a hard-water area. Alternatively, canned beans may be used for this dish, which will then only take 20 minutes to prepare.

Opposite: *Couronne de Maïs à la Française* (page 84) and *Coulibiac de Riz aux Champignons* (page 90).

La Pissaladière Côte d'Azur

French Riviera-Style Pizza

Serves 4

Generations of Italians have lived on the Riviera since Nice and the province of Savoy belonged to Italy. Naturally they have influenced the gastronomy of this region tremendously, but the French cook is a tough nut to crack and will always have his or her say in a dish, making an amendment here, adding an ingredient there, until the dish becomes yet another addition to the vast and exciting range of French cuisine. A notable example is *Pissaladière*. In name and content its origin as a pizza is recognizable, but the adaptations which have been made to it over the years have rendered it truly French.

Normal bread dough makes a perfect base for *Pissaladière*, just as it does for pizza. Crusty French bread makes a good base, too, and I have even featured a bap version, using this traditional English milk bun. I am even considering what I feel will possibly be the best of all, using a croissant dough mix for a base — but to tell you any more at present would be giving away too much, you will have to wait and see!

So here, for now, is the precious *Pissaladière* recipe which I used to prepare at the Hotel des Pins in Cannes when I was Commis Assistant Chef there in 1937.

Imperial (Metric)	American
1 lb (450g) bread dough (page 176) *or* **brioche dough (page 178)**	**1 pound bread dough (page 176)** *or* **brioche dough (page 178)**
½ lb (225g) button mushrooms	**4 cups button mushrooms**
Juice of 1 lemon	**Juice of 1 lemon**
3 fl oz (90ml) olive oil	**⅓ cup olive oil**
8 stuffed olives, sliced	**8 stuffed olives, sliced**
4 large tomatoes, skinned, seeded and sliced	**4 large tomatoes, skinned, seeded and sliced**
1 large onion, sliced	**1 large onion, sliced**
4 oz (100g) sliced Mozzarella cheese	**4 ounces sliced Mozzarella cheese**
Sea salt and freshly ground black pepper	**Sea salt and freshly ground black pepper**
Freshly chopped oregano	**Freshly chopped oregano**

1. Roll the dough into a ball and brush it with oil. With your hands, flatten and enlarge the ball until you have a disc about 10 inches (25cm) in diameter. Place the dough on an oiled baking sheet and leave to prove for 15 minutes. If your oven is too small to accommodate one big pizza, make two, or even four, small *pissaladière.*
2. Clean and dry the mushrooms and marinate them in lemon juice for 5 minutes.
3. Place the topping on the *pissaladière* in this order: first, sliced mushrooms, and olives, then sliced tomatoes, slices of onion and finally slices of cheese.
4. Bake at 400°F/200°C (Gas Mark 6) for 15 to 20 minutes. Sprinkle with herbs and a little extra oil before serving.

Opposite: *Les Brocolis aux Pommes à la Vendéenne* (page 155).

Les Six Purées Printanières

Six Delicate, Colourful Vegetable Purées

Serves 10

By adding other ingredients to a basic vegetable purée you can lift the flavour, enrich it or complement its protein. Spices, herbs, eggs, cheese and pulses — all have their part to play in this, and combining vegetables with imagination will make for most delicious flavours. Spinach added to peas, for example, will add both colour and flavour; tomatoes will give an acidity to sharpen beans and carrots; eggs and cream will enrich the flavour of a dish, and curd cheese lighten it; and tahini will flavour and emulsify a purée. Chapter 1 demonstrated the many, varied and delicious ways in which cold puréed vegetables can be used as appetizing and nutritious starters; now the hot version adds another use for these light and delicate purées.

Imperial (Metric) For a potato and swede purée:	American For a potato and rutabaga purée:
½ lb (225g) cooked swedes, mashed	**1 cup cooked, mashed rutabaga**
½ lb (225g) cooked potatoes, mashed	**1 cup cooked, mashed potatoes**
2 eggs, beaten	**2 eggs, beaten**
2 oz (50g) ground peanuts	**½ cup ground peanuts**
4 fl oz (120ml) double cream	**½ cup heavy cream**
Sea salt and freshly ground black pepper	**Sea salt and freshly ground black pepper**

1 Combine the swede (rutabaga) and potato together in a saucepan.
2 Add beaten eggs, peanuts, cream and seasoning. Heat gently together and, as soon as it begins to bubble, pour into small soufflé dishes.

Imperial (Metric) For a broccoli and spinach purée:	American For a broccoli and spinach purée:
½ lb (225g) cooked, mashed broccoli	**1 cup cooked, mashed broccoli**
½ lb (225g) cooked, chopped spinach	**1 cup cooked, chopped spinach**
4 oz (100g) curd cheese	**½ cup curd cheese**
Sea salt and freshly ground black pepper	**Sea salt and freshly ground black pepper**
Freshly grated nutmeg	**Freshly grated nutmeg**

1 In a pan, gently heat together the prepared broccoli and spinach and blend in the curd cheese. Season with salt, pepper and nutmeg.
2 When the purée is heated through, pour into individual ramekins.

Imperial (Metric) For a carrot, red pepper and tomato purée:	American For a carrot, red pepper and tomato purée:
½ lb (225g) carrots, peeled and sliced	**8 ounces carrots, peeled and sliced**
½ lb (225g) red peppers, finely diced	**8 ounces red peppers, finely diced**
2 oz (50g) tomato purée	**4 tablespoons tomato paste**
4 oz (100g) cooked, mashed sweet potato	**½ cup cooked, mashed sweet potato**
1 teaspoon honey	**1 teaspoon honey**
Juice of ½ lemon	**Juice of ½ lemon**
Sea salt and freshly ground black pepper	**Sea salt and freshly ground black pepper**
Pinch fresh chopped basil *or* **oregano**	**Pinch fresh chopped basil** *or* **oregano**

1 Boil the carrots and peppers until soft, then mince through a *mouli-légumes* to a fine purée.
2 Reheat in a saucepan with the tomato purée (paste), mashed potato, honey, lemon juice, seasoning and herbs. When hot, pour into soufflé dishes as with the other purées.

Imperial (Metric) For a cabbage and potato purée:	American For a cabbage and potato purée:
½ lb (225g) green cabbage	**8 ounces green cabbage**
½ lb (225g) cooked, mashed potato	**1 cup cooked, mashed potato**
2 oz (50g) butter	**¼ cup butter**
Sea salt and freshly ground black pepper	**Sea salt and freshly ground black pepper**
A little grated Parmesan cheese	**A little grated Parmesan cheese**

1 Wash and shred the cabbage. Boil for 8 minutes, then drain well and chop finely.
2 Blend the cabbage into the mashed potato and heat with the butter in a saucepan.
3 Season to taste and stir in cheese as desired. When hot, pour into soufflé dishes as before.

Imperial (Metric) For a chestnut and onion purée:	American For a chestnut and onion purée:
1 large onion	**1 large onion**
½ lb (225g) tinned chestnut purée	**8 ounces canned chestnut paste**
4 fl oz (120ml) double *or* sour cream	**½ cup heavy *or* sour cream**
Sea salt and freshly ground black pepper	**Sea salt and freshly ground black pepper**
1 tablespoon yeast extract	**1 tablespoon yeast extract**

1 Peel the onion and boil until soft. Chop finely and blend with the chestnut purée.
2 Stir in the cream, seasoning and yeast extract. Heat through and serve in individual ramekins.

Imperial (Metric) For a bean and tomato purée:	American For a bean and tomato purée:
½ lb (225g) tinned baked beans in tomato sauce	**1⅓ cups canned baked beans in tomato sauce**
1 clove garlic	**1 clove garlic**
½ lb (225g) cooked, mashed potato	**1 cup cooked, mashed potato**
2 oz (50g) cream cheese	**¼ cup cream cheese**
Sea salt and freshly ground black pepper	**Sea salt and freshly ground black pepper**

1 Liquidize the baked beans in their sauce with the garlic.
2 Blend with the mashed potato in a saucepan to mix well.
3 Stir in the cream cheese and seasoning and heat. When well warmed, pour into individual soufflé dishes.

Note: Serve the selection of purées warm and let guests help themselves to the ones which take their fancy. Hot French bread is ideal with these for a buffet. For a dinner party, warm a large, shallow serving dish and arrange equal amounts of the different purées in a simple but decorative pattern in the dish, paddling the top with a palette knife so that they touch, thus displaying their contrasting colours, but do not mix them into one another as the effect would be spoiled.

The purées can be served with hard-boiled eggs, turned out of their dishes and coated in light, contrasting sauces, and served with grains, pasta or other vegetables to complete the meal.

La Raviolette Florentina

A Cheese and Spinach Pasta Dish

Serves 4

When the Italian princess Maria de Medici became Queen of France in 1573 she brought with her an army of Italian chefs. This was the beginning of the mutual influence of Italian cooking on French and vice versa. A notable introduction at that time was pasta, which has been used, albeit infrequently, in French classic cuisine ever since. This dish is a variation on one which I created many years ago for the Italian actress Sophia Loren.

Imperial (Metric)	American
For the pasta:	For the pasta:
4 eggs, beaten	**4 eggs, beaten**
1 teaspoon olive oil	**1 teaspoon olive oil**
Pinch each sea salt and grated nutmeg	**Pinch each sea salt and grated nutmeg**
½ lb (250g) fine wholemeal semolina	**2 cups fine wholewheat semolina**
For the filling:	For the filling:
2 oz (50g) cooked spinach, squeezed dry	**2 ounces cooked spinach, squeezed dry**
2 oz (50g) curd cheese	**¼ cup curd cheese**
4 oz (100g) grated Parmesan *or* Cheddar cheese	**1 cup grated Parmesan *or* Cheddar cheese**
Sea salt and freshly ground black pepper	**Sea salt and freshly ground black pepper**
Freshly grated nutmeg	**Freshly grated nutmeg**
4 eggs	**4 eggs**
4 oz (50g) butter, for dish	**½ cup butter, for dish**
2 oz (50g) sliced white mushrooms *or* truffles, for garnish	**1 cup sliced white mushrooms *or* truffles, for garnish**
Extra grated Parmesan cheese, for garnish	**Extra grated Parmesan cheese, for garnish**

1. To make the pasta paste, beat the eggs and combine them with the oil and seasoning in a bowl. Sprinkle on the semolina, beating to form a smooth dough. Roll the dough into a ball and rest for 30 minutes.
2. Roll the dough out to a thickness of ⅛ inch (3mm) and cut, with a fancy pastry cutter, eight rounds about 6 inches (15cm) in diameter.
3. For the filling, chop the spinach finely and blend it into the curd cheese. Add the grated cheese, seasoning and one beaten egg, mixing to a smooth, well-mixed paste. Divide into four equal balls.
4. On a pastry board dusted with a little semolina, lay four rounds of pasta.
5. Place a ball of filling onto each pasta round. Make a well in the top of each filling and very carefully crack an egg into each well.
6. Wet the edges of the pasta with water and place another round of pasta over the top, crimping the edges to seal the filling in completely.
7. Grease a shallow baking dish with half the butter. Place the filled raviolettes in the dish. Cover them level with boiling salted water. Boil for 4 to 6 minutes and then drain well in a clean cloth.
8. Use half the remaining butter to grease a baking dish. Place the raviolettes on the dish, sprinkle with mushrooms or truffles and dot with the rest of the butter. Lastly, sprinkle with a little Parmesan cheese.
9. Brown under the grill for 3 to 4 minutes. Serve piping hot, each raviolette in an individual dish.

6 *Les Plats de Garniture*

Side Dishes

Up until the Nineteen-sixties, chefs everywhere abided strictly by the rigid rules of classic French *haute cuisine* with regard to vegetable garnishes. The styles and preparation were firmly laid down, with the appropriate traditional name to identify the ingredients. For instance, a garnish whose name included the term *Alsacienne* would contain sauerkraut; *Boulangère* would be sliced potatoes cooked with onions; *Bretonne* would be beans in a tomato sauce; *Clamart* — peas; *Doria* — cucumber; *Dubarry* — cauliflower; *Florentine* would indicate spinach; *Parmentier* would contain potato cubes; *Conti* would be lentils and *Bruxelloise* (more obviously) Brussels sprouts. The list is endless but Escoffier listed as many as 175, and I, in the Fifties, listed twice that amount in my book *Haute Cuisine*.

The Seventies and Eighties have seen a tremendous change taking place in the kitchens of restaurants all over the world. Food has become, at the same time, more simple and more creative. The use of vegetables has gone far beyond a fanciful decoration for a meat, fish or poultry dish. Vegetables have become foods in their own right, to be savoured and appreciated as such. Of course, they still have a very important place as a complement to the main part of the dish, since a chef knows what will best offset a dish in terms of flavour, colour, appearance, texture and nutrition, and many a *nouvelle* creation will be served already decorated with delicate mangetout (snow) peas or whatever the chef has chosen — and Heaven help the customer who wants spinach instead! Still, it shows the importance now placed on the vegetable side dish, rather than the very secondary emphasis given to the rigid garnishes of the old style of cooking.

However, as will be easily seen from the pages of this book, most chefs would be sad to lose the old names altogether and *Niçoise*, *Bourgeoise*, Richelieu and the rest will always have an important and evocative place in any menu, although more often accompanied by a simple, descriptive name too, nowadays. This is surely the best of both worlds, and the fine new approach to the preparation, cooking and presentation of vegetables will not suffer for an elegant *and* a simple name!

In this chapter you will find dishes which make a perfect accompaniment to your main course. There are also many dishes here which will make a good, simple supper dish if you choose or, for that matter, an interesting and elegant first course. The choice is up to you — I feel sure you will enjoy making your decisions, sampling, experimenting and ringing the changes to create delicious meals for all occasions.

Courgettes Gratinées au Riz Andalouse

Courgettes (Zucchini) Stuffed with Rice Pilaff

Serves 4

Courgettes (zucchini), like other members of the same family including marrow (squash), cucumber and other gourds, have very little nutritive value and so must be combined with other ingredients which will make up a balanced dish. Fortunately, these vegetables lend themselves to being stuffed and baked and their flavour is complemented by a great many more nutritional ingredients, such as cheese, brown rice and other grains, resulting in a wealth of dishes and styles which derive from the marrow (squash) family in general. Gone are the days when tasteless marrow (squash) was stuffed with tasteless meat to produce a watery, unappetizing mush, as used to be the case in Britain not very long ago. Now the influence of a more multinational situation has made available vegetables which the Mediterranean countries have taken for granted for many years. This dish makes a perfect accompanying vegetable, or will provide a tasty supper for two.

Imperial (Metric)	American
4 courgettes (about ½ lb/225g each)	**4 zucchini (about 8 ounces each)**
3 fl oz (90ml) olive oil	**⅓ cup olive oil**
1 medium onion, chopped	**1 medium onion, chopped**
2 cloves garlic, chopped	**2 cloves garlic, chopped**
1 green chilli, sliced	**1 green chili, sliced**
1 red pepper, seeded and diced	**1 red pepper, seeded and diced**
5 oz (125g) long grain brown rice	**⅔ cup long grain brown rice**
Pinch curry powder	**Pinch curry powder**
Pinch paprika	**Pinch paprika**
Sea salt and freshly ground black pepper	**Sea salt and freshly ground black pepper**
1 pint (600ml) water	**2½ cups water**
1 teaspoon yeast extract	**1 teaspoon yeast extract**
1 tablespoon tomato purée	**1 tablespoon tomato paste**
6 stuffed olives, sliced	**6 stuffed olives, sliced**
2 oz (50g) grated hard cheese	**¼ cup grated hard cheese**
4 fl oz (120ml) extra olive oil, for baking	**½ cup extra olive oil, for baking**

1. Wash the courgettes (zucchini) but do not peel. Dry and cut in half lengthwise.
2. Cut out some of the pulp with a knife or Parisienne cutter, leaving enough flesh to retain a firm shape. Retain the pulp and seeds.
3. Cook the filling: in a saucepan, heat the oil and sauté the onion, garlic, chilli and pepper for 4 minutes without browning. Add the pulp from the courgettes (zucchini).
4. Stir in the rice so that it absorbs the oil evenly. Stir in the spices and seasoning and then add the water, yeast extract, tomato purée (paste) and olives.
5. Stir all the ingredients together well, cover and cook for 40 to 50 minutes, until the rice is tender and the water absorbed.
6. Fill the courgette (zucchini) cavities with the rice mixture and place in a shallow, buttered earthenware dish, with a little oil. Sprinkle with cheese.
7. Bake the courgettes (zucchini) for 20 minutes at 400°F/200°C (Gas Mark 6).

Variations:
Larger marrows (squash) can be cooked in the same way, but should be peeled and blanched before stuffing. Cucumbers, too, can be used — prepare exactly the same way as for courgettes (zucchini).

Endives Lilloise

Braised Chicory (Endive) with Cheese and Eggs

Serves 4

The chicory plant, or endive as it is known in France and America, has a slightly bitter taste which does not appeal to everybody but is very popular with gourmets. It can be eaten raw as a salad with a garlic or blue cheese dressing, baked in its own juices with a little lemon juice, or boiled until tender and then sautéd in butter. At Lille, near the Belgium border, where my brother Pierre lives, chicory (endive) is cultivated in caves because the darkness keeps them beautifully white.

Imperial (Metric)	American
8 heads chicory	**8 heads Belgian endive**
5 oz (150g) butter	**⅔ cup butter**
Sea salt	**Sea salt**
4 hard-boiled eggs	**4 hard-boiled eggs**
2 tablespoons chopped parsley	**2 tablespoons chopped parsley**
Freshly ground black pepper	**Freshly ground black pepper**
2 oz (50g) wholemeal breadcrumbs	**1 cup wholewheat breadcrumbs**
2 oz (50g) grated hard cheese	**½ cup grated hard cheese**
1 lemon	**1 lemon**

1. Wash the chicory (endive) and trim off the root.
2. Place 2 oz (50g/¼ cup) butter in a saucepan with a good pinch of sea salt, and the juice of half the lemon. Put the chicory (endive) in the pan and cover level with water. Boil for 40 minutes.
3. Drain the chicory (endive) and gently press out excess moisture.
4. Heat another 2 oz (50g/¼ cup) butter in a frying pan and sauté the chicory (endive) until golden-brown on all sides. Place them in a shallow baking dish.
5. Shell the eggs, pass them through a sieve and mix them with the parsley and season with black pepper.
6. Heat the remaining butter and sauté the breadcrumbs until golden. Sprinkle these over the chicory (endive).
7. Sprinkle the egg and parsley over the top of this and top with grated cheese. Brown quickly under the grill. Sprinkle with finely grated lemon rind and squeeze the juice of a quarter of the lemon over the top if liked. Serve immediately.

La Bouquetière Versailles

A Vegetable Selection

Serves 4
Illustrated opposite page 112.

There are always occasions when you will be entertaining guests who you know are hard to please, or when you don't know what their preferences and dislikes are. This selection of vegetables is the perfect solution: all are appealing to look at, delicious in flavour, and present a good contrast of tastes, textures and colours. For this *bouquetière* I have selected artichoke bottoms stuffed with pea purée; mushroom caps with cream cheese and peanut butter; broccoli fritters; tomatoes stuffed with mixed vegetables and peas in a cream sauce, but the variations are endless.

Imperial (Metric)	American
4 artichoke bottoms, fresh or tinned	**4 artichoke bottoms, fresh or canned**
½ lemon	**½ lemon**
2 oz (50g) cooked and puréed peas, seasoned	**¼ cup cooked and puréed peas, seasoned**
4 tartlet cases, baked blind (see page 44)	**4 tartlet cases, baked blind (see page 44)**
2 oz (50g) cooked and puréed carrots, seasoned	**¼ cup cooked and puréed carrots, seasoned**
16 small asparagus spears	**16 small asparagus spears**
4 large mushrooms	**4 large mushrooms**
2 oz (50g) curd cheese	**¼ cup curd cheese**
1 hard-boiled egg, chopped	**1 hard-boiled egg, chopped**
2 oz (50g) peanuts, ground to a paste	**4 tablespoons peanuts, ground to a paste**
Sea salt and freshly ground black pepper	**Sea salt and freshly ground black pepper**
Chopped garlic	**Chopped garlic**
1 egg, beaten	**1 egg, beaten**
3 oz (75g) wholemeal flour	**¾ cup wholewheat flour**
½ pint (300ml) mixed milk and water	**1⅓ cups mixed milk and water**
4 oz (100g) broccoli florets	**4 ounces broccoli florets**
4 oz (100g) diced mixed vegetables, such as peppers and carrots, plus peas and sweetcorn	**1 cup diced mixed vegetables, such as peppers and carrots, plus peas and sweetcorn**
4 large tomatoes	**4 large tomatoes**
¼ pint (150ml) double cream	**⅔ cup heavy cream**
4 oz (100g) cooked French beans	**4 ounces cooked string beans**
8 rings red pepper	**8 rings red pepper**

1. If using fresh artichoke bottoms, cut all the leaves off four artichokes, remove the chokes, rub the bottoms with lemon and boil for 10 minutes. Fill each bottom with a little pea purée and set aside.
2. Fill the baked tartlet cases with carrot purée and set aside.
3. Trim and lightly scrape the asparagus spears, tie into a bundle and boil for 10 minutes, and then refresh in cold water. Cut off most of the stalks and keep for use in soups. Reserve the tips.
4. Wash the mushrooms and remove the stalks. Chop the stalks finely and blend with the cheese, egg, peanuts, seasoning and garlic to taste. Fill each mushroom cap with the mixture. Bake for 5 minutes in a buttered ovenproof dish to cook the filling. Set aside.
5. Prepare a batter by mixing together in a bowl the beaten egg, flour and milk and water. Clean the broccoli florets and season with salt, pepper and lemon juice. Coat them in a little flour, then in the batter and deep-fry for 4 minutes until golden-brown. Drain and keep hot.

6 Boil the mixed vegetables for 5 minutes. Remove the top quarter of each tomato, scoop out the seeds and pulp and keep for use in sauces or soups. Fill the hollow tomatoes with the vegetables mixed with the cream. Bake at 400°F/200°C (Gas Mark 6) for 8 minutes. Set aside.
7 Place small bundles of green beans in rings of red pepper. Do the same with the asparagus tips.
8 Take a long oblong or oval dish or platter and arrange the vegetable dishes decoratively around the plate, alternating colours and styles as much as possible. Fill the centre of the dish with a bunch of watercress. Serve and let guests help themselves to a selection.

Variation:
For a more substantial dish, the centre could be filled with vegetable fritters. For the illustration opposite page 112, we used cauliflower fritters (page 46), but almost any vegetable could be used to make an attractive centrepiece.

Les Choux à l'Ananas

Sauerkraut with Pineapple

Serves 4

Part of the region of Alsace is German by blood, culture and language, but is French politically. The best dishes of this area are hard to beat gastronomically. The French love the Germanic use of cabbage in the traditional dish of sauerkraut, but it is a hard job to convince some other nations of the virtues of fermented cabbage as a food. I have been told that fields of cabbage are dumped and left to rot in Britain every year because of lack of pickers and customers. However, this is a delicious dish, well worth trying as a side dish to a simple main course, or as a supper dish by itself served with just buttered boiled new potatoes, or perhaps hard-boiled eggs. It is good, too, served as a salad with a blue cheese dressing. Reheated with juniper berries and a little white wine it is excellent as well. Serve in the hollowed-out pineapple halves for an attractive effect.

Imperial (Metric)	American
1 medium pineapple	**1 medium pineapple**
2 lb (900g) tinned sauerkraut	**5 cups canned sauerkraut**
2 oz (50g) butter	**¼ cup butter**
1 medium onion, chopped	**1 medium onion, chopped**
Sea salt and freshly ground black pepper	**Sea salt and freshly ground black pepper**
4 fl oz (120ml) single cream	**½ cup light cream**

1 Split a fresh, ripe pineapple in two, remove its woody core and scoop out the pulp with a grapefruit knife. Chop or shred it well. Reserve the skins for serving, if wished.
2 Wash the sauerkraut in plenty of cold water and drain it thoroughly.
3 Heat the butter in a large saucepan and sauté the onion without browning for 3 minutes.
4 Add the pineapple pulp, sauerkraut and seasoning. Cook for 4 minutes.
5 Stir in the cream and boil gently for 10 minutes. Serve hot with boiled new potatoes, or in any of the ways suggested above.

Variation:
Fresh white or green cabbage could be substituted for the sauerkraut.

Les Pommes Crépinettes

Potato Pancakes

Serves 10

In my family there is constant competition to produce the best variety of these delightful pancakes. On both sides of the Channel we have the same liking for them, but our recipes are somewhat different, so I will give you both the French variety, and my Anglicized version. Try both and decide which you like best.

Imperial (Metric) French version:	American French version:
1 lb (450g) potatoes	**1 pound potatoes**
2 eggs, beaten	**2 eggs, beaten**
½ pint (300ml) milk	**1⅓ cups milk**
4 oz (100g) wholemeal flour	**1 cup wholewheat flour**
Sea salt and freshly ground black pepper	**Sea salt and freshly ground black pepper**
2 oz (50g) chopped onion	**⅔ cup chopped onion**
2 oz (50g) cooked sweetcorn kernels	**⅔ cup cooked sweetcorn kernels**
1 clove garlic, chopped	**1 clove garlic, chopped**
1 tablespoon freshly chopped parsley	**1 tablespoon freshly chopped parsley**
½ lb (225g) mixed oil and butter	**1 cup mixed oil and butter**

1. Peel, wash, dry and coarsely grate the potatoes, or cut into matchstick strips by hand. Wash and drain well.
2. Blend the eggs and milk into the flour to form a smooth batter. Season and add the chopped onion, sweetcorn, garlic, parsley and the potato strips.
3. Heat half the oil and butter in a 6 inch (15cm) pan and drop in tablespoons of the mixture, to make four small pancakes. Fry gently on both sides until golden-brown. Drain on absorbent paper. Repeat until all the ingredients are used up. Serve piping hot, sprinkled with a little salt if wished.

Imperial (Metric) English version:	American English version:
1 lb (450g) potatoes	**1 pound potatoes**
2 eggs, beaten	**2 eggs, beaten**
2 oz (50g) wholemeal flour	**½ cup wholewheat flour**
Sea salt and freshly ground black pepper	**Sea salt and freshly ground black pepper**
Celery salt (see page 110)	**Celery salt (see page 110)**
Vegetable oil for frying	**Vegetable oil for frying**

1. Peel, wash, dry and finely grate the potatoes. Place the grated potato in a bowl and add the beaten eggs and flour to form a smooth, firmish batter of a dropping consistency (firmer than the French version). Season with salt, pepper and celery salt.
2. Heat a little oil in a 6 inch (15cm) pan and drop in four separate tablespoons of batter. Cook to golden-brown on both sides. Repeat until all the ingredients have been used up. Your cakes should be not more than 2 inches (5cm) in diameter, firmer and more filling than the French, and plainer in flavour, but just as enjoyable.

Les Trois Sauvages

Three Types of Wild Mushroom in a Wine and Cream Sauce with Saffron

Serves 4

The use of wild mushrooms as a garnish has caught the imagination of the younger chefs in both France and Britain. Fresh or dried, these mushrooms produce an excellent flavour and make a luxurious garnish. A simple sauce of wine, cream and saffron is an ideal complementary flavouring and is not at all difficult to prepare. Dried mushrooms of the type needed for this recipe can be bought in many delicatessens and health shops. They must be soaked for 1 hour to restore them to their original size. In this dish I have used *cèpes* of the Boletus variety, morels which are a spongy mushroom with cavities like a sponge, and English field mushrooms, but there are many more varieties which could be used.

Imperial (Metric)	American
4 oz (100g) fresh *cèpes* *or* 1½ oz (35g) dried	**4 ounces fresh *cèpes* *or* 1½ ounces dried**
4 oz (100g) fresh morels *or* 1½ oz (35g) dried	**4 ounces fresh morels *or* 1½ ounces dried**
4 oz (100g) fresh field mushrooms	**4 ounces fresh field mushrooms**
2 oz (50g) mixed oil and butter	**¼ cup mixed oil and butter**
1 small onion *or* 3 shallots, chopped	**1 small onion *or* 3 shallots, chopped**
1 small clove garlic, chopped	**1 small clove garlic, chopped**
1 teaspoon wholemeal flour	**1 teaspoon wholewheat flour**
2 tablespoons white port *or* white wine	**2 tablespoons white port *or* white wine**
1 large pinch ground saffron	**1 large pinch ground saffron**
Sea salt and freshly ground black pepper	**Sea salt and freshly ground black pepper**
Small pinch thyme	**Small pinch thyme**
Pinch each paprika and turmeric	**Pinch each paprika and turmeric**
4 fl oz (120ml) single cream	**½ cup light cream**
2 oz (50g) butter	**¼ cup butter**
16 spring onions	**16 scallions**

1. If dried, soak the mushrooms in water until twice their size. If fresh, clean, dry and trim the stalks. Slice the mushrooms.
2. Heat the mixed oil and butter in a pan and sauté the onion and garlic for 4 minutes without browning.
3. Sprinkle on the flour and stir to absorb the fat. Add the wine and the saffron. Stir in the seasoning, herbs and spices and cook gently for 5 minutes.
4. Blend in the cream and continue to cook for a further 5 minutes. Strain the sauce.
5. Heat the butter in a pan and cook the three different types of mushroom in turn, for 3 minutes each. Drain and arrange on a serving dish.
6. Tie the spring onions (scallions) in a bundle and boil for 8 minutes. Drain, squeeze gently and arrange on the serving plate between the mushrooms. Pour a little sauce onto each pile of mushrooms. Serve with toasted wholemeal bread or fresh wholemeal rolls to mop up the juices.

Les Mangetouts aux Graines de Sésame

Mangetout (Snow) Peas with Sesame Seeds

Serves 4
Illustrated opposite page 113.

In all the fashionable restaurants there is a craze for mangetout (snow) peas. They are to be seen wherever food is expensive! To comply with this trend I offer you a simple and comparatively inexpensive way of preparing them which will impress your fashion-conscious guests. All kinds of flavourings are suited to these little pea pods, as is the most simple melted butter dressing. They are delicious served hot or cold. My version, with strips of ginger, fennel, carrots and celery, served hot, complements the fresh colour and flavour of this lightly cooked vegetable.

Imperial (Metric)	American
2 lb (1 kilo) mangetout peas	**2 pounds snow peas**
2 oz (50g) carrots	**2 ounces carrots**
2 oz (50g) celery	**2 ounces celery**
2 oz (50g) fennel	**2 ounces fennel**
2 oz (50g) butter	**¼ cup butter**
2 oz (50g) onion, sliced	**2 ounces onion, sliced**
1 oz (25g) fresh ginger, peeled and chopped	**1 ounce fresh ginger, peeled and chopped**
Sea salt and freshly ground black pepper	**Sea salt and freshly ground black pepper**
1 teaspoon raw cane sugar	**1 teaspoon raw cane sugar**
1 tablespoon soya sauce	**1 tablespoon soy sauce**
1 teaspoon wine vinegar	**1 teaspoon wine vinegar**
2 teaspoons sesame seeds, lightly toasted	**2 teaspoons sesame seeds, lightly toasted**

1. Head and tail the peas and plunge into boiling salted water for 5 minutes. Drain.
2. Cut the carrots, celery and fennel into julienne strips and blanch for 3 minutes in boiling water. Drain well.
3. In a sauté pan heat the butter and quickly stir-fry the onion, ginger and the julienne vegetables for 4 minutes. Add the pea pods to reheat.
4. When the vegetables are all heated through, season to taste and stir in the sugar, soya sauce and vinegar. Cook for 2 more minutes, stirring all the time, sprinkle with sesame seeds and then serve immediately on a heated plate.

Note: The ginger could first be liquidized with the soya sauce and 2 tablespoons oil if it seems at all dry and tough. This 'spreads' the flavour more evenly throughout the dish, too.

If you cut the carrots, celery and fennel into very fine julienne strips, you can omit the blanching procedure.

Les Salsifis Poulette

Salsify in a Wine and Cream Sauce

Serves 4

Salsify, or oyster plant, is very popular in France and Italy but is out of fashion in Britain and America. Many years ago this tuber was one of the many eaten regularly by country people all over Europe. Now, most of these are wild plants which people do not even realize are edible, and salsify has been overlooked by British cooks and greengrocers. It is a great shame and I hope that salsify, and its 'wild' relations will soon experience a revival of interest. Salsify looks like a long, thin, smooth parsnip, but is often confused with another tuber, scorzonera or black salsify, which is closely related to white salsify but has a black skin. For this recipe the white-skinned variety is used.

Imperial (Metric)	American
For the salsify:	For the salsify:
2 fl oz (60ml) white wine vinegar	**¼ cup white wine vinegar**
2 lb (900g) salsify	**2 pounds salsify**
Sea salt	**Sea salt**
1 oz (25g) wholemeal flour	**¼ cup wholewheat flour**
4 tablespoons vegetable oil	**4 tablespoons vegetable oil**
For the sauce poulette:	For the sauce poulette:
1 oz (25g) butter	**2 tablespoons butter**
1 oz (25g) wholemeal flour	**¼ cup wholewheat flour**
4 fl oz (120ml) white wine	**½ cup white wine**
3 egg yolks	**3 egg yolks**
4 fl oz (120ml) sour cream	**½ cup sour cream**
Juice and grated rind of ½ lemon	**Juice and grated rind of ½ lemon**
Sea salt and freshly ground black pepper	**Sea salt and freshly ground black pepper**
Freshly grated nutmeg	**Freshly grated nutmeg**
1 tablespoon freshly chopped parsley	**1 tablespoon freshly chopped parsley**

1. Put 2 pints (1.2 litres/5 cups) water in a basin with the vinegar.
2. Peel and wash the salsify. Cut into small strips and soak in the acidulated water for 30 minutes to prevent the salsify discolouring.
3. Put another 2 pints (1.2 litres/5 cups) water in a large pan with a pinch of salt.
4. Blend the flour with the oil to make a paste and stir this paste into the water until thoroughly blended in. Boil the salsify for 25 minutes. Drain, reserve ½ pint (300ml/1⅓ cups) salsify liquor, refresh in cold water and drain again. Keep warm in an earthenware dish while the sauce is prepared.
5. For the sauce, heat the butter in a saucepan and add the flour. Cook for 3 minutes without browning. Add the reserved salsify liquor and the wine and cook until the sauce has thickened.
6. In a bowl beat the egg yolks lightly and blend in the cream until well mixed. Add the lemon juice and rind and seasoning.
7. Gradually add ¼ pint (150ml/⅔ cup) sauce to the egg mixture and then add back all the egg mixture into the pan of sauce, stir well and check the seasoning. Add grated nutmeg to taste.
8. Pour this sauce over the salsify and serve with a sprinkling of chopped parsley.

Celeri au Yaourt et Roquefort

Braised Celery with a Yogurt and Roquefort Sauce

Serves 4

Celery seeds have a fragrant aroma which is delicious for flavouring sauces and hard-boiled eggs — gourmets like celery seeds or celery salt with quails' or gulls' eggs in particular. To make celery salt, pound together in a mortar, or grind in a coffee mill, 1 teaspoon celery seeds to every 4 oz (100g/⅔ cup) sea salt.

Fresh green celery leaves make a pleasant addition to salads, and the root of the plant can be boiled and served as a vegetable, but it is the stalks of the celery plant which are used most often, in soups, salads, as *crudités*, or braised and served hot with a sauce as in this recipe.

Imperial (Metric)	American
2 heads celery	**2 heads celery**
2 tablespoons white wine vinegar	**2 tablespoons white wine vinegar**
1 oz (25g) wholemeal flour	**¼ cup wholewheat flour**
2 tablespoons vegetable oil	**2 tablespoons vegetable oil**
2 oz (50g) butter	**¼ cup butter**
For the sauce:	For the sauce:
1 oz (25g) butter	**2½ tablespoons butter**
1 oz (25g) wholemeal flour	**¼ cup wholewheat flour**
Sea salt and freshly ground black pepper	**Sea salt and freshly ground black pepper**
Freshly grated nutmeg	**Freshly grated nutmeg**
2 oz (50g) grated Roquefort cheese	**½ cup grated Roquefort cheese**
4 fl oz (120ml) natural yogurt	**½ cup plain yogurt**
3 tablespoons water	**3 tablespoons water**
1 teaspoon cornflour	**1 teaspoon cornstarch**
1 tablespoon freshly chopped parsley, for garnish	**1 tablespoon freshly chopped parsley, for garnish**
2 hard-boiled eggs, shelled and chopped, for garnish	**2 hard-boiled eggs, shelled and chopped, for garnish**

1. Trim the celery heads, removing any discoloured or damaged parts, and reserving the leaves for use in stocks. Cut the sticks of celery into pieces about 2 inches (5cm) long. Wash under running water.
2. Put 2 pints (1.2 litres/5 cups) water into a pan with the vinegar. Blend together the flour and oil and stir this into the boiling water.
3. Add the cut celery to the water and boil for 10 minutes, then refresh in cold water. Reserve ½ pint (300ml/1⅓ cups) of the celery liquor.
4. Heat the butter in a large saucepan and arrange the celery pieces in the bottom, packed close together. Add water to just come level with the celery and boil for 35 minutes until tender.
5. For the sauce, melt the remaining butter in a pan and add the flour. Cook, stirring, to make a roux, for 3 minutes without browning.
6. Gradually stir in the reserved celery stock and, when thick and smooth, add the salt, pepper and nutmeg and the cheese.
7. Blend the yogurt and water together with the cornflour (cornstarch). Gradually pour this mixture into the hot, but not boiling, sauce.

8 Reheat to boiling point and simmer gently for 4 minutes. Strain and check seasoning.
9 Remove the celery from the pan and drain. Arrange in a shallow serving dish and coat with the sauce. Sprinkle with parsley and chopped egg and serve immediately.

Les Petits Pois à la Française

Peas Cooked with Button Onions and Lettuce in Butter

Serves 4

The British tend to resist any adventurous methods of cooking peas. Fresh peas must be boiled with a few fresh mint leaves and that is all. Of course, mushy peas are also a traditional British dish, too, but that is about the extent of the variety in British pea-based dishes! I think it is the colour which puts many people off our traditional way of cooking peas. For people who expect peas to be vivid green bullets a first glimpse of *Petits Pois à la Française* will be a bit of a shock. The yellowy-brown colour which comes with longer, slower cooking, however, is accompanied by a wonderful development of flavour which any gourmet will tell you is worth reconsidering your aesthetic judgement for. Although usually encountered as a side dish, this is often served as a course in France and will make a tasty supper dish, served with a baked potato.

Imperial (Metric)	American
2 lb (900g) freshly picked green peas	**2 pounds freshly picked green peas**
12 button onions	**12 button onions**
1 small round-headed lettuce	**1 small round-headed lettuce**
4 oz (100g) butter	**½ cup butter**
1 teaspoon raw cane sugar	**1 teaspoon raw cane sugar**
Sea salt and freshly ground black pepper	**Sea salt and freshly ground black pepper**
1 tablespoon wholemeal flour	**1 tablespoon wholewheat flour**

1 Shell the peas and collect them in a bowl. Wash and drain them.
2 Peel and rinse the button onions.
3 Wash and separate the lettuce leaves. Discard any spoilt ones and shred the rest.
4 Heat three-quarters of the butter in a small saucepan and sauté the onions for 3 minutes without browning.
5 Add the lettuce and cook for 1 minute, then add the peas. Add just enough water to come level with the vegetables. Season with the sugar, salt and pepper. Cook gently until the vegetables are tender — about 15 to 20 minutes.
6 Blend the remaining butter with the flour to make a paste (this is called *beurre manié* in culinary terms). Stir this into the boiling liquid to thicken it. Check seasoning and serve on a plate, preferably with a border of *duchesse* potatoes.

Variations:
To cater for British tastes, a little freshly chopped mint could be sprinkled onto the dish. The dish could be liquidized with 1 pint (300ml/2½ cups) milk to make a soup, or drained and sieved to make a purée to fill artichoke bottoms as in the *Bouquetière* dish (page 104).

Pommes Amandine

Piped Potatoes with Almonds

Serves 4

A mixture of mashed potato, butter and egg is known as *duchesse* in culinary parlance. It is used as a piped mixture to decorate the edges of a dish, to cover the top of dishes, or is made into small pyramids or crowns or piped swirls to serve instead of normal, whole potatoes. My almond-flavoured *duchesse* mixture is used as a shell to hold a mixture of vegetables in cream sauce. The shells are sprinkled with toasted flaked almonds and baked or gently browned under the grill (broiler) before being filled.

The same mixture can, when cold, be shaped into croquettes of any shape, coated in flour, then beaten egg, then breadcrumbs, and fried until golden.

Imperial (Metric)	American
1½ lb (650g) potatoes	**1½ pounds potatoes**
2 oz (50g) butter	**¼ cup butter**
3 egg yolks	**3 egg yolks**
Sea salt and freshly ground black pepper	**Sea salt and freshly ground black pepper**
2 oz (50g) ground almonds	**½ cup ground almonds**
3 oz (75g) cooked green peas	**½ cup cooked green peas**
3 oz (75g) sweetcorn kernels	**½ cup sweetcorn kernels**
4 fl oz (120ml) thick white sauce	**½ cup thick white sauce**
4 oz (100g) lightly toasted flaked almonds	**1 cup lightly toasted slivered almonds**

1. Wash, peel and rewash the potatoes. Quarter and boil in salted water for 25 minutes until cooked. Drain.
2. Reheat the potatoes very gently for 4 minutes to dry them out. Then sieve or mash very thoroughly to a smooth purée. Return this to the saucepan with the butter and warm it through.
3. Stir in the beaten egg yolks and seasoning to mix well, then add the ground almonds.
4. On a greased baking tray, pipe 'nests' of potato mixture: start from the centre and pipe out spirally to make the base, then pipe a ring on top, around the edge, to make a little wall to keep the filling in. You should make 8 nests. Dry under the grill (broiler) for a few minutes but do not allow to colour too much.
5. In a saucepan blend the peas, corn and sauce together and season to taste. Fill the nests with this mixture and sprinkle with almonds. Bake at 400°F/200°C (Gas Mark 6) for 4 minutes and serve hot.

Note: The potato shells could be brushed with beaten egg for a better colour, or melted butter for extra flavour.

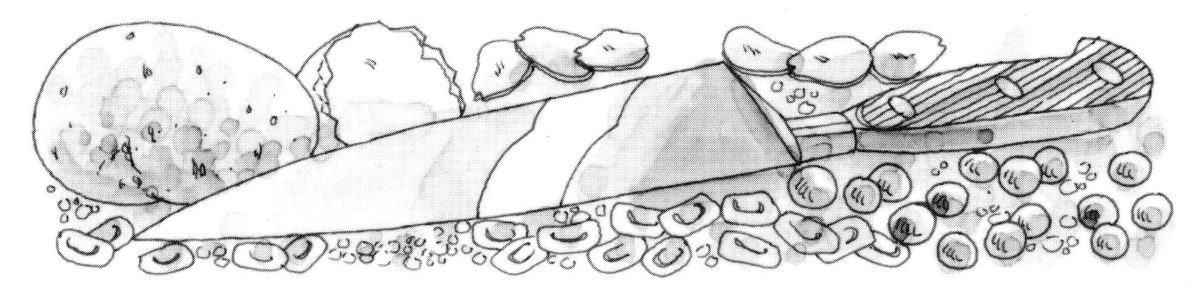

Opposite: *La Bouquetière Versailles* (page 104).

BEURRE
FRAIS

Les Pommes Nouvelles Smitane

Boiled New Potatoes with Sour Cream and Chives

Serves 4

The subject of whether new potatoes should be scraped of their skins is a matter of some debate these days. An *haute cuisine* chef, cooking for discerning customers, will almost certainly peel the fine skin from new potatoes because of the look of the dish. A more informal *bistro*-type restaurant, on the other hand, may well leave them on with no complaint from customers who are usually pleasantly surprised by the extra flavour — if, that is, they do not already eat them that way at home, since it certainly makes things much easier for the busy cook if the chore of scraping potatoes is dispensed with. It is all a matter of taste and aesthetics. Just don't forget to wash your new potatoes extra well if you intend to leave their skins in place! It is worth noting that, although old potatoes are cooked from cold water, new potatoes should be put into boiling water from the start.

Imperial (Metric)	American
2 lb (900g) small new potatoes	**2 pounds small new potatoes**
2 oz (50g) butter	**¼ cup butter**
1 small onion, chopped	**1 small onion, chopped**
1 teaspoon wholemeal flour	**1 teaspoon wholewheat flour**
¼ pint (150ml) sour cream	**⅔ cup sour cream**
Sea salt and freshly ground black pepper	**Sea salt and freshly ground black pepper**
2 tablespoons chopped fresh chives	**2 tablespoons chopped fresh chives**

1. Scrape the potatoes and rinse them, or wash them thoroughly. Plunge them into plenty of boiling salted water and cook for 20 minutes, or until cooked, and then drain well.
2. Heat the butter in a saucepan and sauté the onion until soft but not browned. Stir in the flour to absorb the butter.
3. Gradually add the sour cream. Season and simmer gently, stirring, to produce a smooth sauce.
4. Place the potatoes in a serving dish, coat with the sauce and sprinkle with the chives. Serve hot or cold.

Opposite: *Les Mangetouts aux Graines de Sésame* (page 108).

Pomme Suzette au Cognac

Baked Potato Stuffed with Mushrooms Flavoured with Brandy and Cream

Serves 4

The best choices for baking are old (late-season), floury potatoes. The ideal size is around 8 ounces (225g) per potato. The simple baked potato can be varied endlessly by its treatment once cooked. There is the classic knob of butter, with just a little sea salt and freshly ground black pepper, or cream cheese and chives. Then there are all the many 'stuffings', where the potato is halved once cooked and the cooked pulp scooped out, mixed with other ingredients, replaced in the shells and reheated in the oven. You can create anything from an accompanying vegetable to a full scale all-in-one supper dish. This dish, like all baked potato variations, is very easy to prepare, but is most luxurious in flavour and is a little bit different from the usual way of stuffing a potato shell, making it especially appealing in appearance, too.

Imperial (Metric)	American
4 large potatoes	**4 large potatoes**
4 oz (100g) butter	**½ cup butter**
Sea salt and freshly ground black pepper	**Sea salt and freshly ground black pepper**
1 lb (450g) white button mushrooms	**1 pound white button mushrooms**
1 small onion, chopped	**1 small onion, chopped**
4 tablespoons brandy	**4 tablespoons brandy**
1 pinch saffron	**1 pinch saffron**
4 tablespoons double cream	**4 tablespoons heavy cream**
Juice of ½ lemon	**Juice of ½ lemon**
1 teaspoon cornflour	**1 teaspoon cornstarch**
Freshly grated nutmeg	**Freshly grated nutmeg**
1 tablespoon freshly chopped parsley	**1 tablespoon freshly chopped parsley**

1. Wash the potatoes well and dry thoroughly. Wrap each potato in foil, place them in a roasting tin and bake for 1 hour at 400°F/200°C (Gas Mark 6).
2. Remove the potatoes from the oven and from their foil, cut in half lengthways and scoop out all the pulp.
3. Put all the potato pulp in a bowl and mash or sieve it to a smooth purée. Add half the butter and season with salt and pepper.
4. Place the mashed potato in a piping bag. Carefully pipe a border round the edge of each potato shell, leaving a central cavity in each one. This is to be filled with sauce. You can make the potato border as simple or as decorative as you like.
5. Clean and dry the mushrooms, trimming off any parts of the stalk which are sandy or earthy. Leave small mushrooms whole, halve or quarter any larger ones.
6. Heat the remaining butter in a small saucepan and sauté the onion until soft but not browned. Add the mushrooms and cook gently for 4 minutes.
7. Strain off all the juice which will have been produced into another saucepan and boil it for 3 minutes, until reduced by half. Add the brandy, saffron and cream and boil for 4 minutes until syrupy. Add the lemon juice.
8. Blend the cornflour (cornstarch) with 4 tablespoons of water and stir this into the sauce. Cook to thicken. Check the seasoning and add nutmeg.
9. Place some mushrooms and some sauce into the cavity of each potato.

10 Return the potatoes to the oven for 4 minutes to dry the potato border. Serve sprinkled with chopped parsley.

La Purée de Rutabaga aux Betteraves

Swede (Rutabaga) and Beetroot (Beet) Purée with Honey and Nuts

Serves 4

While no one would deny that fresh raw, or lightly cooked vegetables are most important and should be eaten frequently, a purée makes a pleasant change of texture for a meal, when prepared well and attractively presented. It can also be very nutritious, because all purées are best when enriched with eggs or cream and butter, which adds protein as well as improving the flavour and texture of the puréed vegetable. The best method of puréeing vegetables is to toss them in butter before boiling in the minimum of water, then pass them through a sieve or *mouli-légumes* (which gives a better texture than a blender or food processor) and reheat with cream or butter or beaten egg. This purée can be varied with different combinations of vegetables. All are prepared in the same way, only cooking times vary. All purées can be made into soups by diluting with stock or milk to the desired consistency.

Imperial (Metric)	American
1 lb (450g) beetroot	**1 pound beets**
1 lb (450g) swedes	**1 pound rutabaga**
4 oz (100g) butter	**½ cup butter**
2 oz (50g) chopped onion	**⅓ cup chopped onion**
2 oz (50g) honey	**4 tablespoons honey**
Sea salt and freshly ground black pepper	**Sea salt and freshly ground black pepper**
2 oz (50g) peanuts, toasted and ground to a paste with a little oil or water	**4 tablespoons peanuts, toasted and ground to a paste with a little oil or water**
3 fl oz (90ml) double cream	**⅓ cup heavy cream**

1. Wash, peel, thinly slice and rewash the beetroot (beets) and swedes (rutabaga).
2. Heat half the butter in a large pan and stir-fry the onion until soft but not brown. Add the vegetables and cook for 4 minutes.
3. Cover the vegetables level with water, stir in the honey and add seasoning. Boil for 25 minutes until the vegetables are soft. Drain the liquid and keep for use in soups.
4. Sieve the vegetables to a smooth purée.
5. Heat the rest of the butter in a pan and add the purée to reheat. Simmer for 8 minutes, add the ground peanuts and check seasoning.
6. Finally, blend in the cream and serve.

La Grand Friture de Légumes Cannoise

A Varied Selection of Fried Vegetables

Serves 6-8

All over the world, the French *pommes frites* are accepted as being the best type of potato chip created — even the Americans acknowledge this with their 'French fries'. Far from being a smoky, greasy affair, frying is an art in which the vegetable cooked is sealed by the hot oil long before it has time to absorb any great amount, and all the flavour and juices of the vegetable are sealed in too. A good quality vegetable oil will not produce clouds of black smoke like old-fashioned animal fats, and will allow the true taste of each vegetable to shine through undisguised and unspoilt. Sesame, soya, sunflower, or corn are all good choices of oil. The smaller the item to be cooked, the hotter the oil must be, and the quicker cooking time will be. Large pieces will have to be cooked in oil of about 330-350°F/165-175°C. Large chips are best 'blanched' first — that is, cooked for 5 minutes, without browning, at 285°F/140°C, drained and then cooked again at 350-370°F/175-185°C. After frying, any excess oil will drain away onto kitchen paper. The right temperature fat will produce crisp, golden food, not a greasy, soggy mess. Try to get a '*friture*', a proper copper-bottomed frying pot, rather than using an ordinary saucepan for deep-frying, and don't top up your frying oil. Strain it after use and then keep it for shallow frying or roasting — and *never* fill your *friture* more than half full of oil. Follow these rules and your *Grand Friture* will make a spectacular accompaniment to any dish.

I have selected four different vegetables for this dish — two more could be added from Chapter 3 — *Champignons et Chou-Fleurs Frits* (page 46), mushrooms and cauliflowers. But here, for now, are classic French *pommes frites*, onion rings coated with a simple milk and flour 'batter', aubergines (eggplants) in breadcrumbs, and courgettes (zucchini) in batter. Thus you have a selection of flavours, shapes and textures as well as coatings from which your guests can make a choice. For this amount of fried vegetables, you will need about 3 pints (1.5 litres/7½ cups) vegetable oil.

Imperial (Metric) For pommes frites:	American For pommes frites:
1 lb (450g) potatoes	**1 pound potatoes**

1 Wash and peel the potatoes. Cut into slices ½ inch thick and 2 inches (5cm) long. Then cut these strips into chips 2 inches (5cm) by ½ inch (1cm) by ½ inch (1cm).

2 Wash the chips and dry them thoroughly. Heat the oil and plunge the *frites* in a wire basket, into the oil. Cook without colouring for 4-5 minutes and then remove and drain. Just before you wish to eat them, plunge them back into very hot oil and cook for 1 minute or less until golden and crisp.

Imperial (Metric) For the onion rings:	American For the onion rings:
2 large onions	**2 large onions**
½ pint (300ml) milk	**1⅓ cups milk**
3 oz (75g) wholemeal flour	**¾ cup wholewheat flour**
Sea salt and freshly ground black pepper	**Sea salt and freshly ground black pepper**

1 Peel and slice the onions into ⅛ inch (2mm) thick rings, crossways. Separate into rings.

2 Pour the milk into a soup plate and dip the rings into the milk to wet them thoroughly.

3 Season the flour with the salt and pepper and then coat each onion ring completely in seasoned flour.

4 Heat the oil to 370°F/185°C or higher and deep-fry the onion rings for 30 seconds and then drain immediately and serve.

Imperial (Metric) For the aubergine fritters:	American For the eggplant fritters:
2 large aubergines (½ lb/225g each)	**2 large eggplants (8 ounces each)**
3 oz (75g) wholemeal flour	**¾ cup wholewheat flour**
Sea salt	**Sea salt**
Pinch powdered garlic	**Pinch powdered garlic**
1 egg, beaten	**1 egg, beaten**
4 oz (100g) wholemeal breadcrumbs	**2 cups wholewheat breadcrumbs**

1 Slice the aubergines (eggplants) thickly (about ¼ inch/5mm), slantwise. Wash well and leave in cold water for 10 minutes. Dry with a cloth.
2 Season the flour with salt and garlic powder and coat each slice of aubergine (eggplant) on both sides.
3 Then dip each slice first into beaten egg and then into the breadcrumbs.
4 Heat the oil as for the onion rings and fry the slices for 45 seconds and drain on kitchen paper.

Imperial (Metric) For the courgette frites:	American For the zucchini frites:
4 courgettes	**4 zucchini**
3 oz (75g) wholemeal flour	**¾ cup wholewheat flour**
Sea salt and freshly ground black pepper	**Sea salt and freshly ground black pepper**
½ pint (300ml) batter (page 46)	**1⅓ cups batter (page 46)**

1 Cut each courgette (zucchini) into four sticks lengthwise, with top and tail trimmed off.
2 Season the flour with salt and pepper and then toss the courgette (zucchini) sticks in this. Then dip each stick into the batter.
3 Heat the oil as before and plunge the courgettes (zucchini) in and deep-fry for 2 minutes. Drain well and dry on kitchen paper.

To serve:
When all your vegetables are cooked, place a simple doily on a flat plate and arrange all the vegetables in a pretty pile, either mixed decoratively together or in layers, according to taste. If you have worked quickly they will all still be hot and crisp. Decorate the edges of the dish with lemon quarters, or serve with a dish of Sauce Tartare (page 47) on the side.

The mushroom and cauliflower fritters (page 46) may be used as well, particularly if you are entertaining several people. This 'fry-up' is ideal as a side dish at an out-of-doors barbecue meal, or for a children's party.

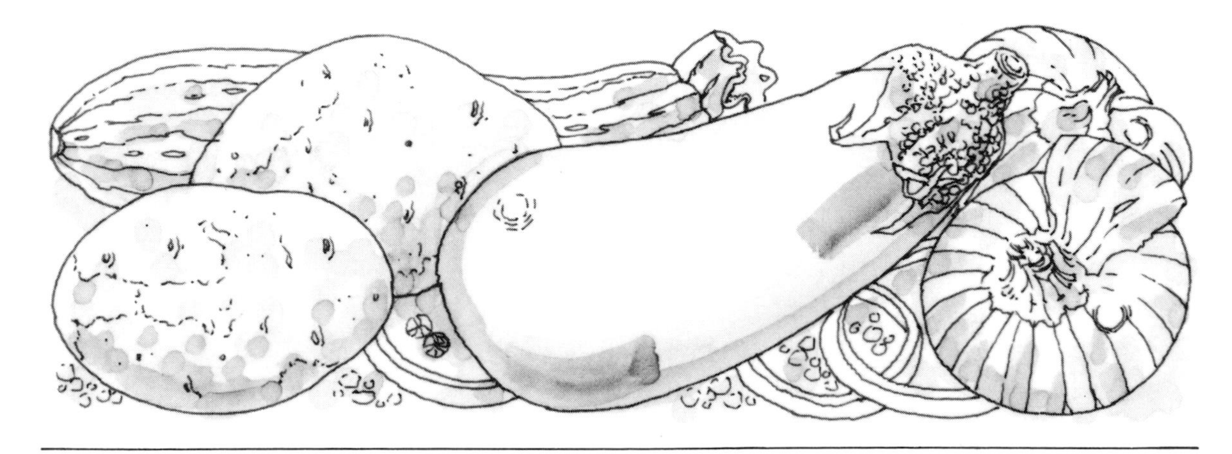

Les Haricots Panachés Tarbaise

Two Types of Bean in a Rich Dressing

Serves 4

Beans were one of the first cultivated crops, some varieties being grown in Switzerland and northern Italy as early as the Bronze Age, and the Ancient Egyptians took them as an emblem for life itself. In the seventeenth century beans were eaten as a cure for baldness, and have always been eaten mashed with garlic as a remedy for coughs and colds.

Flageolets are the finest, most delicious of all the dried varieties of beans, and tiny French (snap) beans are the best fresh type. They are often served together in France, the pods and the seeds providing an interesting contrast of texture, flavour and colour.

Imperial (Metric)	American
½ lb (225g) flageolet beans	**1 cup flageolet beans**
1 onion, studded with 2 cloves	**1 onion, studded with 2 cloves**
½ carrot	**½ carrot**
Sprig thyme	**Sprig thyme**
½ lb (225g) fresh, small French beans	**8 ounces fresh, small snap beans**
For the dressing:	For the dressing:
2 oz (50g) chopped onion	**⅓ cup chopped onion**
1 teaspoon Dijon mustard	**1 teaspoon Dijon mustard**
1 hard-boiled egg, shelled and chopped	**1 hard-boiled egg, shelled and chopped**
3 tablespoons white wine vinegar	**3 tablespoons white wine vinegar**
3 tablespoons walnut oil	**3 tablespoons walnut oil**
3 tablespoons natural yogurt	**3 tablespoons plain yogurt**
Sea salt and freshly ground black pepper	**Sea salt and freshly ground black pepper**
1 tablespoon chopped fresh chives	**1 tablespoon chopped fresh chives**
1 clove garlic, chopped	**1 clove garlic, chopped**
Juice and finely grated rind of 1 lemon	**Juice and finely grated rind of 1 lemon**
2 tablespoons chopped fresh parsley	**2 tablespoons chopped fresh parsley**

1. Soak the flageolet beans overnight in distilled or boiled water. Wash and drain.
2. Boil in plain water, skimming off any scum which rises to the surface. After 2 hours, by which time the beans should be nearly cooked, add the onion, carrot and thyme. Cook for 30 minutes more, by which time the beans should be done. The beans should at all times just simmer gently, covered with a lid. Discard the vegetables and drain the flageolets. Place them in a serving bowl and keep hot.
3. Top and tail the French (snap) beans. Boil in salted water for 6 to 8 minutes and drain. Place in the bowl with the flageolets.
4. Put all the dressing ingredients into a blender and liquidize them.
5. Toss the hot beans in the cold dressing and serve immediately.

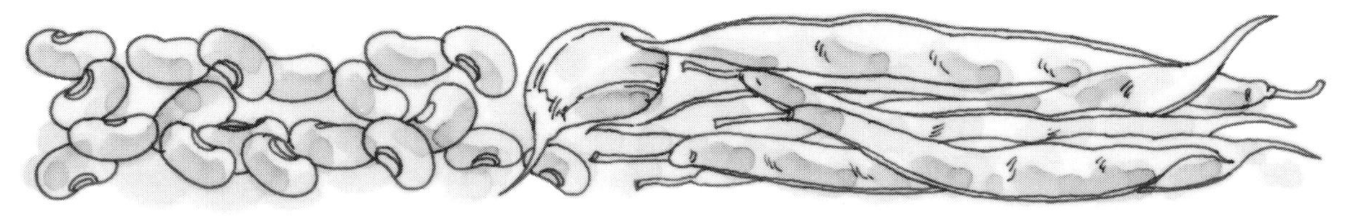

Macaroni Champs Elysées

A Medley of Macaroni and Vegetable Strips with Mangetout (Snow) Peas

Serves 4

Pasta is delicious served in the Summer as a salad dish with fresh, lightly-cooked vegetables or with pulses. (It is just as good in Winter, too, of course!) When you need a carbohydrate-based side dish which is not too heavy, a pasta salad, hot or cold, is ideal. Macaroni is a useful size and shape to mingle with the pleasantly *al dente* vegetables. Always cook the pasta in plenty of salted water and drain very well. Plenty of lemon juice is needed in this dish to really sharpen up the flavour of the mild pasta and fresh vegetables.

Extra pasta will keep well in the refrigerator for up to a week. Before use, reheat it in boiling water for a few minutes, then drain well and sauté in butter before adding your chosen sauce.

Imperial (Metric)	American
4 oz (100g) carrots	**4 ounces carrots**
4 oz (100g) celery	**4 ounces celery**
4 oz (100g) French beans	**4 ounces snap beans**
4 oz (100g) red pepper	**4 ounces red pepper**
4 oz (100g) mangetout peas	**4 ounces snow peas**
4 oz (100g) onion	**4 ounces onion**
4 oz (100g) wholemeal macaroni	**1 cup wholewheat macaroni**
4 oz (100g) butter	**½ cup butter**
Sea salt and freshly ground black pepper	**Sea salt and freshly ground black pepper**
3 fl oz (90ml) cream	**⅓ cup cream**
Juice of 1 lemon	**Juice of 1 lemon**
4 oz (100g) grated Gruyère cheese	**1 cup grated Gruyère cheese**

1 Peel and wash the carrots. Cut into very fine strips. Cut the celery to a similar thickness. Top and tail the beans. Split and seed the pepper and cut into thin strips. Top and tail the mangetout (snow) peas. Slice the onion into thin rings.
2 Blanch all the vegetables except the onion in boiling salted water for 5 minutes. Drain well.
3 Boil the macaroni in boiling salted water for 12 minutes or until *al dente*. Refresh in cold water and then drain well.
4 Heat the butter in a large pan and toss all the vegetables except the onion together. Season and place in a dish.
5 In any butter remaining in the pan, sauté the onion for 4 minutes until soft. Drain.
6 Pour the cream into the pan and bring to the boil. Add the lemon juice and seasoning. Stir this mixture in with the vegetables and the pasta and serve immediately, with grated cheese stirred in at the last minute.

7 *Les Salades Simples et Composées*

Simple and Mixed Salads

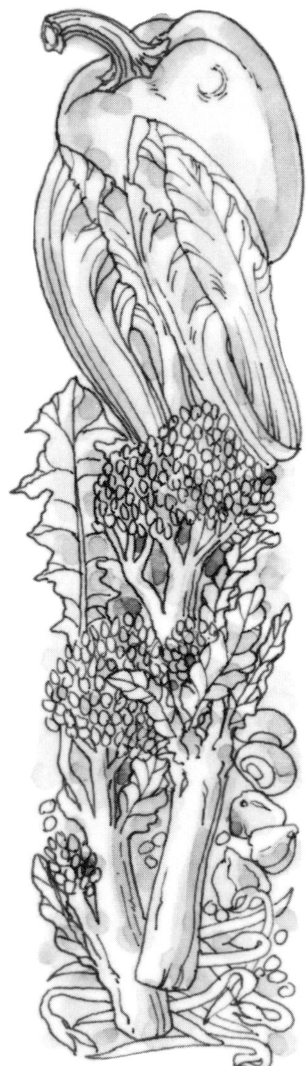

There are those for whom a lifelong experience of salads has been the occasional exposure to a few pieces of iceberg lettuce (so named for the similarity of flavour!) on the side of a restaurant plate. One can forgive them for not realizing the wealth of flavours, colours and textures which can be added to a salad, simply by varying the leaf ingredients, let alone all the other possibilities. But anyone who loves good food, and vegetarians and wholefooders in particular, should try to use this cornucopia to the full. So many leaves can be used to make a delicious salad: I can recall as a child picking wild dandelion leaves from our village green for inclusion in a salad. This is quite common in France, and is catching on in Britain though dandelions are still, for most people, just a weed. (If you decide to try dandelion leaves, do pick young tender ones, away from main roads or potentially sprayed crops to avoid pollution.) Other leaves include cress, chicory (endive), Chinese leaves, radiccio (a beautiful red-leafed lettuce), corn salad or lamb's lettuce, spinach and chard — and, of course, lettuce in all its varieties.

All vegetables can be added to salads, from the standard tomatoes and cucumber, to root vegetables, cauliflower or broccoli florets, mushrooms and herbs. Grains, pulses and nuts make wonderful additions, too, for a main course salad, and fruits should not be forgotten, as they give a salad an exotic flavour which is most refreshing.

Sprouted Seeds

I feel these deserve a special mention here, as they are a wonderful form of food and are a delicious addition to any salad. Sprouting increases the vitamin content of seeds tremendously — between four and ten times over the course of four days. Alfalfa sprouts in particular are extremely healthy. They contain many minerals and amino acids as well as vitamins, and they aid in the formation of digestive enzymes. Almost any whole, natural seed will sprout, and all are full of flavour and life. In fact, many people believe that sprouted seeds are the best form of food of all, because of this fact that they are actually 'alive' when eaten.*

Salad Oils

Everyone has their favourite oil for salad dressings, and these tastes vary regionally and nationally, as well as personally. The best of all oils for salads is, in my opinion, walnut oil. It is, however, very expensive, but it can be mixed half-and-half with peanut oil, to lower the cost while retaining the same wonderful flavour. Sesame oil, too, has a distinctive flavour, and is especially good to use if you are making a salad with an eastern flavour. The popularity of Vietnamese cooking in France has brought with it a growing use of sesame oil. Peanut oil (known in France as *arachide* oil) is most popular in the north of France, whereas in the south the only oil considered worth using is olive oil. This, too, is expensive, and some people consider its flavour a little strong for salads, but for others it is an indispensable part of a vinaigrette or mayonnaise. Safflower and sunflower oils are many people's choice of salad oil and make a good, mild-flavoured base for a dressing, but soya oil and corn oil are best kept for cooking.

Of course, all oils are high in calories and, for slimmers, tend to defeat the object of eating a salad in the first place. There are many alternatives, such as soured cream and low fat yogurt, which replace oil quite acceptably. Avocado pulp can also be used in a dressing because of its high oil content, as has been discussed earlier in this book.

Vinegars

All manner of substances can be used to make vinegar, including malt, cider, molasses and wine. Vinegar made from good, strong cider is as good as wine vinegar and, many would say, better for the health, and is always better than malt vinegar for any of the purposes in this book. Malt vinegar is prepared from an infusion of malt and cereal which is fermented with yeast to produce alcohol. The vinegar produced is almost always dark in colour, always extremely strong, and will tend to swamp the subtle ingredients in these recipes.

Wine vinegar is made from soured red or white wine, many of the best varieties coming from the Orléans area in France. There is also a type of vinegar called spirit vinegar, which is produced by an intermediate distillation at a point between the alcoholic fermentation and the acetification of the liquid. This type of vinegar is most often used for the making of pickles and sauces.

As with oils, the type of vinegar used is largely up to the chef; however, the choice is not so wide. I would only advocate the use of cider or wine vinegar for salad dressings, since they add flavour but do not overpower the delicate flavours of the vegetables being used. Perhaps the best way of trying out these flavours is to taste them for yourself — that way you will come to know which oil and which vinegar suits a salad best.

Brillat-Savarin wholeheartedly praised the salad. Gourmets have always recognized the use of a delicate *mélange* of leaves and herbs, and perhaps a few root vegetables, as a refresher between courses to stimulate the palate in preparation for indulgences still to come, but now salads are being accepted as a course, and even a meal, in themselves. They can be as full of goodness and flavour as you choose to make them. Take an example from the recipes in this chapter and learn to see your salads as creations worthy of real enjoyment, not to be hidden shamefacedly at the edge of a plate. Your palate and your health will benefit!

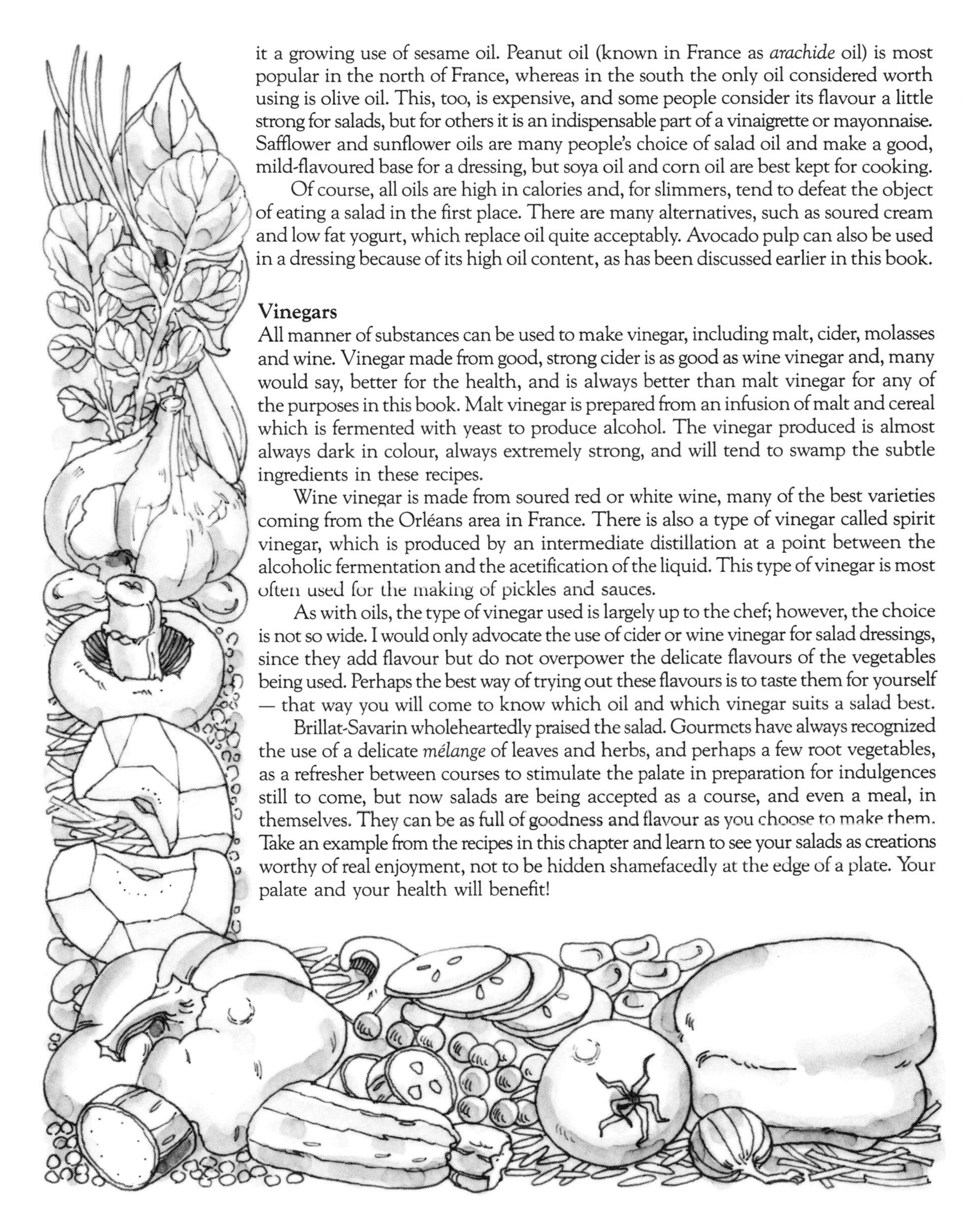

* For more information about sprouting seeds, see *The Complete Sprouting Book* by Per and Gita Sellmann (Thorsons, 1984).

La Salade au Fromage du Cantal

Cantal Cheese Salad

Serves 4

Many types of cheese are used to complement green salads, either as a part of the dressing (blue cheese is well known in this context) or as a part of the garnish, cut into small cubes. Either way, the result is a delicious and nutritionally very good meal or accompanying dish. In France, the main course is usually followed by a salad and then the cheeseboard, before dessert, so this particular salad combines the two courses into one.

I have used Cantal for this salad. It is a hard, pressed cheese which, when fresh, can have a crumbly texture like that of a mature English Cheddar or Wensleydale, or Greek Féta.

Imperial (Metric)	American
For the dressing:	For the dressing:
3 tablespoons cider vinegar	**3 tablespoons cider vinegar**
2 tablespoons walnut *or* **olive oil**	**2 tablespoons walnut** *or* **olive oil**
½ teaspoon sea salt	**½ teaspoon sea salt**
Freshly ground black pepper	**Freshly ground black pepper**
½ onion, chopped	**½ onion, chopped**
1 clove garlic, peeled	**1 clove garlic, peeled**
1 wedge lemon	**1 wedge lemon**
1 large sprig parsley, washed and dried	**1 large sprig parsley, washed and dried**
2 tablespoons crumbled Cantal cheese	**2 tablespoons crumbled Cantal cheese**
For the salad:	For the salad:
1 lettuce with a good heart	**1 lettuce with a good heart**
1 red pepper, seeded and chopped	**1 red pepper, seeded and chopped**
1 green pepper, seeded and chopped	**1 green pepper, seeded and chopped**
1 tomato, sliced	**1 tomato, sliced**
1 small onion, sliced into rings	**1 small onion, sliced into rings**
¼ cucumber, sliced	**¼ cucumber, sliced**
4 oz (100g) Cantal, Féta *or* **mature Cheddar cheese, cut into ¼ inch (5mm) cubes**	**½ cup Cantal, Féta** *or* **mature Cheddar cheese, cut into ¼ inch cubes**
1 tablespoon freshly chopped parsley	**1 tablespoon freshly chopped parsley**

1. Place all the ingredients for the dressing into a blender (including the lemon wedge, rind and all) and liquidize. Do this some time in advance so that the flavours have a chance to mingle.
2. Clean the lettuce leaf by leaf and drain in a salad basket or a cloth by shaking well.
3. Place the lettuce leaves and the diced peppers in a large salad bowl (preferably wooden). Shake the dressing well in a corked bottle or screw-capped jar and sprinkle half of it onto the lettuce and peppers and toss well.
4. Make a well in the centre of the lettuce and pepper mixture. Around the top, arrange a decorative, alternating pattern of tomato, onion and cucumber slices and black olives.
5. Place the cubes of cheese in the centre of the salad and splash the rest of the dressing over the cheese and other salad ingredients.
6. Sprinkle with parsley and serve immediately, either as a main course or as the last course of a meal. Serve with crusty wholemeal bread to mop up the dressing.

La Salade Auvergnate

Potato and Watercress Salad from the Province of Auvergne

Serves 4

In terms of flavour, watercress has become a great favourite with the new generation of chefs. Liquidized with mayonnaise, white sauce or yogurt it adds a very special flavour to a sauce, as well as a most attractive colour. We older cooks are inclined to prefer using it raw, its leaves mingling attractively with the other ingredients, such as in this salad from Auvergne. The Auvergne is famous for its Cantal cheese, which we used in the previous recipe. Here it is featured again, but this time in a more substantial salad with new potatoes. The watercress adds colour to the pale, creamy-yellow hues of the salad. It is best to peel the potatoes in this recipe as they will absorb the dressing much better through their flesh than through their skins.

Imperial (Metric)	American
For the dressing:	For the dressing:
2 tablespoons wine vinegar	**2 tablespoons wine vinegar**
4 tablespoons walnut oil	**4 tablespoons walnut oil**
1 teaspoon Dijon mustard	**1 teaspoon Dijon mustard**
Sea salt and freshly ground black pepper	**Sea salt and freshly ground black pepper**
2 small shallots, chopped	**2 small shallots, chopped**
6 leaves watercress	**6 leaves watercress**
For the salad:	For the salad:
1½ lb (750g) new potatoes, washed	**1½ pounds new potatoes, washed**
1 small bunch watercress	**1 small bunch watercress**
5 oz (150g) Cantal cheese, cut into ¼ inch (5mm) cubes	**⅔ cup Cantal cheese, cut into ¼ inch cubes**

1 Place all the dressing ingredients in a blender and liquidize. Reserve, to allow the flavours to develop and mingle.

2 Boil the potatoes for 20 to 25 minutes, until tender. As soon as they are cool enough to handle, peel their skins, dice the potatoes and place them in a salad bowl.

3 Clean the watercress thoroughly and remove any tough stalks. Stir in with the potatoes, add the cheese and mix all the ingredients well.

4 Stir in the dressing; toss the salad to coat everything evenly and serve.

Note: New potatoes will absorb the dressing best while still warm, and the salad is best served, too, while the potatoes are warm, contrasting with the other, cold, ingredients.

La Salade de Poireau à la Rouennaise

Leek Salad

Serves 4

In this dish, the leeks are cooked and served in a way normally reserved for asparagus. Tender young leeks, well prepared, can be easily as delicious a dish as luxurious (and expensive) fresh asparagus spears. To make the dish more nutritional I have created a dressing using nuts and eggs, which will add protein to the salad.

Imperial (Metric)	American
For the dressing:	For the dressing:
4 fl oz (120ml) dry white wine	**½ cup dry white wine**
1 teaspoon Dijon mustard	**1 teaspoon Dijon mustard**
1 raw egg yolk	**1 raw egg yolk**
2 hard-boiled eggs, shelled and chopped	**2 hard-boiled eggs, shelled and chopped**
2 oz (50g) roasted peanuts	**4 tablespoons roasted peanuts**
2 tablespoons peanut oil	**2 tablespoons peanut oil**
3 fl oz (90ml) sour cream	**⅓ cup sour cream**
Juice and grated rind of 1 lemon	**Juice and grated rind of 1 lemon**
1 clove garlic, chopped	**1 clove garlic, chopped**
1 tablespoon fresh chopped parsley and mint	**1 tablespoon fresh chopped parsley and mint**
Sea salt and freshly ground black pepper	**Sea salt and freshly ground black pepper**
1 teaspoon coriander seeds	**1 teaspoon coriander seeds**
For the salad:	For the salad:
16 fresh young leeks	**16 fresh young leeks**

1. Combine all the dressing ingredients in a blender, and liquidize to a well-emulsified, creamy dressing. Reserve until ready to use.
2. Trim the roots from the leeks, remove any damaged or wilted leaves and trim away part of the green leaves, but not all.
3. Cut down the centre of the leeks from the top of the green leaves just as far as the start of the white. Wash carefully under running water, to get rid of all the dirt which is hidden in the leaves.
4. Drain the leeks and then tie in bundles of four. Boil in salted water for 12 to 15 minutes. Drain well and untie. Squeeze each leek very gently to remove excess water, but do not squeeze out all the juice.
5. Arrange four leeks on each serving plate. Either serve hot with the dressing separately, or cold likewise, or pour on a little dressing, thus allowing the leeks to cool in the dressing. They will absorb more this way.

Note: A dish of boiled new potatoes makes an ideal accompaniment to this dish, or serve with plenty of wholemeal bread to mop up the dressing.

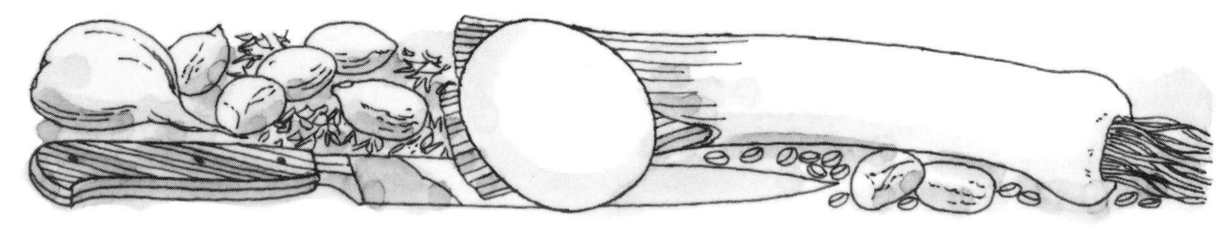

La Salade de Mâche Ducastaing

Corn Salad, Beetroot (Beet) and Celery Salad with a Wine and Blue Cheese Dressing

Serves 4

There are many names, in both French and English, for this delicious little salad vegetable. In France it is *mâche* or *doucette*, in English it is known as corn salad or lamb's lettuce. It grows all over Europe in late Winter and Spring, although it is, sadly, a rare sight in greengrocers' shops. It has always been used as a spring tonic by country people, and its fresh root is the basis for a homoeopathic remedy.

This recipe combines it with equal mixtures of celery, beetroot (beet) and celeriac, in an orange and cheese-flavoured dressing, which incorporates the very special French flavour of *St Raphael*, the quinine-flavoured aperitif.

Imperial (Metric)	American
For the dressing:	For the dressing:
1 tablespoon brandy *or* orange liqueur	**1 tablespoon brandy *or* orange liqueur**
1 tablespoon *St Raphael* aperitif	**1 tablespoon *St Raphael* aperitif**
Juice and grated rind of 1 orange	**Juice and grated rind of 1 orange**
1 tablespoon wine vinegar	**1 tablespoon wine vinegar**
2 tablespoons peanut oil	**2 tablespoons peanut oil**
2 egg yolks	**2 egg yolks**
1 oz (25g) mashed Roquefort cheese *or* any blue cheese except Gorgonzola	**4 tablespoons mashed Roquefort cheese *or* any blue cheese except Gorgonzola**
1 small shallot, chopped	**1 small shallot, chopped**
2 tablespoons single cream	**2 tablespoons light cream**
½ tablespoon horseradish sauce	**½ tablespoon horseradish sauce**
Sea salt and freshly ground black pepper	**Sea salt and freshly ground black pepper**
For the salad:	For the salad:
½ lb (225g) corn salad	**8 ounces corn salad**
½ lb (225g) celery, cleaned	**8 ounces celery, cleaned**
½ lb (225g) cooked beetroot, peeled	**8 ounces cooked beet, peeled**
½ lb (225g) celeriac root, peeled	**8 ounces celeriac root, peeled**
Orange rind to taste, cut into fine strips	**Orange rind to taste, cut into fine strips**
20 shelled walnuts	**20 shelled English walnuts**

1. Put all the dressing ingredients into a blender and liquidize. Set aside for the flavours to mingle and develop.
2. Clean the corn salad and trim off any roots. Leave in sprigs.
3. Cut the celery and beetroot (beet) into julienne strips (about the length and thickness of matchsticks).
4. Soak the celeriac in water acidulated with a little white wine vinegar and cut into julienne strips only at the last minute.
5. Place the orange strips in a little water and blanch for 5 minutes, then refresh in cold water.
6. Combine all the salad ingredients except the orange strips in a salad bowl and toss with the dressing (but do not drench the ingredients with it). Sprinkle the strips of orange rind over the top.

Variation:
The salad could be garnished with orange segments instead of strips of peel.

La Salade Flamande aux Choux Rouges

Flemish Red Cabbage Salad

Serves 4
Illustrated opposite page 128.

A *sauerkraut* of cabbage, that is a fermented mixture of red or white cabbage, is very popular in Europe, particularly in its Eastern regions. This salad uses red cabbage, but you might like to substitute white for a more traditional *sauerkraut*-type base. I think you will find that a vinaigrette-based dressing is better for tenderizing the cabbage than the typical mayonnaise-based one. If you use white cabbage, you may prefer to use a milder cheese than Roquefort or similar blue cheeses. If so, use Cheddar, Cantal, Edam, Port Salut, Gouda or Féta — whichever you choose will be equally flavoursome and nutritional. Some people find that cabbage has an untoward effect upon their digestive systems — they will be delighted to know that grated carrot is used in almost all coleslaw recipes to combat just this occurrence, and that pickling the cabbage in the dressing for at least an hour before eating will diminish the inconvenience, too!

Imperial (Metric)	American
For the dressing:	For the dressing:
3 tablespoons cider vinegar	**3 tablespoons cider vinegar**
3 tablespoons peanut *or* **sunflower oil**	**3 tablespoons peanut** *or* **sunflower oil**
1 medium onion, chopped	**1 medium onion, chopped**
2 cloves garlic, peeled	**2 cloves garlic, peeled**
1 oz (50g) Roquefort cheese *or* **other blue cheese of choice, crumbled**	**¼ cup Roquefort cheese** *or* **other blue cheese of choice, crumbled**
Sea salt and freshly ground black pepper	**Sea salt and freshly ground black pepper**
1 teaspoon grainy mustard	**1 teaspoon grainy mustard**
1 tablespoon honey	**1 tablespoon honey**
For the salad:	For the salad:
1 small red cabbage (about 1 lb/450g)	**1 small red cabbage (about 1 pound)**
2 large carrots, peeled and grated	**2 large carrots, peeled and grated**
4 oz (100g) firm blue cheese, cut into small cubes	**½ cup firm blue cheese, cut into small cubes**
2 Golden Delicious apples	**2 Golden Delicious apples**
2 tablespoons chopped fresh parsley	**2 tablespoons chopped fresh parsley**
2 tablespoons chopped fresh chives *or* **spring onions**	**2 tablespoons chopped fresh chives** *or* **scallions**

1. Put all the ingredients for the dressing into a blender and liquidize for a few seconds until the dressing is emulsified and thin. Set aside until needed, for the flavours to mingle and develop.
2. Quarter the cabbage and remove the woody core. Cut the leaves into very thin shreds and place in a salad bowl.
3. Combine the grated carrot with the shredded cabbage and stir in the cubed cheese. Toss with dressing and leave for 1 hour to marinate.
4. Just before serving, cut each apple into quarters, and then cut each quarter across into triangles. Toss with the salad and sprinkle with parsley and chives. Serve at once.

La Salade de Concombre à la Menthe

Cucumber Salad in a Mint Dressing

Serves 8

Cucumber has been cultivated for over 3,000 years. According to Pliny, the Emperor Tiberius had it on his table at all times. It was popular with another ruler, too — Henry VIII was apparently very fond of it. Cucumber has diuretic properties and its flesh is good for making skin smooth and white.

Mint is one of the most popular herbs, whether for savoury dishes such as this one, or as a flavouring for sweets and chocolates. Its scent alone is enough to stimulate the appetite. It was traditionally believed to prevent raw milk from souring — this is immaterial in this particular dish, since it is combined with yogurt! This salad is perfect on a hot Summer's day. The cooling combination of mint and yogurt refreshes the palate — and indeed the whole person — completely.

Imperial (Metric)	American
Juice and grated rind of 1 lemon	**Juice and grated rind of 1 lemon**
2 cloves garlic, peeled	**2 cloves garlic, peeled**
10 fresh mint leaves	**10 fresh mint leaves**
1 tablespoon raw cane sugar *or* **honey**	**1 tablespoon raw cane sugar** *or* **honey**
¼ pint (150ml) natural yogurt	**⅔ cup plain yogurt**
Sea salt and freshly ground black pepper	**Sea salt and freshly ground black pepper**
1 tablespoon freshly chopped parsley	**1 tablespoon freshly chopped parsley**
2 large green cucumbers	**2 large green cucumbers**

1 Place all the ingredients except the cucumbers into a blender and liquidize to a smooth creamy dressing.
2 Peel the cucumber, if wished, and cut into thin diagonal slices. Place in individual bowls and cover with dressing.

Variations:
This salad is good served with spicy dishes, or with plain boiled potatoes. The cucumbers could be liquidized along with the dressing ingredients, and the resulting blend served as a sauce with hot potato salad, hot boiled baby carrots or hot French (snap) beans.

La Salade Miraculeuse de la Vierge Marie

Lentil and Mushroom Salad

Serves 4

When I was a child, it was customary in my family to go on pilgrimages to Lourdes — we must have been at least ten times during my youth. The event was part holiday, part a religious dedication. I remember very well the modest little *pension de famille* where we used to stay. The food they served was simple but good, this salad being a particular favourite of mine. Sometimes my grandmother would make a batch of this salad herself, and pack it up for us to eat on the overnight train journey from Amiens to Lourdes. During such journeys we would sing hymns and pray for any sick relatives, or for our sins which as a child seemed so numerous! Anyway, we always seemed to feel much better for it.

Imperial (Metric)	American
For the dressing:	For the dressing:
2 shallots, chopped	**2 shallots, chopped**
2 spring onions, cleaned and chopped	**2 scallions, cleaned and chopped**
1 tablespoon fresh chopped chervil *or* **mint**	**1 tablespoon fresh chopped chervil** *or* **mint**
3 tablespoons olive oil	**3 tablespoons olive oil**
3 tablespoons wine vinegar	**3 tablespoons wine vinegar**
Sea salt and freshly ground black pepper	**Sea salt and freshly ground black pepper**
For the salad:	For the salad:
½ lb (225g) green lentils	**1⅓ cups green lentils**
1 medium onion	**1 medium onion**
2 cloves	**2 cloves**
1 *bouquet garni* (sprig thyme, stick celery and bay leaf, tied in a bunch)	**1 *bouquet garni* (sprig thyme, stalk celery, and bay leaf, tied in a bunch)**
2 cloves garlic	**2 cloves garlic**
2 large carrots, peeled and sliced	**2 large carrots, peeled and sliced**
½ pint (300ml) red wine	**1⅓ cups red wine**

1 Put all the ingredients for the dressing in a blender and liquidize to a smooth sauce. Reserve until needed.
2 Pick over the lentils for stones or other impurities. Soak in boiled or distilled water for 2 hours.
3 Peel the onion and stud it with the cloves.
4 Drain the lentils and place them in a large saucepan with the onion, *bouquet garni*, garlic and carrots. Cover with water and boil for 40 minutes.
5 Drain the lentils again and this time reheat in the red wine for 15 minutes. Season with sea salt and black pepper. Cool, without draining.
6 Clean the mushrooms and trim the stalks if sandy or earthy. Dry well and slice. Marinate them in 2 tablespoons of the dressing for 10 minutes.
7 Drain the lentils, stir in the mushrooms and the rest of the dressing and serve.

Opposite: *La Salade Flamande aux Choux Rouges* (page 126) and *La Taboulée des Croisades* (page 132).

La Salade Fort de France

Green Banana Salad from Martinique

Serves 4

When I was doing my National Service in the French navy, we visited the island of Martinique and I recall some superb meals there made with the local produce. This salad is an example of the French influence upon the regional style of cooking.

Green bananas, or plantains are, to the people who grow them, as potatoes are to us — a staple starch food. Like all these foods, they must be cooked — thus they are very different from the yellow bananas we know and should not be confused with them. Personally, I always feel we eat bananas before they are ripe enough. I prefer them when the flesh is turning brown and is at its most rich and sweet — many people throw them away at this point! To give you an example of the delicious flavour of a banana at this stage of ripeness, I have incorporated one into my dressing for this salad. Do try it, you will be delighted with the flavour.

Imperial (Metric)	American
For the dressing:	For the dressing:
1 teaspoon Dijon mustard	**1 teaspoon Dijon mustard**
½ oz (12g) fresh ginger, peeled	**½ ounce fresh ginger, peeled**
Juice and grated rind of 2 limes	**Juice and grated rind of 2 limes**
4 tablespoons peanut oil	**4 tablespoons peanut oil**
Sea salt and freshly ground black pepper	**Sea salt and freshly ground black pepper**
1 small green chilli, sliced	**1 small green chili, sliced**
1 small eating banana, *very* ripe	**1 small eating banana, *very* ripe**
For the salad:	For the salad:
2 lb (900g) green plantain bananas	**2 pounds green plantain bananas**
Juice of 1 lime	**Juice of 1 lime**
4 oz (100g) shelled green peas	**⅔ cup shelled green peas**
1 large carrot, peeled and diced	**1 large carrot, peeled and diced**
1 stick celery, chopped	**1 stalk celery, chopped**
1 iceberg or cos lettuce	**1 iceberg or Romaine lettuce**

1. Place all the salad dressing ingredients into a blender and liquidize to a creamy, smooth dressing. Place in the refrigerator until needed.
2. Peel the plantain and cut into pieces. Boil in salted water with the lime juice for 15 minutes, until tender. Drain well.
3. In a pan, boil together the peas, carrot and celery for 5 minutes. Drain.
4. Combine the plantain with the other vegetables in a salad bowl. Toss with dressing and chill for 1 hour. Serve with lettuce leaves all around the bowl.

Variations:
Fresh banana could be used if plantain is unavailable (but do not boil, of course!). A lemon mayonnaise with 4 tablespoons of apple purée added makes a good alternative dressing.

Opposite: *La Salade Princesse Anne* (page 134).

La Salade Montparnasse

A Mixed Vegetable Salad in Mayonnaise with Asparagus

Serves 4

In my student days in Paris, I and my fellow students would frequent the bistros of the Latin Quarter for our lunches. We could never afford the expensive meat-based dishes, but a mixed vegetable salad, augmented with an egg and with asparagus when in season, was an absolute treat and we never felt deprived of good food or nourishment.

I note that many children are very fond of mixed chopped vegetables in a salad dressing as a spread for sandwiches — well this is, I suppose, the grown-up, gourmet version!

This type of salad demands a perfect mayonnaise sauce, so follow the instructions carefully if you are a novice.

Imperial (Metric)	American
For the mayonnaise:	For the mayonnaise:
1 teaspoon Dijon mustard	**1 teaspoon Dijon mustard**
½ teaspoon sea salt	**½ teaspoon sea salt**
Large pinch freshly ground black pepper	**Large pinch freshly ground black pepper**
3 egg yolks	**3 egg yolks**
½ pint (300ml) peanut *or* **sunflower oil**	**1⅓ cups peanut** *or* **sunflower oil**
1 tablespoon warmed white wine vinegar	**1 tablespoon warmed white wine vinegar**
1 teaspoon honey	**1 teaspoon honey**
1 tablespoon mixed fresh chopped parsley and mint	**1 tablespoon mixed fresh chopped parsley and mint**
1 medium onion, finely chopped	**1 medium onion, finely chopped**
For the salad:	For the salad:
4 oz (100g) carrots	**4 ounces carrots**
4 oz (100g) potatoes	**4 ounces potatoes**
4 oz (100g) turnips	**4 ounces turnips**
4 oz (100g) French beans	**4 ounces snap beans**
4 oz (100g) shelled green peas	**⅔ cup shelled green peas**
4 oz (100g) sweetcorn kernels	**⅔ cup sweetcorn kernels**
2 oz (50g) white mushrooms *or* **truffles**	**2 ounces white mushrooms** *or* **truffles**
4 hard-boiled eggs	**4 hard-boiled eggs**
16 asparagus spears	**16 asparagus spears**

1. To make the mayonnaise, place the mustard, seasoning and egg yolks in a bowl and whisk together for 2 minutes. When it has begun to thicken up, start adding the oil — in drops at first, rather than a stream, beating each drop in well and whisking all the time. As it thickens you can add the oil a little more quickly, in a thin stream. When you have a thick mayonnaise, add the warm vinegar to thin it down slightly, and then stir in the rest of the mayonnaise ingredients. Set aside, covered.
2. Peel and wash the root vegetables. Cut them into ¼-inch (5mm) cubes. Boil each vegetable separately in salted water for 5 minutes, or until just tender but still crisp. Boil the peas and corn likewise. Refresh and drain all the vegetables.
3. Put all the cooked vegetables in a salad bowl and stir in half the mayonnaise.
4. Clean the mushrooms and slice thinly. If using truffles, boil them for 5 minutes in ¼ pint (150ml/⅔ cup) sherry or Madeira. Add to the salad.

5 Peel and halve the hard-boiled eggs and place, cut side down, on top of the salad. Coat with mayonnaise, thinned down a little if necessary with a spoonful of hot water.
6 Scrape the asparagus stalks thinly with a potato peeler. Tie in bundles of eight and boil in salted water for 10 minutes. Refresh and allow to cool.
7 When the asparagus is cold, untie the bundles and arrange the spears around the salad bowl. If the stalks are very long, just the tips could be used as garnish and the spears cut up and stirred into the salad.

La Salade d'Endives des Ardennes

Chicory (Endive) Salad with Fruit and Nuts

Serves 4

This salad combines the distinctive, slightly bitter flavour of chicory (endive), so much beloved by gourmets, with the sweetness of apple and dried fruit and the rich flavour of walnuts by amalgamating them in a creamy dressing. It is a truly delicious combination. For a more pronounced nutty taste, a few walnuts are blended in with the dressing, and the walnut flavour will be further enhanced if the nuts are lightly toasted before blending.

Imperial (Metric)	American
For the dressing:	For the dressing:
Juice and grated rind of 1 lemon	**Juice and grated rind of 1 lemon**
4 shelled walnuts	**4 shelled English walnuts**
¼ pint (150ml) single cream *or* **yogurt**	**⅔ cup light cream** *or* **yogurt**
Sea salt and freshly ground black pepper	**Sea salt and freshly ground black pepper**
Pinch ground ginger	**Pinch ground ginger**
Pinch raw cane sugar	**Pinch raw cane sugar**
1 teaspoon French mustard	**1 teaspoon French mustard**
1 hard-boiled egg, shelled and chopped	**1 hard-boiled egg, shelled and chopped**
For the salad:	For the salad:
4 large heads chicory	**4 large heads endive**
1 apple, Cox's or Golden Delicious	**1 apple, Cox's or Golden Delicious**
16 shelled walnuts	**16 shelled English walnuts**
2 oz (50g) sultanas, soaked in water *or* **wine**	**⅓ cup golden seedless raisins, soaked in water** *or* **wine**

1 Put all the dressing ingredients into a blender and liquidize. Set aside for the flavours to develop and mingle.
2 Trim the end of each head of chicory (endive) and remove any damaged or wilted outer leaves. Cut across into thick slices. (Do not wash after they have been sliced as they lose flavour and colour.)
3 Wash and core the apple, quarter and then slice each wedge into thin triangular slices.
4 Combine in a salad bowl the chicory (endive), walnuts and apple. Toss with the dressing.
5 Drain the sultanas (golden seedless raisins) and scatter them over the top of the salad.

La Taboulée des Croisades

Cracked Wheat Salad with Tomatoes and Olives

Serves 4
Illustrated opposite page 128.

Ever since the days of the Crusades, when French and English monarchs were constantly engaged in battles in the Middle East, there have been close connections between France and the Arab world — not always so warlike, fortunately, and from this involvement France has absorbed and adapted many spicy, interesting dishes. The process has been mutual, of course, and French cooking is very popular in many parts of the Middle East. *Taboulée* is one such dish which has been eagerly adopted into the cuisine of France. It is equally popular in fashionable Paris and in the cosmopolitan parts of southern France such as the port of Marseilles.

Cracked wheat, also known as bulghur, is a coarsely ground wheat which has been partially cooked and then dried. This method was developed in countries where raw grain would be eaten by insects before it could be prepared for the table!

Imperial (Metric)	American
For the dressing:	For the dressing:
Juice and grated rind of 2 lemons	**Juice and grated rind of 2 lemons**
3 fl oz (75ml) olive oil	**1/3 cup olive oil**
2 cloves garlic, peeled	**2 cloves garlic, peeled**
10 shelled walnuts	**10 shelled English walnuts**
2 fl oz (50ml) natural yogurt	**1/4 cup plain yogurt**
Sea salt and freshly ground black pepper	**Sea salt and freshly ground black pepper**
For the salad:	For the salad:
2 oz (50g) mixed butter and olive oil	**1/4 cup mixed butter and olive oil**
1 medium onion, chopped	**1 medium onion, chopped**
1/2 lb (225g) cracked wheat	**1 1/3 cups cracked wheat**
1 1/4 pints (750ml) water	**3 1/4 cups water**
Sea salt and freshly ground black pepper	**Sea salt and freshly ground black pepper**
4 oz (100g) baked beans	**2/3 cup baked beans**
4 medium tomatoes, sliced	**4 medium tomatoes, sliced**
8 black olives	**8 black olives**
1 cos lettuce	**1 Romaine lettuce**

1 Place all the ingredients for the dressing in a blender and liquidize to a smooth cream. Pour into a bottle or jar and refrigerate until needed.
2 Heat the oil and butter in a large saucepan and sauté the onion until translucent but not brown. Add the cracked wheat and stir to coat all the grains with fat — about 5 minutes. Add water and boil for 15 to 20 minutes, stirring occasionally. Drain and allow to cool. Season.
3 Stir in the dressing and the baked beans.
4 Turn the *taboulée* out into a fairly shallow bowl. Decorate the top with tomato slices and olives.
5 Separate the lettuce into leaves and rinse very thoroughly under cold running water. Drain well. If wished, refrigerate for a little while to make the leaves extra crisp.
6 Arrange the leaves around the edge of the bowl, or serve separately. Alternatively, spread the leaves out on a serving plate and top with small mounds of *taboulée*. Either way, the leaves are used to scoop up the salad, in much the same way as *crudités* with a dip.

La Salade de Fèves des Marais

Broad (Windsor) Bean Salad with Fennel

Serves 4

Broad beans make a most delicious salad, especially when they are very young. If you are unsure of the age of the beans, shell them and cook them as described below, but bite one before continuing with the salad. If the skin is tough, as is often the case with older beans, it really is worth removing it. This is no real hardship for four portions and your salad will be the better for it.

Fennel is delicious eaten raw, but for this salad you may wish to boil the slices for 5 minutes first. This is best if your head of fennel seems a tough one, and also if you are unsure whether your guests like this vegetable's distinctive aniseed taste, as this is diminished by boiling.

Imperial (Metric)	American
For the dressing:	For the dressing:
1 medium onion, chopped	**1 medium onion, chopped**
1 tablespoon fresh chopped summer savory, tarragon and parsley	**1 tablespoon fresh chopped summer savory, tarragon and parsley**
1 teaspoon Dijon mustard	**1 teaspoon Dijon mustard**
2 tablespoons peanut oil	**2 tablespoons peanut oil**
2 tablespoons cider vinegar	**2 tablespoons cider vinegar**
Juice and grated rind of 1 lemon	**Juice and grated rind of 1 lemon**
Sea salt and freshly ground black pepper	**Sea salt and freshly ground black pepper**
4 fl oz (120ml) sour cream	**½ cup sour cream**
1 tablespoon honey	**1 tablespoon honey**
For the salad:	For the salad:
2 lb (900g) broad beans in their pods	**2 pounds Windsor beans in their pods**
3 oz (75g) tinned sweetcorn kernels	**½ cup canned sweetcorn kernels**
2 heads fennel, sliced into julienne strips	**2 heads fennel, sliced into julienne strips**
4 tomatoes, skinned, seeded and chopped	**4 tomatoes, skinned, seeded and chopped**
1 tablespoon fresh chopped parsley	**1 tablespoon fresh chopped parsley**

1. Put all the dressing ingredients into a blender goblet and liquidize to a smooth cream. Reserve in the refrigerator until needed.
2. Shell the beans and boil in lightly salted water for 20 minutes, until tender.
3. Drain the beans and remove their skins if necessary.
4. Combine the beans with the sweetcorn and fennel in a large salad bowl.
5. Stir the dressing into this mixture and leave to soak for 1 hour.
6. Just before serving, top the salad with the chopped tomato pulp and sprinkle with parsley.

Variation:
This dish could be varied by the addition of cooked wholemeal pasta shells or macaroni to produce a very nourishing main course salad.

La Salade Princesse Anne

A Salad of Fruits and Leaf Vegetables with a Spicy Dressing

Serves 4
Illustrated opposite page 129.

I have twice been presented to Princess Anne at Royal shows where I have been asked to demonstrate. I have always felt most honoured that Her Royal Highness should take such an interest, and present this recipe as a token of my gratitude.

In the 1950s, when I was Executive Chef and Catering Manager of the famous Fortnum and Mason in Piccadilly, London, we catered for many Royal occasions. It was often a point of great interest that I chose to use fruits in my salads. These days it is more common, but then it was most innovative.

Imperial (Metric)	American
For the dressing:	For the dressing:
1 teaspoon Dijon mustard	**1 teaspoon Dijon mustard**
1 tablespoon sweet chutney	**1 tablespoon sweet chutney**
1 teaspoon raw cane sugar	**1 teaspoon raw cane sugar**
2 tomatoes, skinned, seeded and chopped	**2 tomatoes, skinned, seeded and chopped**
1 teaspoon tomato purée	**1 teaspoon tomato paste**
1 pinch ground mixed spice	**1 pinch ground mixed spice**
Juice and grated rind of 1 orange	**Juice and grated rind of 1 orange**
5 tablespoons tarragon vinegar	**5 tablespoons tarragon vinegar**
3 tablespoons sunflower oil	**3 tablespoons sunflower oil**
1 clove garlic, peeled	**1 clove garlic, peeled**
2 oz (50g) pecan nuts	**2 ounces pecan nuts**
1 small onion, chopped	**1 small onion, chopped**
¼ teaspoon celery seeds	**¼ teaspoon celery seeds**
2 tablespoons parsley leaves	**2 tablespoons parsley leaves**
4 tablespoons natural yogurt	**4 tablespoons plain yogurt**
For the salad:	For the salad:
1 small lettuce (round head)	**1 small lettuce (round head)**
8 tender young dandelion leaves	**8 tender young dandelion leaves**
3 oz (75g) fresh spinach leaves	**3 ounces fresh spinach leaves**
1 small radiccio	**1 small radiccio**
4 oz (100g) beansprouts	**2 cups beansprouts**
2 spring onions, sliced	**2 scallions, sliced**
2 mint leaves, chopped	**2 mint leaves, chopped**
4 thin slices fresh pineapple	**4 thin slices fresh pineapple**
2 pawpaws, peeled and seeded, and cut into small cubes	**2 pawpaws, peeled and seeded, and cut into small cubes**
4 thin slices watermelon	**4 thin slices watermelon**
4 fresh figs	**4 fresh figs**
½ lb (225g) cottage cheese	**1 cup cottage cheese**

1 Place all the dressing ingredients into a blender and liquidize to a thin creamy dressing. Reserve in the refrigerator until needed.

2 Separate all the salad leaves. Wash and drain one type at a time — do not mix them.

3 In a very large bowl, mix the green lettuce, dandelion and spinach leaves (torn roughly if very large). Toss with about a third of the salad dressing.
4 In the centre of the green salad, arrange the red radiccio leaves. Around these arrange the beansprouts, sprinkled with spring onions (scallions).
5 Sprinkle the salad with mint and drizzle on a little more dressing, to lightly coat the radiccio, beansprouts, spring onions (scallions) and mint.
6 On a large flat dish, arrange the pineapple slices neatly. Top each slice with some cubed pawpaw.
7 Arrange the slices of watermelon prettily between the pineapple slices.
8 Place a bowl of cottage cheese in the centre of the plate, with the figs around it.
9 Put the rest of the dressing in a sauceboat. Each guest will help himself to leaf salad, fruit salad and cheese and add further dressing according to taste. This is ideal for a small buffet party, especially in Summer.

Variation:
A small quantity of lemon jelly could be beaten into the cottage cheese, just before it sets, to make a lemony mousse.

La Salade de Tomates au Cognac

Brandied Tomato Salad

Never add a dressing to a tomato salad too far in advance. This applies also to lettuce-based salads — a dressing will draw the juices out of tomatoes, making the salad watery if left too long, and wilts lettuce. Rice, root vegetable and pulse based salads often benefit from having the dressing added while the cooked ingredients are still hot, because the effect of cooling a hot ingredient in cold dressing causes it to soak up more of the flavourful dressing, and the resulting salad is, overall, more enjoyable.

It is interesting to note that the more acid-tasting the tomato, the higher the vitamin C content. This vitamin is destroyed by cooking, so a tangy tomato salad is a tasty Summer treat which will boost your vitamin C levels nicely!

Imperial (Metric)	American
For the dressing:	For the dressing:
Juice and grated rind of 1 lemon	**Juice and grated rind of 1 lemon**
2 tablespoons walnut oil	**2 tablespoons walnut oil**
4 fl oz (120ml) natural yogurt	**½ cup plain yogurt**
1 teaspoon French mustard	**1 teaspoon French mustard**
1 teaspoon honey	**1 teaspoon honey**
Juice of ½ orange and ½ lemon	**Juice of ½ orange and ½ lemon**
1 tablespoon wine vinegar	**1 tablespoon wine vinegar**
Sea salt and freshly ground black pepper	**Sea salt and freshly ground black pepper**
For the salad:	For the salad:
2 lb (900g) tomatoes	**2 pounds tomatoes**
2 oranges, peeled and segmented	**2 oranges, peeled and segmented**
4 fl oz (120ml) brandy	**½ cup brandy**
2 tablespoons chopped fresh chives	**2 tablespoons chopped fresh chives**
1 green pepper, sliced into rings	**1 green pepper, sliced into rings**

1. Place all the dressing ingredients in a blender and liquidize to a smooth creamy mixture. Set aside until needed, in the fridge.
2. Slice the tomatoes horizontally and place on a large, flat serving dish, overlapping slightly.
3. Arrange orange segments around the tomatoes.
4. Pour the brandy over the salad and leave to marinate for 10 minutes.
5. Drain off the brandy without disturbing the salad, and add the brandy to the dressing and shake well to mix.
6. Pour the dressing over the salad, sprinkle with the chives and decorate with pepper rings. Serve immediately.

8 *Les Friandises de Fromage*

Cheese Dishes

I do not think anyone would argue that, as with wine, France produces the finest cheeses in the world, in terms of both quality and variety. From the simplest farmhouse table to the greatest Paris restaurants, cheese is taken very seriously indeed. There is not a family in France who would think it odd to have a selection of seven cheeses on the table: two soft, like Petit-Suisse and perhaps a fresh *chèvre* (goat's milk cheese); two ripened, like Brie or Coulommiers or Camembert; two hard, cooked cheeses such as Comté or Cantal; and a blue cheese such as Roquefort.

In fact, in just such a simple cheeseboard, one has represented all the main types of cheese production, from the fresh, uncooked result of curdling milk with an enzyme, be it animal or plant, or an acid like vinegar, to the type of cheese which is ripened, its soft outer crust being formed during this time by the action of a safe mould on the surface of the cheese, to the pressed, cooked cheese with its firm, smooth paste scattered, perhaps, with even-sized holes from the fermentation which takes place early on in the making, to the immense variety of 'blue' cheeses, in which the mould is introduced deep into the cheese with wires to create the familiar blue-green veins which gourmets love so well (when all blue cheeses were ripened in caves, as Roquefort still is, this veining happened quite naturally, by the way).

Then, from these basic types, come literally hundreds of variations, each one totally distinguishable by its own special character, perhaps because of the milk from which it is made, the techniques and conditions by which it is prepared, blended, moulded or matured, and even because of the character of the people of the region from which it comes, or the flavours of the other local produce which it is meant to complement. Many of these cheeses never leave France — many, indeed, never leave the region or even the village in which they are made, and only the fortunate traveller will have the chance of tasting this most local of produce, washed down with a glass of a truly local wine (the sort which doesn't 'travel' either).

However, all the pleasures of the cheeseboard are only half the story. This chapter presents just a sample of the other half — the wealth of wonderful dishes which can be created from our many cheeses, using just other natural, country produce such as eggs, fresh vegetables and grains. So here you will find the simplest, yet most successful and enduring of country dishes like Fondue Lorraine, to the most sublime of classical cuisine, such as *Quenelles de Fromage* in a saffron sauce. Select a bottle of your favourite French wine and take your choice of delicious dishes.

La Fondue Lorraine

French Cheese Fondue

Serves 12

Fondues are usually associated with Switzerland because, over the centuries, that is where they have found their 'home'. However, all the provinces along the Swiss and German borders, Alsace, Lorraine and Savoy, have their own version of this increasingly popular dish. No one really knows who invented the fondue, although it has been suggested that the reason for its development was to use up cheeses which had certain defects, such as abnormally large holes or cracks, which were still good to eat but which could not be sold fresh.

The combination of cheeses used in a fondue is a matter of taste, as are the other ingredients used, such as which wine to choose. Of French cheeses, Comté and Beaufort are a good choice, but any hard cheese will produce an acceptable fondue. The basic principle is that one cheese should be full fat and the other a lower fat cheese.

To make a good fondue it is best to have a proper pot, known as a *caquelon*, made of heatproof earthenware with a glazed interior. These are now very easy to find in the shops, and are usually sold along with a small spirit burner which is necessary to keep the fondue at the correct temperature. Your guests each have a long fondue fork, onto which they spear cubes of bread, or pieces of raw vegetable such as mushrooms, which are then swirled in the rich, cheesy sauce and eaten. One pot is sufficient for a small dinner party, but any more than six guests will really require more than one pot. Too many people trying to dip cubes of bread at once will result in a messy fondue and disgruntled guests.

Imperial (Metric)	American
1 lb (450g) Beaufort cheese	**2 cups Beaufort cheese**
1 lb (450g) Comté cheese	**2 cups Comté cheese**
1 lb (450g) Emmenthal cheese	**2 cups Emmenthal cheese**
3 cloves garlic	**3 cloves garlic**
¼ pint (150ml) water	**⅔ cup water**
1¾ pints (1 litre) *Pouilly Fuissé* or other dry white wine	**4½ cups *Pouilly Fuissé* or other dry white wine**
Freshly ground black pepper	**Freshly ground black pepper**
3 fl oz (90ml) Kirsch	**⅓ cup Kirsch**
1 tablespoon cornflour *or* **potato flour (*fécule*), blended with 2 fl oz (60ml) water**	**1 tablespoon cornstarch** *or* **potato flour (*fécule*), blended with ¼ cupful water**
1 large, slightly stale wholemeal loaf	**1 large, slightly stale wholewheat loaf**

1. Cut all the cheese into very thin slices (do not grate).
2. Liquidize the garlic in a blender with the water.
3. Pour the garlic liquid into the fondue pot along with the wine and heat gently on the stove.
4. When the garlic and wine solution comes to the boil, gradually stir in the cheeses, stirring all the time, until you have a smooth, thick sauce.
5. Season the sauce with plenty of black pepper and stir in the Kirsch.
6. Add the starch and water mixture to the pot and stir it in thoroughly. The fondue is now ready to be transferred to the spirit burner on your dining table.
7. Serve the fondue with the bread cut into 1-inch (2.5cm) cubes, and any other 'dippable' foods which you fancy.

Variations:
Many books have been written just covering all the variations on this simple but delicious dish. For example,

to the mixture, you could add 3 egg yolks and 5 oz (150g/1½ cups) sliced white mushrooms (or even truffles). Or a sprinkling of chopped blanched almonds, or of celery seeds, is very tasty. It is a perfect dish for experimentation: use your own favourite cheeses and wines, and stir in different flavourings as you like. A very economical — though not very French — fondue can be made with mature Cheddar cheese and cider or beer!

You can do all sorts of things with the mixture itself, once it is made, as a change from the traditional way of serving and eating it. Try it spread on *croûtons*, or poured into baked potatoes — it is delicious whatever way you serve it.

Les Croustillants de Brie Champenois

Brie Fritters

Serves 4

Talleyrand, the statesman and gourmet, dubbed Brie the King of Cheeses, and it was said by his critics that the only master he never betrayed was Brie!

There are many different types of Brie, but the main three are Brie de Meaux, Brie de Melun and Brie de Coulommiers. Brie de Meaux is made on farms. It is considered by many to be the 'true' Brie, and the one to which Talleyrand was so devoted. Brie de Melun is made in small dairies by traditional methods. It has a more pronounced flavour and smell than Brie de Meaux, and is slightly more salty and more sharp. Brie de Coulommiers is usually factory-made and is enriched with cream to make it smooth and mild. It is in season from October to May, whereas the other two are best from October to June.

Imperial (Metric)	American
1 lb (450g) piece of Brie, not too ripe	**1 pound piece of Brie, not too ripe**
2 oz (50g) wholemeal flour	**½ cup wholewheat flour**
2 eggs, beaten	**2 eggs, beaten**
3 oz (75g) mixed wholemeal breadcrumbs and crumbled flaked almonds	**1 cup mixed wholewheat breadcrumbs and crumbled slivered almonds**
½ pint (300ml) vegetable oil	**1⅓ cups vegetable oil**

1 Cut the Brie into eight triangles of roughly equal size.
2 Coat each piece in flour, then in beaten egg and lastly in the breadcrumb and almond mixture.
3 Heat the oil until just about smoking and then shallow-fry the fritters until golden brown — this only takes a minute — and then serve immediately.

Variation:
Any soft cheese of this type can be prepared similarly: Camembert is the obvious other one, but Pont l'Evêque, Caprice des Dieux and many others are just as good.

Les Beignets de Fromage à la Jurassienne

Rich Cheesy Fritters

Serves 4

These delicious little fritters are a traditional dish of the beautiful Jura region of France, which produces Comté cheese. Because the cheese is bound with a thick egg-based white sauce, they do not melt and fall apart on being fried, as you might imagine they would. The advantage of this type of dish is that any cheese can be used, even if it is getting a little past its best, so you could finish up the cheeseboard from a Saturday night dinner party by having *beignets de fromage* for supper on Sunday. Surprisingly perhaps, cheese prepared in this way is more digestible than when it is eaten raw. You could serve them on their own, without the apple fritters, but I find these provide a pleasant, sweet-sharp contrast to the rich and creamy *beignets*.

Imperial (Metric)	American
4 oz (100g) butter	**½ cup butter**
4 oz (100g) wholemeal flour	**1 cup wholewheat flour**
1¾ pints (1 litre) milk	**4½ cups milk**
Sea salt and freshly ground black pepper	**Sea salt and freshly ground black pepper**
Grated nutmeg	**Grated nutmeg**
½ lb (450g) grated Comté, Gruyère or other hard cheese	**2 cups grated Comté, Gruyère or other hard cheese**
5 eggs	**5 eggs**
2 oz (50g) wholemeal flour	**½ cup wholewheat flour**
6 oz (150g) wholemeal breadcrumbs	**3 cups wholewheat breadcrumbs**
2 oz (50g) crushed flaked almonds	**½ cup crushed slivered almonds**
2 large Golden Delicious apples	**2 large Golden Delicious apples**
Vegetable oil for shallow frying	**Vegetable oil for shallow frying**

1. Heat the butter in a large saucepan and stir in the flour to make a roux. Cook for a few minutes, without browning, stirring constantly.
2. Gradually whisk the milk into the roux. Do this in four stages, making sure the mixture is smooth at the end of every stage; you are less likely to end up with a lumpy sauce this way.
3. Season the sauce well with salt, pepper and nutmeg, and then stir in the cheese.
4. Separate four of the eggs. Beat the yolks lightly in a bowl and then stir in ½ pint (300ml/1⅓ cups) sauce, to make a thick paste. Then stir this into the pan of sauce, stirring well to amalgamate completely.
5. Pour this mixture into a deep, flat earthenware dish, measuring 8×4 inches (20×10cm). Leave to cool and harden, refrigerating once it is cool enough.
6. When the paste is quite cold, turn it out onto a pastry board and cut into 2-inch (5cm) squares.
7. Spread the flour on a flat dish. Mix the breadcrumbs with the almonds and spread them on a flat dish, too.
8. Lightly beat the whole egg with the egg whites, just enough to mix them together, and pour them onto another dish.
9. Peel and core the apples, and cut into thick slices.
10. Pass first the *beignets* then the apple slices through the flour, then coat in the egg mixture and then the breadcrumb and nut mixture.
11. Heat the oil in a deep frying pan (skillet) and sauté the fritters for ½ minute on each side, until golden-brown. Drain on kitchen paper and transfer to a serving dish and keep warm. Sauté the apple

fritters for 2 minutes until golden-brown. Drain on kitchen paper and arrange around the beignets as a garnish. Serve immediately.

La Gougère Bourguignonne

Choux Pastry with Cheese

Once mastered, the technique of making choux pastry is very easy and, like a soufflé, it is always just the thing to impress your guests. However, once you have tried it, I think you will find it so simple and so delicious that you will not want to save it for dinner parties or special occasions. A *gougère* makes a tasty light meal at any time of day — best enjoyed with a glass of Chablis!

Imperial (Metric)	American
½ pint (300ml) water	**1⅓ cups water**
4 oz (100g) butter	**½ cup butter**
Sea salt	**Sea salt**
½ lb (225g) wholemeal flour	**2 cups wholewheat flour**
5 eggs, beaten	**5 eggs, beaten**
Freshly ground black pepper	**Freshly ground black pepper**
Pinch celery seeds	**Pinch celery seeds**
4 oz (100g) Gruyère cheese	**½ cup Gruyère cheese**
1 oz (25g) butter, for the mould	**2 tablespoons butter, for the mold**
1 tablespoon wholemeal flour, for the mould	**1 tablespoon wholewheat flour, for the mold**

1. Put the water and the butter into a saucepan and heat to boiling point, with a pinch of salt.
2. As the buttery water boils, tip in all the flour at once, very quickly, and stir fast to blend it all together. Keep stirring, over the heat, until the mixture forms a smooth, very thick paste which comes away cleanly from the sides of the pan in a solid mass.
3. Remove the paste from the heat and cool for 4 minutes.
4. Add the beaten eggs to the paste a little at a time, making sure they are well blended. Stop adding egg when the mixture is of a very thick but pourable consistency — 'holding a thread', as it is known in culinary terms.
5. Add pepper and celery seeds.
6. Cut half the cheese into small cubes, and grate the rest. Add first the grated cheese and then the cubes to the mixture, making sure the cubes are evenly distributed throughout.
7. Grease a ring mould or savarin mould with the remaining butter and sprinkle with flour. Pour the paste into this mould evenly.
8. Bake on the middle shelf of a preheated oven at 400°F/200°C (Gas Mark 6) for 30 to 35 minutes. Turn out onto a flat dish and serve cut into portions.

Variations:
Most other hard cheeses, English or French, could be used for this dish. Almonds or aniseeds could be sprinkled onto the mixture before baking. The dish looks even more attractive baked in individual ring moulds, if you have them.

Le Soufflé au Fromage Vert-Pré

A Watercress Cheese Soufflé

Serves 8

Originally, soufflés were served in flour-and-water pastry cases in which they were baked (the case itself was not eaten). This practice has long been replaced with the more convenient soufflé dish or ramekin. I think it rather a shame, and it makes for a very effective dinner party dish if you serve your soufflé in an (edible) pastry case. So long as you bake the pastry blind first, the case and the soufflé will be cooked in the same time. Still, for this recipe I will assume that you are using the more standard individual ramekins for your soufflés. For hints on the art of soufflé-making, see the *Carrot and Broccoli Soufflé* recipe on page 50.

Imperial (Metric)	American
3 oz (75g) softened butter for ramekins	**⅓ cup softened butter for ramekins**
4 tablespoons grated Parmesan cheese	**4 tablespoons grated Parmesan cheese**
1 oz (25g) dry wholemeal breadcrumbs	**¼ cup dry wholewheat breadcrumbs**
1 oz (25g) butter	**2 tablespoons butter**
1½ oz (40g) wholemeal flour	**⅓ cup wholewheat flour**
½ pint (300ml) single cream, warmed to 180°F/80°C	**⅔ cup light cream, warmed to 180°F**
1 oz (25g) spinach purée, squeezed dry	**¼ cup spinach purée, squeezed dry**
1 clove garlic, chopped	**1 clove garlic, chopped**
2 tablespoons chopped watercress leaves	**2 tablespoons chopped watercress leaves**
Sea salt and freshly ground black pepper	**Sea salt and freshly ground black pepper**
Pinch cayenne pepper	**Pinch cayenne pepper**
Pinch freshly grated nutmeg	**Pinch freshly grated nutmeg**
4 egg yolks	**4 egg yolks**
6 egg whites	**6 egg whites**

1 Butter the individual soufflé dishes thickly. Stir half the Parmesan cheese into the breadcrumbs and use this mixture to coat the buttered interiors of the ramekins.

2 Heat the second portion of butter in a saucepan and stir in the flour. Cook for 1 minute, stirring, but do not allow to brown. Slowly stir in the cream, a quarter at a time, making sure that it is well absorbed into the *roux*. You should end up with a smooth, thick sauce.

3 Add the spinach, garlic and watercress to the sauce. Stir in half of the remaining cheese and add seasonings to taste.

4 Stir the egg yolks into the sauce and remove from the heat as soon as the first bubble appears. Cover with a tight lid to keep warm while you prepare the egg whites.

5 Put the egg whites into a large mixing bowl with a pinch of salt and whisk until it holds stiff peaks.

6 Stir a quarter of the egg white into the sauce to lighten it, mixing it in very thoroughly. Then add the rest bit by bit, using a metal spoon with a cutting motion. Do not try to make it completely smooth — it doesn't matter if the whites are not completely blended, it would make the soufflés less fluffy if they were.

7 Pour the mixture into the ramekins, leaving a rim of only ⅛ inch (3mm) at the top. Make a shallow trench with the back of a teaspoon around this rim. This ensures that the soufflé top will rise level and makes a more attractive finished dish.

8 Level the tops of the soufflés with a palette knife and mark a criss-cross pattern on the tops. Sprinkle

with the remaining Parmesan and bake in the centre of the oven at 425°F/225°C (Gas Mark 7) for 12 to 15 minutes, by which time the soufflés will be well risen and set.

Variation:
The alternative, suggested in the introduction to this recipe, is to bake your soufflé in a pastry case. Bake blind either a 9-inch (23cm) or two 6-inch (15cm) diameter pastry cases (2 inches/5cm deep in either event), then pour in your soufflé mixture and bake as in point 8, above. This old-fashioned way of serving soufflés is now rather novel and should be revived — apart from anything else it is an insurance in case of the soufflé being ready before your guests are, since it will still look good in this presentation, even if it is not as risen as normal.

Les Galettes Fécampoise

Camembert Cakes

Serves 8

Camembert was perfected by a Madame Harel in 1790, during the French Revolution. This soft cheese is fermented by the bacillus *Camembertii* and, when coagulated, it is pressed at a temperature of 18°C into the familiar rounds or semi-circles which are synonymous with French cheese for many people. As with Brie, there are many different types of Camembert. Camembert Fermier, made on the farm, is quite a rarity even in France but is worth seeking out as it is more rich and fruity in flavour than the far more common commercially produced Camembert. Another type is Camembert *affiné*, which develops an orangy skin as the cheese gets really ripe. This is for cheese fans only as it gets very smelly at that stage too!

These little cakes from Normandy make a delicious luncheon dish with a crisp salad and a bottle of chilled Normandy cider.

Imperial (Metric)	American
4 oz (100g) softened butter	**½ cup softened butter**
½ lb (225g) medium-ripe Camembert	**1 cup medium-ripe Camembert**
3 eggs, beaten	**3 eggs, beaten**
1 lb (450g) self-raising wholemeal flour	**4 cups self-raising wholewheat flour**
Sea salt	**Sea salt**
Pinch cayenne pepper	**Pinch cayenne pepper**
½ teaspoon cumin seeds	**½ teaspoon cumin seeds**
1 egg yolk	**1 egg yolk**
2 tablespoons water	**2 tablespoons water**
Extra wholemeal flour for dusting	**Extra wholewheat flour for dusting**

1 Cream the butter and cheese together to a smooth paste.
2 Add the beaten eggs and the flour a little at a time, and then the spices and seasonings. The paste should be the consistency of shortcrust pastry. Roll into a ball and rest it for an hour or two.
3 Dust a pastry board with flour. Divide the dough into small pieces about the size of an egg. Roll them out on the board into rounds ¼ inch (5mm) thick.
4 Place the rounds on a greased baking sheet and brush with a wash made from the egg yolk and water, mixed together. Bake at 400°F/200°C (Gas Mark 6) for 15 to 20 minutes.

La Flamiche de Melun

Brie Turnover

Serves 4

Every region of France has its own variations of this type of cheese pastry. You could use shortcrust pastry to make this dish, but a puff pastry will produce a lighter, yet richer, dish.

Imperial (Metric) For the puff pastry:	American For the puff pastry:
½ lb (225g) wholemeal bread flour	**2 cups wholewheat bread flour**
Pinch sea salt	**Pinch sea salt**
½ lb (225g) butter	**1 cup butter**
4 fl oz (120ml) water	**½ cup water**
1 tablespoon lemon juice	**1 tablespoon lemon juice**
Extra wholemeal flour for dusting	**Extra wholewheat flour for dusting**
1 egg, beaten, for glazing	**1 egg, beaten, for glazing**

1. Sift the flour and salt into a large bowl. Reserve the bran for some other dish.
2. Rub a quarter of the butter into the flour.
3. Make a well in the mixture and add the water and lemon juice. Knead the mixture to a dough and roll into a ball.
4. Slash the top of the dough in a cross shape, cover with a damp cloth and leave to rest for 30 minutes.
5. While the dough is resting, knead the butter until it is the same consistency as the pastry dough, and then roll it out on a floured board to a neat oblong ⅛ inch (3mm) thick. You will need to flour the butter and the rolling pin, as well as the board, very carefully so that the butter does not stick.
6. Roll out the dough to the same thickness as the butter. Place the butter piece on top of the dough and fold the two layers three times. Roll again into an oblong, fold into three again and rest the dough for 20 minutes.
7. Repeat this procedure twice more, then wrap in clingfilm and chill until needed.

Imperial (Metric) For the filling:	American For the filling:
2 oz (50g) softened butter	**¼ cup softened butter**
3 oz (75g) ripe Brie de Melun	**3 ounces ripe Brie de Melun**
2 oz (50g) wholemeal flour	**½ cup wholewheat flour**
1 egg, beaten	**1 egg, beaten**
Sea salt *or* **celery salt (page 110)**	**Sea salt** *or* **celery salt (page 110)**
Freshly ground black pepper	**Freshly ground black pepper**

1. While the pastry is chilling, blend together in a bowl the butter and cheese until well mixed.
2. Add the flour and egg to form a very soft, fairly smooth paste. Season to taste.

To assemble the dish:

1. On a floured board, roll out the pastry into an oblong 10 inches (25cm) long and 5 inches (12cm) wide. It should be about ⅛ inch (3mm) thick.

2 Cut the pastry into two squares. Place one square on a greased baking tray. Brush its edges with a little beaten egg.
3 Place the filling in the centre of the square and cover it with the other square of pastry, crimping the edges with the fingers to seal well.
4 Mark the top of the turnover with a criss-cross pattern and brush with egg wash.
5 Bake in a preheated oven at 400°F/200°C (Gas Mark 6) for 25 to 30 minutes.

Variations:
A peeled and chopped apple could be added to the cheese filling for a more tangy flavour. This filling could equally well be used in little quichelettes.

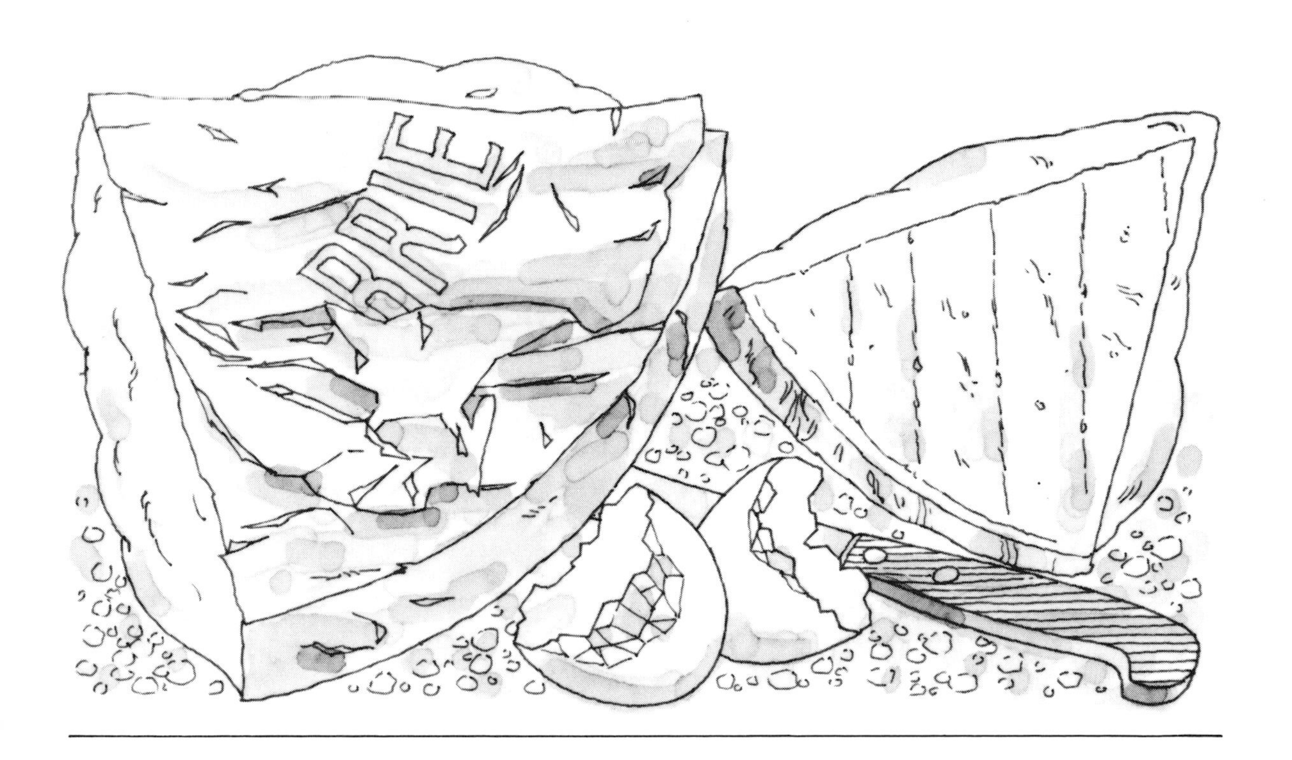

Le Fromage du Poitou

Goat's Cheese Flan

Goats are sometimes called 'poor man's cows' — how derisive! Not only is goat's milk healthier than cow's milk, causing fewer allergic reactions, but also gourmets almost always prefer goat's cheese to cow's milk varieties. The general name for any type of goat's milk cheese is *chèvre*, but this covers a wide range of textures and strengths of flavour, from mild, soft fresh cheeses to hard, well aged and strongly-flavoured ones. The Loire is well known for its goat cheeses, but most regions of France have at least one variety. This recipe comes from Poitou on the western coast of France.

Imperial (Metric)	American
For the sweet shortcrust pastry:	For the sweet shortcrust pastry:
½ lb (225g) wholemeal flour	**2 cups wholewheat flour**
4 oz (100g) butter	**½ cup butter**
1 oz (25g) raw cane sugar	**2 tablespoons raw cane sugar**
1 egg, beaten	**1 egg, beaten**
For the filling:	For the filling:
½ lb (225g) goat's cheese, crust removed	**1 cup goat's cheese, crust removed**
4 tablespoons double cream	**4 tablespoons heavy cream**
3 oz (75g) wholemeal flour	**¾ cup wholewheat flour**
3 oz (75g) cornflour	**¾ cup cornstarch**
2 tablespoons orange liqueur	**2 tablespoons orange liqueur**
Pinch sea salt	**Pinch sea salt**
5 eggs, separated	**5 eggs, separated**
4 oz (100g) diced angelica	**½ cup diced angelica**
5 oz (150g) finely ground raw cane sugar	**⅔ cup finely ground raw cane sugar**

1. Prepare the pastry by rubbing in the flour and butter to the consistency of fine breadcrumbs. Stir in the sugar and beaten egg to form a smooth dough. Roll into a ball and rest for 1 hour.
2. Blend together the goat's cheese and cream. Gradually stir in the two types of flour, then the liqueur, salt, beaten egg yolks and finally the angelica. Make sure everything is thoroughly mixed.
3. Beat the egg whites with a pinch of salt. When they hold firm peaks, start adding the sugar, a spoonful at a time, beating the egg whites back to a firm stage each time. Fold this carefully into the cheese mixture.
4. Roll out the pastry and line a well-greased flan ring. Fill the pastry case with the cheese filling.
5. Bake in a preheated oven at 400°F/200°C (Gas Mark 6) for 45 minutes to 1 hour, until golden. Serve hot or cold with a light fruit salad.

Les Boulettes de la Belle-Hélène

Cheese Dumplings Baked in a Yogurt Pastry

Makes about 60

These little cheese savouries can be used for all sorts of occasions. This quantity is ideal as an appetizer before a dinner party, or as a savoury course during the meal, or as part of a selection of *hors d'oeuvres* or as a dish in a finger buffet. The combination of the bland cream cheese, the tasty chives or spring onions (scallions) and the distinctive flavour of the aniseeds, all wrapped up in a delicious and unusual yogurt pastry makes for a dish to stimulate the palate of even the most discerning gourmet.

Imperial (Metric)	American
For the pastry:	For the pastry:
1 teaspoon sea salt	**1 teaspoon sea salt**
2 tablespoons baking powder	**2 tablespoons baking powder**
1 lb (450g) wholemeal flour	**4 cups wholewheat flour**
1 egg	**1 egg**
¼ pint (150ml) natural yogurt	**⅔ cup plain yogurt**
2 tablespoons vegetable oil	**2 tablespoons vegetable oil**
¼ pint (150ml) melted butter	**⅔ cup melted butter**
1 beaten egg, plus a little water, for wash	**1 beaten egg, plus a little water, for wash**
For the filling:	For the filling:
1 lb (450g) dryish cream cheese	**2 cups dryish cream cheese**
Sea salt and freshly ground black pepper	**Sea salt and freshly ground black pepper**
1 teaspoon aniseeds	**1 teaspoon aniseeds**
1 egg, beaten	**1 egg, beaten**
1 tablespoon chopped fresh parsley	**1 tablespoon chopped fresh parsley**
2 tablespoons wholemeal flour	**2 tablespoons wholewheat flour**
3 tablespoons chopped chives *or* **spring onions**	**3 tablespoons chopped chives** *or* **scallions**

1. Sift the salt, baking powder and flour together in a bowl.
2. In another bowl, beat together the egg, yogurt, oil and butter until well mixed.
3. Stir the flour into the liquid mixture to form a smooth, soft dough. Roll into a ball and set aside in a cool place for 15 minutes.
4. Combine all the ingredients for the filling to form a smooth but firm paste.
5. On a pastry board, divide the pastry dough into balls about the size of a plum, weighing about ½ ounce (15g) each.
6. Press a hole in each ball and insert a teaspoon of cheese filling. Seal the dough around the filling to make a ball again.
7. Place the balls onto greased baking trays and egg wash them. Bake at 400°F/200°C (Gas Mark 6) for 15 to 20 minutes. Serve hot or cold.

Les Profiteroles au Roquefort

Blue Cheese Choux Buns

Illustrated opposite page 176.

For most people, a profiterole is a sweet dish, filled with cream or *crème pâtissière* and coated in chocolate or spun sugar. These certainly make a delicious occasional indulgence, but the savoury version is becoming more and more popular as health-conscious lovers of good food cut down on rich, sweet desserts in favour of small portions of a savoury dish to end their meal. These little profiteroles are ideal as cocktail party snacks, too. The weight-watching gourmet should beware, of course, of thinking that because the sugar and the chocolate sauce are absent these choux buns can be indulged in *ad infinitum* — the cream and cheese filling, combined with the choux pastry exterior and the spicy wine and cheese glaze don't make this a dish for slimmers!

Imperial (Metric)	American
For the choux pastry:	For the choux pastry:
¼ pint (150ml) water	**⅔ cup water**
Sea salt	**Sea salt**
2½ oz (65g) butter	**5 tablespoons butter**
5 oz (150g) wholemeal flour	**1¼ cups wholewheat flour**
3 large eggs, beaten	**3 large eggs, beaten**
For the filling:	For the filling:
½ lb (225g) cream cheese	**1 cup cream cheese**
2 oz (50g) crumbled Roquefort cheese	**½ cup crumbled Roquefort cheese**
1 teaspoon mixed celery and mustard seeds	**1 teaspoon mixed celery and mustard seeds**
Sea salt and freshly ground black pepper	**Sea salt and freshly ground black pepper**
5 tablespoons whipped cream *or* **butter**	**5 tablespoons whipped cream** *or* **butter**
For the glaze:	For the glaze:
½ lb (225g) Gruyère cheese, grated	**2 cups grated Gruyère cheese**
3 fl oz (75ml) dry white wine *or* **cider**	**⅓ cup dry white wine** *or* **cider**
1 teaspoon tomato purée	**1 teaspoon tomato paste**
1 large pinch each turmeric and paprika	**1 large pinch each turmeric and paprika**

1. To make the choux pastry, heat the water, salt and butter together in a saucepan and, when boiling, tip in all the flour at once and stir quickly until the paste comes away in one smooth ball from the sides of the pan. Remove from the heat and beat in the eggs a little at a time, to obtain a mixture of a smooth, dropping consistency.
2. Fill a piping bag with the mixture and pipe onto a greased baking tray little buns the size of plums. Bake in a preheated oven at 400°F/200°C (Gas mark 6) for 12 to 15 minutes. Remove from the oven and cool.
3. Combine in a bowl the cream cheese, the Roquefort cheese and the seasonings. Blend in the cream or butter and then place the mixture in a piping bag with a small nozzle.
4. Make a little hole in each choux bun and then pipe full of filling. Set the buns aside.
5. Melt the Gruyère cheese in a pan with the wine and tomato purée (paste). When it is a smooth sauce, add turmeric and paprika to taste.
6. With a two-pronged fork, take one bun at a time and dip in the cheese glaze to just half-way up the bun. Place the profiteroles on a serving dish, glazed side upwards and serve as soon as they are all ready.

Variation:
Instead of the glaze, a little grated Gruyère cheese could simply be sprinkled onto the profiteroles before serving.

Les Ramequins à la Potagère

Cream Cheese Custards with Lettuce and Watercress

Cream cheese has a rich, yet bland, flavour. Nonetheless it makes a perfect base ingredient for a great many dishes, and can be enlivened by the addition of all manner of ingredients, from other cheeses to vegetables, herbs and spices. It is a very versatile ingredient which can be lightened with beaten egg whites and whipped cream or blended with creamed potato for a heavier mix. It lends itself to all kinds of uses: as a filling for pancakes, pastries and tarts, as a stuffing for mushrooms and many other vegetables, and for pastas, and as a sauce for a variety of dishes. In this dish it adds its creaminess to a delicately flavoured custard.

Imperial (Metric)	American
1 small bunch watercress	**1 small bunch watercress**
1 small soft-headed lettuce	**1 small soft-headed lettuce**
½ lb (225g) cream cheese	**1 cup cream cheese**
5 eggs, beaten	**5 eggs, beaten**
1 teaspoon sea salt	**1 teaspoon sea salt**
Freshly ground black pepper	**Freshly ground black pepper**
Freshly grated nutmeg	**Freshly grated nutmeg**
½ pint (300ml) milk	**1⅓ cups milk**
2 oz (50g) softened butter	**¼ cup softened butter**
¼ pint (150ml) single cream	**⅔ cup light cream**
3 tablespoons fresh chopped parsley	**3 tablespoons fresh chopped parsley**

1 Pick over the watercress and remove yellowed leaves and tough stalks. Wash and drain and then cut into thin shreds.
2 Wash and drain the lettuce leaves, removing any wilted or damaged ones, and then cut into thin shreds too.
3 In a bowl, beat together the cheese and eggs to make a soft, well-blended mixture. Season to taste with salt, pepper and nutmeg.
4 Gradually stir the milk into this mixture. When you have a smooth, creamy mixture, add the shredded watercress and lettuce.
5 Liberally coat six ramekins with softened butter and then fill them to the brim with the cheese and leaf mixture. Place the ramekins in a baking tray half filled with hot water.
6 Bake the custards at 350°F/180°C (Gas Mark 4) for 15 to 20 minutes.
7 Unmould the custards onto individual dishes. Boil the cream quickly and pour over the custards. Sprinkle with parsley and serve.

Les Crépinettes aux Champignons Opéra

Pancakes (Crêpes) Stuffed with Cheese-stuffed Mushrooms

Serves 4

Pancakes, or *crêpes* as we call them, have always been popular in France as the basis for a meal. They can be made using different types of flour and to hold any filling from the most simple to the quite luxurious. They are sold at fairs and festivals as a snack with a sprinkling of sugar and *Grand Marnier* liqueur, or a spreading of jam for the children, and the *crêperies* so typical of Brittany are now flourishing in towns all over France. This dish is certain to be a great success with your guests because of the wonderful combination of flavours and textures, but also because of the novelty of a stuffing within a stuffing.

Imperial (Metric)	American
1 quantity pancake batter (page 34)	**1 quantity crêpe batter (page 34)**
Vegetable oil for frying pancakes	**Vegetable oil for frying crêpes**
4 oz (100g) butter	**½ cup butter**
1 medium onion, chopped	**1 medium onion, chopped**
8 large, cupped field mushrooms (about 1 lb/450g in total), stems removed and chopped	**8 large, cupped field mushrooms (about 1 pound in total), stems removed and chopped**
2 oz (50g) mixed walnuts and flaked almonds	**½ cup mixed English walnuts and slivered almonds**
2 oz (50g) seedless raisins soaked in 2 tablespoons cognac	**⅓ cup seedless raisins, soaked in 2 tablespoons cognac**
2 oz (50g) cream cheese	**¼ cup cream cheese**
2 oz (50g) blue cheese	**¼ cup blue cheese**
1 egg, beaten	**1 egg, beaten**
Sea salt and freshly ground black pepper	**Sea salt and freshly ground black pepper**
2 oz (50g) grated hard cheese	**½ cup grated hard cheese**

1 Prepare the batter as instructed on page 34. Heat the oil in a pan and fry 8 equal-sized pancakes (crêpes). Set aside on kitchen paper.
2 Heat half the butter in a saucepan and sauté the onion and mushroom stems until soft but not browned. Then add the nuts and drained raisins (reserving the soaking brandy) and cook for 2 minutes. Remove from the heat.
3 Cream together the cream cheese and the blue cheese to form a paste, then stir in the onion, nut and raisin mixture. Cool this mixture slightly and then blend in the beaten egg and the reserved brandy. Season to taste.
4 Wash and dry the mushroom caps. Fill each cap with some cheese mixture and smooth flat with a knife.
5 Melt the remaining butter in a small pan and dip each mushroom cap in this.
6 Take a pancake (crêpe) and place a mushroom, filling upward, on it. Fold neatly around the mushroom to form a little parcel. Repeat with the rest of the pancakes (crêpes) and mushrooms and then place them in a shallow greased baking dish. Brush with more of the melted butter and top with grated cheese.
7 Bake at 400°F/200°C (Gas Mark 6) for 15 minutes, splashing with melted butter two or three times during cooking. Serve straight from the oven, sizzling hot.

Tourte aux Trois Fromages

A Three-Cheese Pie

As well as cream cheese and Gruyère, this recipe uses Cantal cheese, which is thought to be the oldest French cheese of all. Cantal is sometimes called the French Cheddar and, like this great British cheese, it has its commercially-made variety, *Laitier*, which is made all year round in dairies (never huge factories, like some Cheddar), and its 'farmhouse' variety, *Fermier*, which is made during the Summer, and which you will rarely find outside the Auvergne region in which it is produced. It is covered by an *appellation d'origine* — just like a good wine!

Imperial (Metric)	American
4 oz (100g) cream cheese	**½ cup cream cheese**
6 eggs, beaten	**6 eggs, beaten**
4 oz (100g) diced Cantal cheese	**1 cup diced Cantal cheese**
4 oz (100g) diced Gruyère cheese	**1 cup diced Gruyère cheese**
4 oz (100g) walnuts	**¾ cup English walnuts**
1 small onion, chopped	**1 small onion, chopped**
1 tablespoon chopped fresh parsley	**1 tablespoon chopped fresh parsley**
Sea salt and freshly ground black pepper	**Sea salt and freshly ground black pepper**
1½ quantities pastry (page 44)	**1½ quantities pastry (page 44)**

1 In a bowl combine the cream cheese and the beaten eggs.
2 Add the diced cheeses, the nuts, chopped onion and parsley and stir well. Season to taste.
3 On a floured pastry board, roll out half the pastry to ¼ inch (5mm) thickness, in a circle 8 inches (20cm) in diameter. Use this to line a greased 7 inch (18cm) quiche tin.
4 Fill the pastry case with the cheese mixture; brush the edges of the pastry with water.
5 Roll out the other half of the pastry to the same thickness and diameter and place this over the filling, crimping the edges with the wet rim of the base to seal and trimming with a sharp knife.
6 Bake in a preheated oven at 400°F/200°C (Gas Mark 6) for 45 minutes to 1 hour. Serve hot or cold with a green salad.

Crémeux au Coulis de Tomates

A Baked Cheese and Vegetable Pudding with Tomato Dressing

Serves 4

The French word for cheese, *fromage*, comes from the word *forme*, meaning moulded, and is still used in this context in some dishes — the vegetarian diner should watch out on a French menu for dishes such as *fromage de tête*: literally 'head cheese' or brawn! But, as well as *fromage à la crème*, many dishes, especially the *nouvelle* variety, will make much of *fromage frais* or *fromage blanc*, the light, soft, unripened cheese which is used to replace cream to such good advantage for both the palate and the waistline. In this dish, we not only can afford in terms of calories, but require in terms of richness, the luxury of a full cream cheese. The tomato *coulis* is a rich sauce which requires no thickening, and which complements the creamy pudding admirably by its tangy flavour.

Imperial (Metric)	American
For the pudding:	For the pudding:
½ lb (225g) cream cheese	**1 cup cream cheese**
5 eggs, beaten	**5 eggs, beaten**
Sea salt and freshly ground black pepper	**Sea salt and freshly ground black pepper**
Freshly grated nutmeg	**Freshly grated nutmeg**
2 oz (50g) cooked green peas	**⅓ cup cooked green peas**
2 oz (50g) sweetcorn kernels	**⅓ cup sweetcorn kernels**
2 oz (50g) diced red peppers	**⅓ cup diced red peppers**
½ pint (300ml) milk	**1⅓ cups milk**
For the dressing:	For the dressing:
2 fl oz (60ml) olive oil	**¼ cup olive oil**
1 small onion, chopped	**1 small onion, chopped**
1 clove garlic, chopped	**1 clove garlic, chopped**
8 tomatoes, skinned, seeded and chopped	**8 tomatoes, skinned, seeded and chopped**
2 tablespoons tomato purée	**2 tablespoons tomato paste**
½ teaspoon sea salt	**½ teaspoon sea salt**
½ teaspoon raw cane sugar	**½ teaspoon raw cane sugar**
Freshly ground black pepper	**Freshly ground black pepper**
1 tablespoon mixed fresh chopped mint and parsley	**1 tablespoon mixed fresh chopped mint and parsley**

1. Beat together the cheese and eggs, and season generously.
2. Stir in all the vegetables and then blend in the milk thoroughly.
3. Pour the mixture into a lightly greased charlotte mould. Place the mould in a baking tray half filled with hot water. Bake at 350°F/180°C (Gas Mark 4) for 40 to 45 minutes.
4. While the pudding is cooking, prepare the *coulis*. Heat the oil in a saucepan and sauté the onion for 4 minutes. Add the garlic and cook for a further minute.
5. Stir into the onion and garlic mixture the tomato pieces and purée (paste). Cook for 4 minutes, stirring, then season to taste and add the herbs.
6. When the pudding is cooked, turn it out onto a warmed serving dish and pour the sauce around it. Serve immediately.

Les Talmouses de Saint-Denis au Brie

Little Tartlets Filled with a Brie Cheese Soufflé

Makes 24

This is one of the oldest French cheese pastries, dating from the twelfth century. It was created by the people of Sarcelles, who presented them to the Archbishop of Paris accompanied by this little poem:

Des Talmouses de Saint-Denis,
Vous vous portez fort bien aussi,
Comme on voit à votre frimousse,
Qu'on prendrait pour une Talmouse.*

There is a modern version of this dish which uses chopped cheese, blended with a choux pastry, as a filling for a pastry case. I prefer the old-fashioned Talmouse, and it is this recipe which I give you now.

Imperial (Metric)	American
½ lb (225g) Brie cheese	**8 ounces Brie cheese**
½ lb (225g) cream cheese	**1 cup cream cheese**
Sea salt and freshly ground black pepper	**Sea salt and freshly ground black pepper**
Freshly grated nutmeg	**Freshly grated nutmeg**
2 teaspoons raw cane sugar	**2 teaspoons raw cane sugar**
1 tablespoon cornflour	**1 tablespoon cornstarch**
4 egg yolks	**4 egg yolks**
2 egg whites	**2 egg whites**
1 lb (450g) puff pastry (page 144)	**1 pound puff pastry (page 144)**

1 Cut the rind off the Brie as thinly as possible and then pound the cheese to a smooth paste with the cream cheese. Season with salt, pepper, nutmeg and sugar.
2 Blend the cornflour (cornstarch) into the cheese, followed by the egg yolks, to make an evenly mixed smooth cream.
3 Whisk the egg whites until they hold firm peaks and then fold gradually into the cheese mixture.
4 Roll out the pastry and use it to line 24 little tartlet moulds. Prick the base of each pastry case and then fill with the soufflé mixture to two-thirds full.
5 Bake in a preheated oven at 400°F/200°C (Gas Mark 6) for 20 minutes. Serve immediately.

* The Talmouses of Saint-Denis
Keep you in very good health
As one can see from your round, shiny face
Which one would take for a Talmouse.

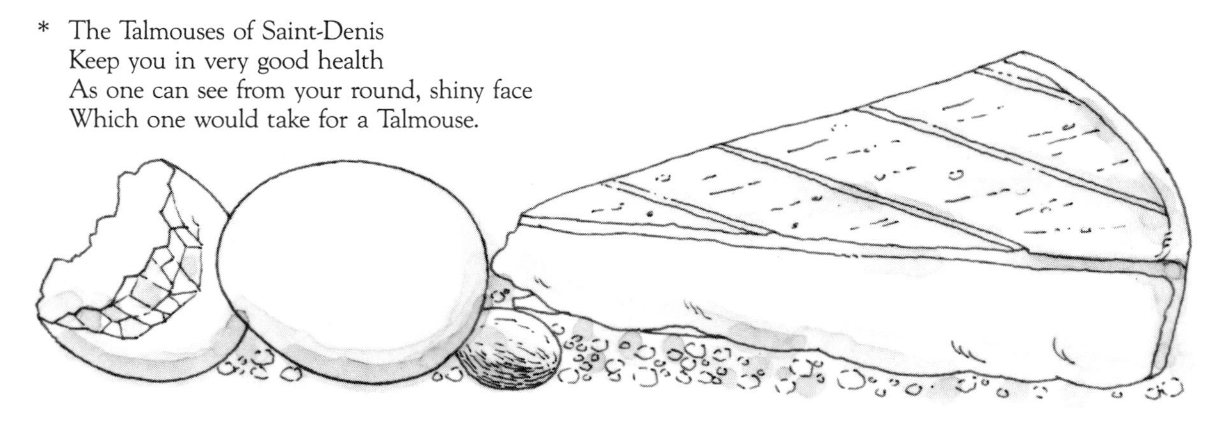

Quenelles de Fromage Sauce Saffran

Cheese Mousse Dumplings in a Saffron Sauce

The word *quenelle* comes from the Saxon word *knyl*, meaning to pound to a paste. From this comes also the German *knödel* and the English verb to knead, and the word noodle. Yet the *quenelle* is neither kneaded nor is it some kind of pasta or noodle — it is, however, usually made from a pounded mixture. In these particular delicate little cheese *quenelles* the curd cheese takes the place of a pounded mixture of fish or meat, and the flavour and texture are the better for it. You will need two ordinary tablespoons to shape your mixture into the right egg-shape. When poached, the *quenelle* should be as light as whipped cream.

Imperial (Metric)	American
1 whole egg plus 2 egg whites	**1 whole egg plus 2 egg whites**
1 lb (450g) curd cheese	**2 cups curd cheese**
Sea salt and freshly ground black pepper	**Sea salt and freshly ground black pepper**
Freshly grated nutmeg	**Freshly grated nutmeg**
Juice and freshly grated rind of ½ lemon	**Juice and freshly grated rind of ½ lemon**
2 oz (50g) wholemeal breadcrumbs	**½ cup wholewheat breadcrumbs**
12 large, fresh leaves spinach	**12 large, fresh leaves spinach**
For the sauce:	For the sauce:
1 oz (25g) butter	**2 tablespoons butter**
1 small onion, chopped	**1 small onion, chopped**
¼ pint (150ml) dry Vermouth	**⅔ cup dry Vermouth**
1 tablespoon tomato purée	**1 tablespoon tomato paste**
Mashed pulp of 1 avocado	**Mashed pulp of 1 avocado**
Sea salt and freshly ground black pepper	**Sea salt and freshly ground black pepper**
Pinch paprika	**Pinch paprika**
Pinch saffron	**Pinch saffron**
¼ pint (150ml) double cream	**⅔ cup heavy cream**

1. Beat the whole egg and the egg whites together with the cheese until smooth. Season with salt, pepper and nutmeg, then add the lemon juice and rind. Blend in the breadcrumbs to form a smooth, thick paste.
2. Divide the paste into 12 egg-shaped portions by moulding with 2 tablespoons. Place the *quenelles* on greaseproof paper on a baking tray and freeze for 10 minutes, then bake at 375°F/190°C (Gas Mark 5) for 15 minutes. Cool.
3. Wash, drain and blanch the spinach leaves. Drain and spread out on a board.
4. Wrap a leaf round each *quenelle* and place on individual serving plates, two per portion.
5. For the sauce, heat the butter in a saucepan and sauté the onion until soft but not browned. Add the Vermouth, tomato purée (paste) and avocado purée.
6. Season the sauce with salt, pepper, paprika and saffron. Boil for 8 minutes.
7. Stir the cream into the sauce and check the seasoning. Cook gently for a further 4 minutes.
8. Pour the sauce over the *quenelles*. Decorate, if liked, with a tomato 'rose' and a spring of dill, and garnish with a slice of toasted brioche.

Note: A tomato rose can be made by thinly peeling a tomato with a potato peeler or a very sharp knife, and then shaping the delicate peel into a rose-bud shape, with the sprig of dill as its leaves. This will complement the rich green of the wrapped *quenelle* to perfection.

Les Brocolis aux Pommes à la Vendéenne

A Gratin of Broccoli and Potatoes

Serves 4
Illustrated opposite page 97.

The Vendée is the province where I was born. Many of the best French country dishes originated in this region, and are still to be found there, prepared to a high degree of excellence. Much of the farmland is of a very high quality, some of the best having been reclaimed from the sea in the eleventh century. This has become the 'market garden' of France, producing a wide range of excellent vegetables. Consequently, our version of the traditional gratin includes more than just the standard potato slices. This recipe gives a broccoli and potato mixture, but almost any vegetable, such as cauliflower, cabbage, Brussels sprouts or leeks, could be substituted for the broccoli.

Imperial (Metric)	American
½ lb (225g) broccoli	**8 ounces broccoli**
½ lb (225g) potatoes, peeled and sliced	**8 ounces potatoes, peeled and sliced**
2 pints (1.15 litres) water	**5 cups water**
3 cloves garlic, chopped	**3 cloves garlic, chopped**

For the sauce:	For the sauce:
2 oz (50g) Normandy or Vendée butter	**¼ cup Normandy or Vendée butter**
2 tablespoons wholemeal flour	**2 tablespoons wholewheat flour**
¼ pint (150ml) stock from vegetables	**⅔ cup stock from vegetables**
¼ pint (150ml) single cream	**⅔ cup light cream**
4 oz (100g) grated hard cheese of choice	**1 cup grated hard cheese of choice**
Sea salt and freshly ground black pepper	**Sea salt and freshly ground black pepper**

1. Trim the broccoli, wash well and drain. Place in a large saucepan with the sliced potatoes, the water and the garlic. Boil for 20 minutes or until the vegetables are tender but not overcooked.
2. Drain the vegetables, reserving ¼ pint (150ml/⅔ cup) liquid for this dish and the rest for stock for other dishes. Place the vegetables in a shallow earthenware baking dish and set aside.
3. Heat the butter in a saucepan and stir in the flour. Cook gently, stirring to make a roux. Do not allow to brown.
4. Gradually add the vegetable stock to the roux, stirring all the time to make a smooth mixture, then slowly add the cream to make a sauce.
5. Stir in half the cheese and season to taste.
6. Coat the vegetables with this sauce and then sprinkle with the remaining cheese. Place under a hot grill (broiler) until sizzling hot and golden-brown. Serve at once.

9 *Les Entremets Chauds et Froids*

Hot and Cold Sweets

Until the eighteenth century the word *entremet* meant a dish served, literally 'between courses' and would usually follow the main meat course. Thus it was not confined to sweet things, often it would be vegetables, for example. Since then the word has come to mean, for the most part, a sweet made with dairy products. On a French menu this course is no longer, as its name would suggest, between courses, as we like in France to serve our dessert after the cheese course — a fashion which is gradually being adopted in other countries. In a more grand, ceremonial dinner the *entremet* assumes its earlier function and is simply a course following on from the main course and preceding the dessert as a sweet.

There are so many traditional French sweets that it would be easy to devote book after book to the subject — indeed many books have been written which do just that. In this chapter you will find several represented, from simple country puddings such as *Clafoutis* and *Le Far Breton* to more classical cuisine such as *Vacherin aux Marrons.* In all cases I have chosen dishes which lend themselves well to a wholefood approach, and indeed which are improved by the use of these natural ingredients. Although, as with all the recipes in this book, we use good, wholesome ingredients in this chapter, it is not a chapter for slimmers! The use of good French cream, eggs and butter is an integral part of most French sweets and, although portions of rich desserts should always be small, most are still fattening. If you or your guests are watching your weight, go for the Pawpaw and Lime Sorbet, or vary it with other fruits, and serve tiny scoops, prettily decorated. This is a reflection of the very successful *cuisine minceur* and neither host or guests will feel deprived of a delicious culinary experience.

Most important in this chapter, too, is the use of fresh seasonal fruits, and fruit from parts of the world which have influenced French cuisine over the centuries. Thus, our cherries and greengages are represented, our pears and apples too, alongside such more exotic flavours as lime and pawpaw. Since we are a nation of wine drinkers it is not too surprising that the technique of marinating fruit in wine has developed to a fine art. Stewed in a good wine, or perhaps in its 'own' liqueur, a fruit takes on a most luxurious flavour and aroma. Dried fruit, a speciality of the South of France, has been well represented here, too. This region has built up quite an industry around its *pâtés de fruits* and *marrons glacés*, both of which are eaten as a dessert at the end of grand banquets in France. Our rich harvest of nuts has not been left out, either, with chestnuts, almonds and the attractive and distinctly-flavoured pistachio featuring in the recipes. *Pistache* ice-cream is every French child's favourite flavour so watch out for the Pistachio Cream if you are serving *Roulade de Marrons Chocolaté* when children are around!

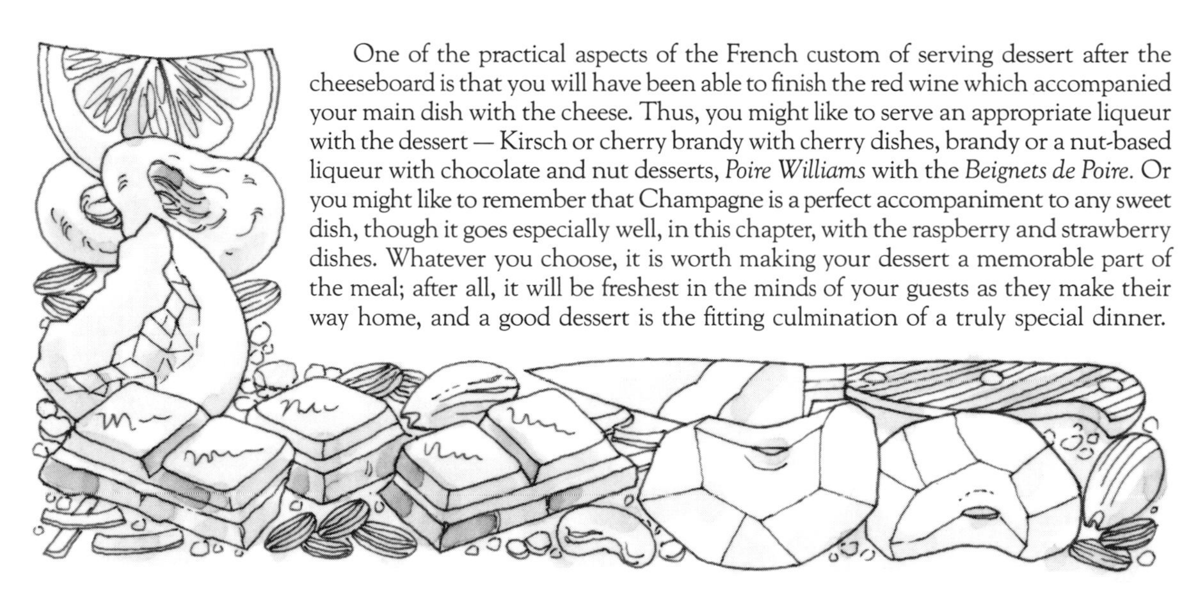

One of the practical aspects of the French custom of serving dessert after the cheeseboard is that you will have been able to finish the red wine which accompanied your main dish with the cheese. Thus, you might like to serve an appropriate liqueur with the dessert — Kirsch or cherry brandy with cherry dishes, brandy or a nut-based liqueur with chocolate and nut desserts, *Poire Williams* with the *Beignets de Poire.* Or you might like to remember that Champagne is a perfect accompaniment to any sweet dish, though it goes especially well, in this chapter, with the raspberry and strawberry dishes. Whatever you choose, it is worth making your dessert a memorable part of the meal; after all, it will be freshest in the minds of your guests as they make their way home, and a good dessert is the fitting culmination of a truly special dinner.

Le Far Breton

A Baked Rum and Raisin Batter Pudding

Bréton cooking is abundant in inexpensive sweet dishes which are quick and easy to make, and extremely nourishing — the *crêpe* being the obvious example. The *far* is a less well-known, but no less enjoyable, example of the cuisine of Brittany. It can be varied endlessly, from a very basic mixture with plain raisins to a more luxurious dish with plums, apricots, cherries or apples, soaked in an appropriate liqueur. For this recipe I have stayed with the traditional raisin filling, but have given it a bit of luxury by soaking the raisins in rum first. Compare this dish with the Limousin *Clafoutis* (page 171). They are similar in their basic ingredients, yet quite unique when cooked. Try both and decide which you like best — most likely you will enjoy both equally, in which case you can cook one or other for your guests as the mood takes you.

Imperial (Metric)	American
5 oz (150g) seedless raisins	**1 cup seedless raisins**
¼ pint (150ml) rum	**⅔ cup rum**
½ lb (225g) wholemeal flour	**2 cups wholewheat flour**
Large pinch sea salt	**Large pinch sea salt**
6 eggs, beaten	**6 eggs, beaten**
2 pints (1.15 litres) milk	**5 cups milk**
4 oz (100g) raw cane sugar, powdered in a grinder	**⅔ cup raw cane sugar, powdered in a grinder**
2 oz (50g) butter	**¼ cup butter**

1 Soak the raisins in the rum for several hours.
2 Put the flour and salt into a large bowl and add the beaten eggs, stirring to mix well.
3 Heat a quarter of the milk to boiling point, then add it gradually to the flour and egg mixture, whisking to make a smooth batter.
4 Stir in the cold milk, the sugar, and the raisins with any residue of rum left from the soaking.
5 Butter a shallow round earthenware baking dish, 8 inches (20cm) in diameter, and pour in the batter.
6 Bake for 1 hour 15 minutes at 375°F/190°C (Gas Mark 5). Cool, and serve cold, cut into slices.

Les Framboises au Sabayon

Raspberries in a Rich Wine Sauce

Serves 4
Illustrated opposite page 161.

The raspberry seems to have come into its own with the advent of the *nouvelle cuisine*, in which many recipes call for the distinctive and delicious flavour of raspberry vinegar. But the flavouring of a good wine vinegar with raspberries to achieve a uniquely piquant taste is really only an extension of the traditional French custom of serving this fruit marinated in red or white wine or even Champagne. This dish marries the fresh, unadorned flavour of the raspberries with a delicate yet intensely-flavoured wine sauce, similar in preparation and origin to the Italian favourite *Zabaglione*.

Imperial (Metric)	American
1 lb (450g) fresh raspberries	**1 pound fresh raspberries**
1 egg white, lightly beaten	**1 egg white, lightly beaten**
2 oz (50g) golden granulated sugar	**⅓ cup golden granulated sugar**
1 drop green vegetable food colouring	**1 drop green vegetable food colouring**
For the sabayon sauce:	For the sabayon sauce:
6 eggs, separated	**6 eggs, separated**
1 whole egg, lightly beaten	**1 whole egg, lightly beaten**
2 oz (50g) raw cane sugar, powdered in a grinder	**⅓ cup raw cane sugar, powdered in a grinder**
Juice and grated rind of ¼ lemon	**Juice and grated rind of ¼ lemon**
¼ pint(150ml) Sauternes or other sweet white wine, slightly warmed	**⅔ cup Sauternes or other sweet white wine, slightly warmed**

1. Pick over the raspberries for imperfect ones, then rinse quickly and drain well.
2. Turn the lightly beaten egg white out onto a flat plate.
3. Spread the sugar on a flat plate, too, and add to it the drop of natural green food colouring. Rub this in thoroughly to the sugar, to tint it an even, leafy green.
4. Take four tall glasses (champagne flutes would be ideal) and dip their rims first in the egg white, then in the sugar to 'frost' the rim with green crystals. Set the glasses aside.
5. In a clean metal basin, place the egg yolks, the whole egg, sugar, lemon juice and rind. Set the bowl over a pan of simmering water and, using a balloon whisk, beat the mixture until it is light and foamy (about 2 minutes should be sufficient, but it may take a little longer — do not scramble the eggs though!).
6. As soon as the mixture is foamy, start to gradually pour in the warmed white wine, whisking all the time. The mixture should thicken to the point where it is thick enough to coat the back of a spoon.
7. At this point, remove the sauce from the heat and continue to whisk, this time over a bowl of rice cubes, for 3 more minutes.
8. Beat the egg whites with a pinch of salt until stiff and fold into the egg-yolk mixture.
9. When the sauce is cool and creamy-thick, set it aside while the raspberries are spooned into each of the prepared glasses to about half full.
10. Top each glass of raspberries with two tablespoons of sabayon sauce. Serve immediately, with the rest of the sauce served separately for guests to top up their glasses with if wished.

Variation:
To serve the sabayon cold, stir in 2 fl oz (60ml/¼ cup) whipped cream before serving.

The raspberries could be marinated in *framboise* liqueur before being covered with the sauce, or the wine in the sabayon could be replaced with this liqueur.

La Tarte Tatin

Caramelized Upside-Down Apple Tart

This delicious dessert was created by two elderly French ladies who ran a very successful restaurant in Paris. It is a classic in France, yet very few chefs in other parts of the world have featured it. I hope this situation will soon be remedied, because it is a very good — and rather special — dessert.

Of all the varieties of apple, the most suited to sweet dishes of this sort are the Cox's Orange Pippin and the French Golden Delicious. Apples are rich in pectin so, once poached, they will help set a cold mousse or a purée of apples and berries.

Imperial (Metric)	American
For the sweet pastry:	For the sweet pastry:
½ lb (225g) wholemeal flour	**2 cups wholewheat flour**
1 pinch mixed spice	**1 pinch mixed spice**
4 oz (100g) butter	**½ cup butter**
1 oz (25g) raw cane sugar, powdered in a grinder	**2 tablespoons raw cane sugar, powdered in a grinder**
1 tablespoon vegetable oil	**1 tablespoon vegetable oil**
1 egg, beaten	**1 egg, beaten**
For the topping:	For the topping:
6 oz (150g) raw cane sugar	**1 cup raw cane sugar**
1 oz (25g) butter	**2 tablespoons butter**
2 fl oz (50ml) water	**¼ cup water**
1 lb (450g) apples	**1 pound apples**

1. Stir the flour and spices together in a bowl and rub in the butter. Then stir in the sugar, oil and beaten egg to make a firm batter. Do not knead, once evenly mixed. Roll into a ball and refrigerate for 30 minutes.
2. Cook the sugar, butter and water together in a pan to make a caramel.
3. Pour this caramel into a heatproof glass flan dish, spreading it out to cover the entire dish.
4. Peel, core and quarter the apples, then slice each wedge in half to give thin slices. Arrange the slices, overlapping slightly, over the caramel. Try to make an attractive pattern with the slices.
5. Roll out the pastry to fit the dish (about ¼ inch/5mm thick) and lay this over the apples.
6. Bake in a preheated oven at 400°F/200°C (Gas Mark 6) for 35 to 40 minutes. Remove from the oven and wait for 6 minutes before proceeding. Run a knife round the dish to loosen the tart, then turn upside-down onto a flat dish. Serve.

Les Beignets de Poires aux Graines de Sésame

Pear Fritters with a Caramel and Sesame Seed Coating

Serves 4
Illustrated opposite.

Classic French cuisine has always included a great many dishes with a caramel finish. The most common one, *crème caramel*, has just about been done to death, although the similar *crème brulée* still retains its appeal for gourmets. This dish combines the richness of a caramel coating with crispy-coated pear fritters and the nutty flavour of sesame seeds. It reflects the interesting combination of French *haute cuisine* with the influence of the immensely popular Vietnamese style of cooking which has had a great influence, particularly with the younger French chefs and diners.

Imperial (Metric)	American
For the beignets:	For the beignets:
2 eggs, beaten	**2 eggs, beaten**
½ pint (300ml) mixed milk and water	**1⅓ cups mixed milk and water**
4 oz (100g) wholemeal flour	**1 cup wholewheat flour**
Pinch sea salt	**Pinch sea salt**
4 large ripe Comice pears	**4 large ripe Comice pears**
2 oz (50g) wholemeal flour	**½ cup wholewheat flour**
Vegetable oil for frying	**Vegetable oil for frying**
For the caramel:	For the caramel:
6 oz (150g) raw cane sugar	**1 cup raw cane sugar**
2 oz (50g) butter	**¼ cup butter**
3 fl oz (90ml) water	**⅓ cup water**
2 oz (50g) sesame seeds	**⅓ cup sesame seeds**
Clear honey, to taste	**Clear honey, to taste**
Mint leaves, for garnish	**Mint leaves, for garnish**

1. Prepare the batter by combining the beaten eggs and milk and water in a bowl and gradually adding the flour and salt to form a smooth batter. Leave it to stand for 30 minutes.
2. Prepare the pears by peeling and coring them, and then cutting into halves, or quarters if large.
3. Coat the pear wedges in flour, then in the batter, and then fry in preheated oil for 2 minutes until golden. Drain well.
4. To prepare the caramel, heat the sugar, butter and water together in a saucepan, boiling until a sugar thermometer reads 300°F/150°C. Add the sesame seeds, then dip the pears into the caramel for a few seconds on either side.
5. Have ready a bowl of ice cubes, so that as each pear fritter is removed from the caramel it can be dipped quickly into the ice. This sets the caramel. Arrange on a plate and decorate with mint leaves.
6. Leave the dish in the refrigerator for 3 hours if you prefer your caramel softer and less brittle, then serve. Or serve straight away, drizzled with honey.

Variation:
Sharp cooking apples or firm but ripe peaches may be substituted for the pears.

Opposite: *Les Beignets de Poires aux Graines de Sésame* (above).

Honey

best served chilled
BLANC
70cl
LIQVOR
67.4° PROOF

Le Soufflé aux Fraises

Strawberry Soufflé

Serves 8

This is an excellent way to use up the left-over egg whites from a Sabayon Sauce, such as in the recipe on page 158, or a rice mould, such as in the recipe on page 164. Strawberries have an infinite variety of uses, although in Britain they are most commonly served with cream. In fact, they can be sliced into a salad with a light, lemon and black pepper dressing (they are very good combined with sliced cucumber this way) and many people like them with just a sprinkling of black pepper. Served as a sweet, they can be puréed to make a sauce for other fruits, or soaked in white wine and then arranged over a sweet shortcrust flan base and glazed to make a delicious tart, or, as in this recipe, puréed as a base for a most exquisite soufflé — a light and flavoursome finish to a rich dinner party. If you can, it is worth obtaining 'wild' or alpine strawberries to make this dish, as their flavour and fragrance is much finer than that of cultivated varieties. It is not difficult to grow your own, and it certainly repays the effort in terms of quality.

Imperial (Metric)	American
2 oz (50g) butter	**¼ cup butter**
¾ lb (325g) raw cane sugar	**2 cups raw cane sugar**
4 fl oz (120ml) water	**½ cup water**
1 lb (450g) strawberries	**4 cups strawberries**
1 tablespoon Grand Marnier	**1 tablespoon Grand Marnier**
7 egg whites	**7 egg whites**

1. Butter the insides of eight individual ramekins and then use 2 oz (50g/⅓ cup) sugar to coat the butter lightly.
2. In a saucepan, boil the water with a further ½ lb (225g/1⅓ cups) sugar until a rich syrup is formed (reading 260°F/140°C on a sugar thermometer).
3. Meanwhile, clean and mash the strawberries, first reserving 8 small, perfect ones for decoration, and pass them through a sieve to remove the seeds.
4. Put this purée in a pan and cook for 5 minutes to reduce the moisture.
5. When the sugar syrup has become very sticky and a drop put in cold water is hard and brittle, add it to the strawberry purée. Cook for 3 more minutes, stir in the liqueur and then set aside to cool.
6. In a very clean and dry mixing bowl, beat the egg whites until they hold firm peaks. Add the last 2 oz (50g/⅓ cup sugar) a teaspoon at a time, beating the egg whites back to firmness between each addition.
7. Stir in half of the strawberry purée, cutting it in with a criss-cross motion until well mixed. Then fold the rest in lightly.
8. Fill the ramekins to the brim with the soufflé mixture. Level the tops and run the back of a teaspoon around the rim to make a channel. This ensures that the top rises level, making a more attractive finished dish.
9. Place the soufflés on a baking sheet and bake in the centre of a pre-heated oven at 400°F/200°C (Gas Mark 6) for 15 to 20 minutes, when they are well risen. Decorate each with a fresh strawberry and serve at once.

Opposite: *Les Framboises au Sabayon* (page 158) and *Marquises au Chocolat* (page 166).

Le Vacherin aux Marrons Chocolatés

A Chocolate-Chestnut Cream in a Nest of Meringue

Serves 8

As with a soufflé, meringues are an ideal way of using up egg whites left over from a dish such as *Framboises au Sabayon* (page 158) which requires only the yolks. In fact, meringues are especially convenient because, stored in an airtight tin, they will keep for several weeks.

This combination of chocolate, puréed chestnuts and meringue is a classic one, with the variation of the meringue being replaced with whipped cream in some dishes. Chestnuts have acquired a luxurious appeal, yet are easy to obtain when in season, and even easier to prepare when — out of season — one purchases a tin of the very high-quality chestnut purées imported from France! Should you wish to prepare your own chestnut purée in season, you must slit the outer hard skin with a sharp knife, roast briefly in a very hot oven to crack the skin wide open, then boil the nut, still in its inner skin, for 5 minutes to allow removal of this second skin. Finally, boil them in their own weight of milk and water mixed until tender, and then purée. Needless to say, most chefs use the ready-made purée, and few diners would be able to tell the difference.

Imperial (Metric)	American
2 lb (900g) chestnut purée	**2 pounds chestnut paste**
4 oz (100g) butter	**½ cup butter**
4 oz (100g) bitter chocolate, melted	**½ cup bitter chocolate, melted**
4 fl oz (120ml) dark rum	**½ cup dark rum**
4 fl oz (120ml) double cream	**½ cup heavy cream**
6 egg whites	**6 egg whites**
¾ lb (350g) golden granulated sugar	**2 cups golden granulated sugar**

1. In a saucepan, combine the chestnut purée with the butter and heat gently until smooth and creamy.
2. Add the melted chocolate and the rum. Mix in well and then set the mixture aside to cool.
3. Whisk the cream until stiff and fold into the cold chestnut-chocolate mixture. Chill while making the meringue nest.
4. In a very clean, dry bowl, beat the egg whites to a firm, peaked state.
5. Powder half the sugar in a grinder, then stir back in with the unowdered half. Add this partially ground sugar, one teaspoon at a time, to the beaten egg whites, beating back to stiffness between each addition. Alternatively, use an electric whisk and beat in the sugar in three stages.
6. When all the sugar has been added and the egg whites hold firm peaks, spoon into a piping bag with a wide star nozzle.
7. Line a baking sheet with silicone paper, or greaseproof paper lightly greased and floured, and mark on this a circle 8 inches (20cm) in diameter.
8. Starting from the centre of the circle, pipe the meringue round in a spiral to the edge. Then pipe a border, two thicknesses high, round the edge to make a 'nest.'
9. Place the baking tray in a very low oven, 250°F/130°C (Gas Mark ½) and allow to dry rather than cook for at least 2 to 3 hours. Then transfer the dry meringue shell onto a serving plate or pretty cake board.
10. Fill a piping bag, fitted with a plain tube ⅛ inch (3mm) in diameter, with the chestnut cream and pipe it into the shell to resemble swirls of spaghetti.

Variations:
The meringue could be made into four individual 3-inch (7cm) shells, which can look very attractive for a dinner party. The filling mixture could also be piped into sweet pastry cases, or onto sponge cakes or ice-cream, or used as a base for poached pears.

La Pascaline Imperiale

A Rich Cheese Mould with a Macedoine of Fruits

Before the Russian Revolution, many French chefs were employed at the court of Tsar Nicholas II, and at the homes of many of the Russian aristocrats. This dish is based on a traditional Russian recipe called *Pashka*, which is served at Easter, but has been adapted by French cuisine as a heritage of those French chefs whose banquets at the Winter Palace and the like are now history. French cream cheeses are so many and delicious that it is no wonder we have adopted this dish as an *haute cuisine* French dessert.

Imperial (Metric)	American
½ lb (225g) French cream cheese	**1 cup French cream cheese**
¼ pint (150ml) set natural yogurt	**⅔ cup set plain yogurt**
4 oz (100g) ground almonds	**1 cup ground almonds**
2 fl oz (60ml) double cream	**¼ cup heavy cream**
4 oz (100g) raw cane sugar, powdered in a grinder	**⅔ cup raw cane sugar, powdered in a grinder**
2 egg whites	**2 egg whites**
Pinch sea salt	**Pinch sea salt**
6 oz (150g) chopped mixed fruits, including: peaches, pears, stoned cherries, pineapple and seedless raisins	**1½ cups chopped mixed fruits, including: peaches, pears, stoned cherries, pineapple and seedless raisins**
3 fl oz (90ml) Kirsch	**⅓ cup Kirsch**

1 Line a charlotte mould with a piece of fine cheesecloth.
2 In a bowl, combine the cream cheese with the yogurt and almonds.
3 Whip the cream with half of the sugar and stir this into the cheese mixture.
4 In a very clean, dry bowl, beat the egg whites and salt until they hold stiff peaks. Then beat in the sugar a little at a time, beating between each addition until stiff again. Fold this mixture into the cheese and cream mixture.
5 Stir the chopped fruit, drained of any excess juices, into the mixture and turn the whole lot into the charlotte mould. Cover with a plate on which must be rested a heavy weight, to press the *Pascaline* firmly. Chill overnight.
6 Remove the mould from the refrigerator, lift out the cheesecloth and give the mixture a firm squeezing to get rid of any residual moisture. Press it back into the charlotte mould for a further hour's chilling, then turn it out onto a serving dish and peel off the cloth. It should keep its shape by this stage. Sprinkle with Kirsch and serve.

Note: This is even more delicious served with a Sabayon Sauce (page 158).

Les Abricots à la Bourdaloue

Baked Rice Mould with Apricots and a Frangipane Cream

Serves 6-8

The best apricots are cultivated in the South of France, in Roussillon, Provence and the Vallée du Rhone. It is one of the fruits most commonly used in confectionery, baking and jams in France, as anyone who has sampled breakfast in a French hotel — coffee, croissants and the ubiquitous apricot jam — will confirm!

This is a rich and filling dessert, but it is also one of the most nutritionally complete sweet dishes you can eat. Many readers will recognize instantly that the rice mould is made along the same lines as the traditional rice pudding. But even rice pudding haters should not let this put them off — it bears no relation to the stodgy, bland and sickly 'nursery' pudding they probably remember from childhood.

Imperial (Metric)	American
For the rice mould:	For the rice mould:
1 pint (600ml) water	**2½ cups water**
½ lb (225g) short grain brown rice	**1 cup short grain brown rice**
2 pints (1.15 litres) milk	**5 cups milk**
4 oz (100g) raw cane sugar	**⅔ cup raw cane sugar**
4 oz (100g) butter	**½ cup butter**
Pinch sea salt	**Pinch sea salt**
1 vanilla pod *or* **3 drops natural vanilla essence**	**1 vanilla bean** *or* **3 drops natural vanilla essence**
6 egg yolks	**6 egg yolks**
For the frangipane cream:	For the frangipane cream:
1 pint (600ml) milk	**2½ cups milk**
4 oz (100g) raw cane sugar	**½ cup raw cane sugar**
2 oz (50g) cornflour	**⅓ cup cornstarch**
1 egg	**1 egg**
3 egg yolks	**3 egg yolks**
4 oz (100g) ground almonds	**1 cup ground almonds**
2 drops natural almond essence *or* **4 tablespoons anisette liqueur**	**2 drops natural almond essence** *or* **4 tablespoons anisette liqueur**
For the apricots:	For the apricots:
18 ripe but firm apricots	**18 ripe but firm apricots**
½ pint (300ml) water	**1⅓ cups water**
4 oz (100g) raw cane sugar	**½ cup raw cane sugar**
2 tablespoons Kirsch	**2 tablespoons Kirsch**

1 To cook the rice, bring the water to the boil, add the rice and cook for 8 minutes. Then drain and discard the water. Bring the milk to the boil with the sugar, then add the rice, half of the butter, salt and vanilla pod (if using vanilla essence, do not add it yet). Cover the pan with a lid and lower the heat. Cook for 30-35 minutes until the rice is well cooked, and almost dry. It will be pasty instead of remaining as individual grains.

2 When the rice is cooked, stir in the egg yolks, away from the heat, and mix in well. Add the vanilla essence if using.

3. Grease a 4 pint (2 litre/10 cup) charlotte or savarin mould with the remaining butter and fill with the rice mixture.
4. Place the mould in a baking tray half-filled with water and bake at 400°F/200°C (Gas Mark 6) for 10 minutes.
5. While the rice mould is cooking, prepare the sauce. Boil the milk and add the sugar to dissolve.
6. In a large bowl, cream together the cornflour (cornstarch) with the egg and the separated yolks, then add the ground almonds and mix well. Pour in about 1 cup of the hot milk, stirring to blend thoroughly.
7. Keeping the rest of the milk at a gentle simmer, add the almond mixture to it, stirring all the time. Boil the sauce for a further 4 minutes to cook the starch completely. Add the almond essence or liqueur.
8. Wash and wipe the apricots. Boil the water and sugar together, then add the apricots and poach for 12 minutes until tender. Drain and halve them, discarding the stones. The syrup can be retained to use again on another occasion, if refrigerated.
9. To serve, turn out the rice mould onto a large, shallow, round dish. Decorate with halved apricots and sprinkle with Kirsch. Serve the frangipane sauce separately. This dish can be served hot, chilled or tepid.

Variations:

Peaches, nectarines, plums, pears or pineapple can be used in place of the apricots. If served cold, the rice could be decorated with whipped cream, glacé cherries, *marrons glacés* or angelica.

The frangipane cream can be used as a topping for an apricot flan, with the fruit being arranged in a pastry shell, then covered in the sauce and baked for 40 minutes, with toasted flaked almonds being sprinkled on before serving. The cream can also be served on its own, or in a glass with fresh berry fruits.

Marquise au Chocolat

Chocolate-Liqueur Cream

Serves 4-6
Illustrated opposite page 161.

Variations on this dish are to be found in all the best restaurants in Paris — or indeed in good French restaurants all over the world, and it is always a favourite, since there are few people who do not find the combination of chocolate, cream and liqueur irresistible. I have been serving the *Marquise* to my customers all my working life, and this particular recipe, using Grand Marnier and brandy to flavour the chocolate cream, has probably been the most popular of all. It is a very rich sweet, so do not be tempted to serve your guests too much as it might become cloying. This recipe will fill four ¼ pint (150ml/⅔ cup) ramekins, but if it is being served at the end of a rich or several-course dinner, it could easily stretch to six servings in smaller dishes without anyone feeling in the least deprived.

Imperial (Metric)	American
4 oz (100g) broken bitter chocolate	**4 ounces broken bitter chocolate**
4 eggs, separated	**4 eggs, separated**
2 fl oz (50ml) Grand Marnier liqueur	**¼ cup Grand Marnier liqueur**
2 fl oz (50ml) brandy	**¼ cup brandy**
4 fl oz (120ml) double cream, whipped	**½ cup heavy cream, whipped**
Pinch sea salt	**Pinch sea salt**

1 Place the broken chocolate in a bowl set over a pan of hot water, so that it melts.
2 Put the egg yolks into another bowl and pour the melted chocolate over them, stirring to blend the mixture well.
3 To this mixture add the liqueurs and the cream. Mix all these ingredients together thoroughly.
4 Beat the egg whites with a pinch of salt. Fold this mixture carefully into the chocolate cream so that it is completely mixed but still light and fluffy.
5 Spoon this mixture into individual ramekins and chill for 2 hours before serving.

Variations:
This cream is delicious served with a *compote* of pears. It can also be heated and used as a sauce for profiteroles, ice-cream or pears *Hélène*. It can be mixed with an equal amount of chestnut purée to make a delicious *Mont Blanc* or used as a filling for a gâteau. Other liqueurs could be substituted for the Grand Marnier — Tia Maria will add a pleasant coffee flavour, for example.

Le Diplomate au Cointreau

A Liqueured Fruit and Sponge Custard

A baked custard is a very simple dish to prepare, but its association with invalid food is, for many people, rather off-putting. This dish, I can assure you, is so far removed from most people's idea of baked custard that it would make even the most resolute custard-hater think again. It is a rich and flavourful dish, attractively presented in moulded form; and the flavour of the glacé fruits — a speciality of the South of France — steeped in an orange liqueur, will delight your guests. Do be sure not to leave out the *marrons glacés*, even if it seems an unnecessary expense. They really do give this dish its uniquely French and decidedly luxurious flavour.

Imperial (Metric)	American
2 oz (50g) butter	**¼ cup butter**
2 oz (50g) chopped glacé fruits such as: *marrons glacés*, cherries, orange and lemon peel and angelica	**½ cup chopped glacé fruits such as: *marrons glacés*, cherries, orange and lemon peel and angelica**
2 fl oz (60ml) Cointreau or other orange liqueur	**¼ cup Cointreau or other orange liqueur**
For the sponge custard:	For the sponge custard:
3 eggs, beaten	**3 eggs, beaten**
2 oz (50g) raw cane sugar	**⅓ cup raw cane sugar**
1 pint (600ml) milk	**2½ cups milk**
2 oz (50g) stale wholemeal sponge cake pieces (see page 168)	**2 ounces stale wholewheat sponge cake pieces (see page 168)**
For the glaze:	For the glaze:
2 oz (50g) raw sugar apricot jam	**4 tablespoons raw sugar apricot jelly**
6 tablespoons water	**6 tablespoons water**
½ teaspoon arrowroot	**½ teaspoon arrowroot**
4 oz (100g) red Morello cherries, to garnish	**1 cup red Morello cherries, to garnish**

1. Butter a 2 pint (1 litre/5 cup) charlotte mould.
2. Rinse excess sugar off the glacé fruits, then leave to soak in liqueur for 1 hour.
3. Stir the beaten eggs and sugar into the milk until the sugar is dissolved, then add the pieces of sponge cake and the glacé fruits along with any remaining liqueur.
4. Pour this mixture into the mould. Place the mould in a baking tray half-filled with hot water, and bake at 375°F/190°C (Gas Mark 5) for 45 minutes. Remove from the oven and leave to cool.
5. While the custard is cooling, prepare the glaze. Heat together the jam and 4 tablespoons of the water.
6. Blend the arrowroot with the rest of the water, and stir this into the hot jam. Cook for 4 minutes to clear the glaze.
7. Turn out the cold custard onto a flat serving dish and pour the glaze over it. Leave for the glaze to cool, then decorate the dish with the cherries and serve.

Le Montmorency au Fromage

A Layered Cherry Cheesecake with Liqueur

Cherries are grown all over France but the best of all come from the Burgundy region and Montmorency in the *Ile-de-France* — in fact, the word *Montmorency* in a French menu always indicates the presence of cherries in the dish concerned. The best variety for this dish is the *griotte* or red Morello cherry, which is sourer than an ordinary eating cherry and adds an appealing piquancy to the dish when baked with the rich cheese topping. This recipe may look rather involved, with its several stages, but each is very simple to execute and, once prepared and assembled, the dish looks quite beautiful and makes a spectacular finish to a special dinner.

Imperial (Metric)	American
1 quantity Sweet Pastry (page 159)	**1 quantity Sweet Pastry (page 159)**
For the sponge:	For the sponge:
1 oz (25g) butter	**2 tablespoons butter**
2 eggs	**2 eggs**
2 oz (50g) raw cane sugar, powdered in a grinder	**⅓ cup raw cane sugar, powdered in a grinder**
2 oz (50g) 81 per cent wholemeal flour	**½ cup 81 per cent wholewheat flour**
For the cherries:	For the cherries:
6 oz (150g) stoned sour red cherries	**1½ cups stoned sour red cherries**
2 fl oz (60ml) mixed Kirsch and cherry brandy	**¼ cup mixed Kirsch and cherry brandy**
For the topping:	For the topping:
3 oz (75g) cream cheese	**⅓ cup cream cheese**
2 fl oz (60ml) double cream, whipped	**¼ cup heavy cream, whipped**
1 tablespoon wholemeal flour	**1 tablespoon wholewheat flour**
2 egg whites	**2 egg whites**
Pinch sea salt	**Pinch sea salt**
2 oz (50g) raw cane sugar	**⅓ cup raw cane sugar**
2 tablespoons raw sugar cherry jam	**2 tablespoons raw sugar cherry jelly**

1. Prepare the pastry as instructed for *Tarte Tatin* (page 159). Set aside to rest.
2. Meanwhile, prepare the sponge. Grease an 8 inch (20cm) sponge tin with half the butter; line with non-stick baking paper, cut to fit the tin.
3. Using an electric beater, whisk the eggs in a large bowl along with the sugar until thick and foamy — about 8 minutes. It helps if the sugar is very slightly warmed before you begin, but do not melt it by overheating.
4. When the eggs and sugar are well beaten, add the flour very gradually, one spoon at a time, mixing in with a rotary movement rather than beating.
5. Pour this mixture into the prepared tin and bake at 375°F/190°C (Gas Mark 5) for 20 to 25 minutes, on the middle shelf. Remove and allow to cool.
6. Put the cherries in a bowl with the liqueurs and leave for at least 10 minutes.
7. Make the cheesecake filling by blending the cream cheese, whipped cream and flour together in a bowl until well blended. Beat the egg whites with a pinch of salt and, when stiff, beat in the sugar.
8. Fold the stiff egg whites into the cheese and cream mixture.

9 Grease a 9 inch (23cm) diameter cake tin, 3 inches (7cm) deep, with the rest of the butter. Line it with the pastry, rolled out to a thickness of ⅛ inch (3mm). Trim the edges.
10 Spread the base of the pastry with the jam, then slice the sponge in half and lay one half on the jam-coated base, cut side upwards. (You will not require the rest of the sponge for this recipe, but it stores well in an airtight tin and can be used in other recipes in this book.)
11 Arrange the cherries over the top of the sponge and sprinkle with the remaining liqueur.
12 Pour the cheesecake mixture evenly over the top of the cherries and bake in a preheated oven at 375°F/190°C (Gas Mark 5) for 30 to 35 minutes.
13 Halfway through cooking, remove the cheesecake from the oven and run a knife around the edge of the cheese filling, otherwise the skin which is forming will cause it to balloon up, rather than rising neatly and evenly.
14 When the cheesecake is golden-brown, remove from the oven and allow to cool before serving.

La Compote du Mendiant

Fruit Compote

This delicious dessert is often to be found in the French countryside, and varies in composition from one region to another. Tea is a perfect medium for soaking the dried fruit — although you will very often find that wine is used, especially the local *vin ordinaire* in the wine-producing regions. In northern France you will even find the dried fruits soaked in beer! To make a more nourishing dessert you should add the juice of 1 orange to the soaking liquid, as dried fruit lose their vitamin C. The *mendiant* of the name is the mendicant friars, whose sombre habit the rich, dark fruits of this dish are said to resemble.

Imperial (Metric)	American
1½ pints (850ml) fresh-brewed tea of choice	**3¾ cups fresh-brewed tea of choice**
2 of each of the following dried fruits: apples, peaches, apricots and prunes	**2 of each of the following dried fruits: apples, peaches, apricots and prunes**
3 oz (75g) seedless raisins	**3 ounces seedless raisins**
1 stick cinnamon	**1 stick cinnamon**
2 oz (50g) raw cane sugar	**⅓ cup raw cane sugar**
6 fl oz (175ml) clear honey	**½ cup clear honey**
Grated rind and juice of 1 lemon	**Grated rind and juice of 1 lemon**
Grated rind and juice of 1 orange	**Grated rind and juice of 1 orange**
Quantity blanched almonds	**Quantity blanched almonds**

1 When the tea has brewed for 5 minutes, pour it over the dried fruit and leave to soak overnight.
2 Stew the fruits in the tea with the cinnamon stick, sugar, honey and peel of the lemon and orange. Cook very gently for 15 to 20 minutes, then allow to cool.
3 Before serving, stir in the lemon and orange juice, and the almonds. Serve in individual bowls as a dessert or as a refreshing breakfast dish. Frangipane Cream (page 164) makes a good accompaniment to a dessert of these dried fruits.

La Papaya à la Citronelle

A Pawpaw and Lime Sorbet

Serves 8

The sorbet is the classic sweet of the *nouvelle cuisine*. Every restaurant aspiring to win popularity will present an arrangement of three little scoops of different sorbets. However, all too often the sorbets will be of the 'bought' variety — all the chef, or his assistant, has to do is arrange a mint leaf here, a spring of berries there, by way of embellishment and the dish is served. This means, too, that a poor chef can get away without being able to prepare more elaborate and difficult sweets. Still, when a sorbet is made by a good chef it can be the perfect way to end a rich meal, or to cleanse the palate between courses for a real gourmet occasion. A good sorbet should have the consistency of snow, not ice. For this, the sugar content should be around 40 per cent of the total weight of fruit. The proportion can be slightly lower, but too much sugar would make it difficult, or even impossible, to freeze. Many fruits can be prepared along the same lines as pawpaw in this recipe. You might like to make a variety of flavours and follow the *nouvelle* style of serving small *quenelles* of each, prettily arranged on simple china.

Imperial (Metric)	American
5 medium-sized, ripe pawpaw	**5 medium-sized, ripe pawpaw**
Juice of 2 limes	**Juice of 2 limes**
10 oz (300g) raw cane sugar	**1⅔ cups raw cane sugar**
4 fl oz (120ml) water	**½ cup water**
2 fl oz (60ml) gin	**¼ cup gin**
2 egg whites	**2 egg whites**
Pinch sea salt	**Pinch sea salt**
2 extra tablespoons raw cane sugar, powdered in a grinder	**2 extra tablespoons raw cane sugar, powdered in a grinder**
Sprigs of red and black currants, for garnish	**Sprigs of red and black currants, for garnish**
Fresh mint leaves, for garnish	**Fresh mint leaves, for garnish**
1 extra lime, for garnish (optional)	**1 extra lime, for garnish (optional)**

1. Cut four of the pawpaw in half lengthwise. Reserve the fifth for a garnish. Scoop the seeds from the cut pawpaw and discard. Then scoop out almost all the flesh, leaving just enough to keep the skin in shape as a shell.
2. Place all the pulp in the goblet of a blender or a food processor along with the lime juice. Blend to a purée.
3. In a pan, heat the sugar and water together gently, then boil for 4 minutes to make a syrup. Add the pawpaw purée and cook for a further 5 minutes.
4. Remove the pawpaw purée from the heat, flavour with the gin and set aside to cool.
5. While the purée is cooling, beat the egg whites with a pinch of salt until they are stiff. Add the sugar and beat again.
6. When the purée is quite cold, fold in the egg whites. Pour the mixture into a freezer tray to a depth of no more than 2 inches (5cm). Freeze for 2 hours.
7. Remove the partially frozen mixture from the tray and beat in a bowl to the consistency of snow, with fine, small crystals. Then pour the sorbet into a plastic container and freeze again, for a further 2 hours.
8. To serve, scoop out large spoons of the sorbet and place in the pawpaw shells (these could be frozen for an hour before serving, if liked). Level the sorbet attractively and decorate with currants and mint

leaves. Place the halves of pawpaw on individual plates and decorate with slices of the reserved pawpaw and slices of lime, if liked, to squeeze over the sorbet if your guests like an especially tangy flavour.

Le Clafoutis aux Reine-Claudes

A Greengage Pudding

The greengage is a type of plum. Its English name comes from Sir Thomas Gage, who introduced this variety into Britain in the early eighteenth century but the English varieties of greengage are certainly not to be compared with the French *Reine-Claude* which is larger, sweeter and possibly the best of all varieties of plum. Do try to seek out the true French fruit for a real treat. If you cannot, this dish, a speciality of the Limousin region of France, will bring out the best in even the more humble greengage. The most common version of this very traditional French dish is with fresh black cherries. It certainly is delicious this way, but the more unusual fruit of Francois I's Queen Claude is worth sampling — and, if you are in a hurry, it is far easier to stone greengages than cherries!

Imperial (Metric)	American
1 lb (450g) greengages	**1 pound greengages**
¼ pint (150ml) brandy	**⅔ cup brandy**
Pinch ground cinnamon	**Pinch ground cinnamon**
3 oz (75g) wholemeal flour	**¾ cup wholewheat flour**
4 oz (100g) raw cane sugar	**⅔ cup raw cane sugar**
4 eggs, beaten	**4 eggs, beaten**
Pinch sea salt	**Pinch sea salt**
2 drops natural vanilla essence	**2 drops natural vanilla essence**
2 fl oz (50ml) vegetable oil	**¼ cup vegetable oil**

1. Wash and dry the greengages, then cut them in half and discard the stones.
2. Place the greengages and the brandy in a bowl with a pinch of cinnamon and leave to soak for 1 hour.
3. In another bowl, combine the flour, sugar and beaten eggs to make a smooth, thick batter. Stir in a pinch of salt and the vanilla essence, and any residue of the brandy which has been soaking the greengages.
4. Coat a shallow earthenware baking dish with the oil. Heat the oven to 400°F/200°C (Gas Mark 6) and then heat the baking dish in the oven for 10 minutes. Pour in half the batter and bake on the top shelf of the oven for 15 to 20 minutes, until well-risen and puffy.
5. Remove the dish from the oven and arrange the greengages on top of the batter. Then cover with the remaining batter and bake for a further 40 minutes on the middle shelf, until golden and risen. Cooking the dish like this ensures that the first part of the batter is cooked crisp and crusty, like an English Yorkshire pudding, and the second layer is softer and more like a set custard.

Mousseline de Pommes au Cassis

Apple and Blackcurrant Mousse

Apples lend themselves well to being combined with a great many fruits, but I think you will find that this blend of sharp cooking apples and tangy blackcurrants is quite unbeatable. You could use eating apples if you prefer a mellower taste, but the cream and eggs do add a certain mildness to the dish which I find is nicely offset by the slight sharpness of the fruits. This is a very refreshing finish to a meal.

Imperial (Metric)	American
1½ lb (650g) cooking apples	**1½ pounds cooking apples**
2 oz (50g) butter	**¼ cup butter**
½ lb (225g) raw cane sugar	**1⅓ cups raw cane sugar**
½ lb (225g) blackcurrants	**2 cups blackcurrants**
4 eggs, separated	**4 eggs, separated**
2 oz (50g) wholemeal cake crumbs (see page 168)	**1 cup wholewheat cake crumbs (see page 168)**
2 teaspoons arrowroot	**2 teaspoons arrowroot**
4 tablespoons water	**4 tablespoons water**
4 fl oz (120ml) whipped cream	**½ cup heavy cream, whipped**
Extra sprigs blackcurrants, for garnish	**Extra sprigs blackcurrants, for garnish**

1. Peel, core and slice the apples. Put them into a saucepan with the butter and three-quarters of the sugar and cook them very gently until they are soft and mushy — about 15 minutes.
2. Pass the apples through a sieve and return the purée to the saucepan.
3. Pick over the fresh currants, removing the stems and any spoilt currants. Wash and drain them, then stir into the apple purée. Alternatively, purée them in a blender and then stir in to the apples, as preferred.
4. Blend the egg yolks and crumbs together and stir into the fruit mixture.
5. Stir the arrowroot and water together, then add to the saucepan and stir in. Reheat the mixture until it bubbles and thickens. Cook for a minute to completely cook the starch, but no longer.
6. Beat the egg whites until stiff, then stir in the remaining sugar and beat again. Fold this mixture into thc hot fruit and mix well. Pour into fluted glasses and chill.
7. Serve topped with whipped cream and with each glass draped with a little sprig of currants.

La Roulade de Marrons Chocolatés

A Chestnut and Chocolate Roll with Pistachio Cream Sauce

Marrons glacés — chestnuts cooked in a rich syrup until crystallized — are probably France's greatest confectionary invention. It seems a shame that these sweet and delicious nuts have such a limited use in many parts of the world, being confined to a roasting over hot coals until charred and spoilt, good for little else than as a hand-warmer on a cold Winter's day. In France we make soups, purées, soufflés, stuffings and cakes from them, as well as subjecting them to the long and involved processes which transform them into *marrons glacés.* This dish uses chestnut purée, which you can make yourself (see instructions on page 162) or can be bought in tins imported from France. This tinned purée is of a very high quality and is one of the few tinned commodities which even top chefs will admit quite readily to using. If you can, though, do try to get some *marrons glacés* with which to decorate your *roulade,* especially if you are serving it as a magnificent finish to an important meal.

Imperial (Metric)	American
2 lb (900g) chestnut purée	**2 pounds chestnut paste**
2 fl oz (50ml) dark rum *or* noisette liqueur	**¼ cup dark rum *or* noisette liqueur**
5 oz (150g) raw cane sugar, powdered in a grinder	**1 cup raw cane sugar, powdered in a grinder**
½ lb (225g) bitter chocolate	**8 ounces bitter chocolate**
¼ pint (150ml) double cream	**⅔ cup heavy cream**
3 egg yolks	**3 egg yolks**
½ pint (300ml) milk	**1⅓ cups milk**
1 teaspoon arrowroot	**1 teaspoon arrowroot**
4 tablespoons water	**4 tablespoons water**
3 oz (75g) shelled and skinned pistachio nuts, chopped	**¾ cup shelled and skinned pistachio nuts, chopped**

1. Mash the chestnut purée and stir in half the liqueur. Mix well.
2. Test the purée for sweetness. Reserving half the sugar for the pistachio cream, add more of the remaining sugar until the mixture is to your taste.
3. In a bowl set over a pan of hot water, melt the chocolate and then blend in the cream. Allow to cool and thicken slightly.
4. On a flat surface lay out a sheet of very clean polythene. Onto this spread the chestnut purée, in a rectangle about 10 by 4 inches (25 by 10cm).
5. Spread the chocolate paste evenly over the chestnut paste.
6. Lifting one end of the sheet, carefully roll the rectangle up, Swiss-roll style. Place in the refrigerator to chill for 20 minutes.
7. Meanwhile, make the pistachio cream. Beat the egg yolks and the reserved sugar together in a bowl. Boil the milk and then pour it slowly onto the yolks, stirring constantly.
8. Blend the arrowroot and water together and then stir this into the egg and milk custard, along with the pistachio nuts.
9. Return the sauce to the pan and reheat for 6 minutes to thicken and cook the sauce. Flavour with the reserved liqueur.
10. Remove the chocolate and chestnut roll from the fridge, cut into slices and serve with the pistachio cream sauce.

10 Les Pains Bénits

Breads

We French love to eat bread and all foreigners seem to agree that our bread is the best in the world. Our *boulangers* bake twenty-two standard varieties of bread, including the especially popular and familiar *baguette* and *ficelle*, but the range of country breads, baked at home all over France, increases this range of traditional French breads many times over. We eat bread with all our meals, from brioches and croissants with our *café au lait* for breakfast (when the bread should always be dunked in the coffee in traditional French style), to the main meal of the day, be it a simple farmworker's soup or stew or a many-coursed gourmet dinner. And our snacks — *casse-croûtes* and *goûters* — are almost always bread-based. Over ½ pound (225g) per day is the standard bread consumption of a French citizen — many eat considerably more.

When made well, with good, wholesome ingredients, bread can be a very nutritious food, and a real pleasure to eat in itself rather than just a base for more flavoursome spreads or toppings. Breads using whole grains, of course, are good sources of fibre and vitamins, and wheat flour, when wholemeal, also contains the valuable wheatgerm. So a simple loaf can be a valuable part of the diet, but its potential does not end there. For a basic dough can be enriched with all manner of other ingredients, such as eggs, milk and cheese, dried fruits, nuts, flours made from pulses such as soya or grains such as rice. Breads such as these can be real storehouses of good things and should be regarded as an indispensable part of healthy eating, not just for vegetarians but for everyone. So much imagination can be used in choosing flavourings for your bread that meals need never be dull or repetitive. Don't forget, either, that bread can be frozen, either when freshly baked or after proving. Provided it is well-wrapped, your bread will be just as good once thawed as if it were newly made, so even a small family or a single person can enjoy the flavour and variety of home-made bread by planning an occasional batch bake of small loaves.

The secret of successful bread making has to be the treatment of your yeast. If you do not treat it right it simply will not perform correctly! Yeast is a living organism which thrives at a temperature of between 72°F/22°C and 82°F/28°C. This means that the water you use to blend the yeast should be between 72° and 75°F (22° and 24°C). The fermentation of the yeast itself will raise this temperature a little more. The room in which the bread is to prove should maintain this sort of temperature, and none of your ingredients should be straight from the fridge, either. Don't go overboard, though, as water or room temperatures of over 84°F/29°C will result in dry, dull bread which goes stale quickly. Follow instructions in the recipes, too, for kneading, proving and 'knocking back'. Do not be tempted to cut corners in these seemingly laborious or time-consuming processes. They are essential for giving the

yeast time to work, giving a good volume and lightness to the dough, and the kneading helps elasticate the gluten in the bread, making for a better textured bread. It also ensures that the ingredients are completely mixed, which is essential for a good loaf. Make sure your oven is heated to the right temperature before putting the loaf in the oven, and test the loaf to ensure it is completely cooked after the specified amount of time, by removing it from its tin and rapping on its base with the knuckles. There should be a distinctly 'hollow' sound — if it sounds dull, replace it in its tin and put it back in the oven for a further 5 minutes or so before testing again.

As is the case with soufflés, choux pastry and the like, there is a certain mystique to breadmaking, inspired no doubt by the legions of people who try it once and fail, and never try again. Yet it is really a basic cooking skill, simple and satisfying, which no cook worth his or her salt should be unable to include in their repertoire. Try the little breakfast rolls first. Once you have mastered these you should feel confident enough to tackle any of the other recipes — just a browse through this chapter will, I hope, tempt your palate enough to convince you that breadmaking is a skill well worth mastering.

Les Petits Pains de Déjeuner

Breakfast Rolls

Makes 18

The best way to learn how to make bread is by preparing a dough suitable for small rolls. This way you learn not only the procedures involved but also the effects of handling the dough, the effects of the yeast, and the baking process. Most importantly, too, you will learn how to mould your dough into attractive shapes. What you have learnt to do well with small amounts can easily be adapted to larger loaves.

Imperial (Metric)	American
1 lb (450g) strong wholemeal flour	**4 cups strong wholewheat flour**
1 oz (25g) fresh baker's yeast	**2 tablespoons fresh baker's yeast**
9 fl oz (255ml) water	**1¼ cups water**
1 teaspoon raw cane sugar	**1 teaspoon raw cane sugar**
2 tablespoons low-fat milk powder	**2 tablespoons low-fat milk powder**
4 oz (100g) hard vegetable fat	**½ cup hard vegetable fat**
1 teaspoon sea salt	**1 teaspoon sea salt**
2 fl oz (60ml) milk	**¼ cup milk**

1 Scoop out 1 tablespoon flour and reserve. Place the rest in a heap on a large pastry board. Make a well in the centre.

2 Crumble the yeast into a third of the water and stir until the yeast is well mixed. Pour this mixture into the well and sprinkle with the reserved flour, the sugar and the milk powder. Leave to ferment for 12 minutes, by which time the yeast mixture should be slightly bubbly.

3 Heat the rest of the water to 80°F/27°C (if you are unsure, or have not made bread before, use a cooking thermometer to check the temperature). Add this water to the yeast mixture in the well of flour and gradually blend the flour into this mixture.

4 When all the flour has been drawn into the liquid (use a fork or your fingers to do this) give the dough a good kneading and then roll it onto a ball. Cover the dough with an inverted bowl, or place in a polythene bag, either of which will retain the temperature of the dough, and leave for 40 minutes.

5 When the dough has rested and risen for 40 minutes, 'punch down' by giving it a good pummelling with the knuckles. Reshape it into a ball, and scatter the top with half the vegetable fat, cut into small pieces.

6 Leave the dough to rise again for 10 minutes, then knead to blend in the fat. Shape into a ball again and this time sprinkle the top of the dough with the salt. Your dough is now ready for shaping into rolls. (If new to breadmaking, you might like to check the temperature of your dough — it should be between 78-84°F/25-29°C.)

7 Divide the dough into 18 equal-sized pieces. Roll each one into a neat ball.

8 Grease a baking tray with the rest of the vegetable fat and arrange the rolls on it. Brush the rolls with a little milk and then leave them to prove for a further 20 to 25 minutes in a warm place.

9 Preheat the oven to 425°F/220°C (Gas Mark 7) and bake the rolls on the middle shelf for 15 to 20 minutes. Serve warm or cold with fresh French butter and perhaps your favourite conserve.

Opposite: *Les Profiteroles au Roquefort* (page 148).

ROQUEFORT
GARANTI
D'ORIGINE ET DE QUALITE
ROQUEF
FULL FAT BLUE VEIN CHEESE
AGED OVER
DAYS
APPELLATION
D'ORIGINE CONTROLEE
ROQUEFORT
FRANCE
QUESO

Le Pain Bis de Campagne

Country Wholemeal (Wholewheat) Bread

Makes 2 loaves, 14 ounces (400g) each
Illustrated opposite.

This is the bread which my grandmother used to make twice a week when I was a child. She would bake it in the communal village oven, as there was no commercial bakery in the village.

This bread can be produced from start to finish in 1½ hours. You can either bake it in two 1 pound (500g) loaf tins or shape it into two loaves of whatever shape you like. My grandmother's loaves were round, but you could plait yours, or make a cottage loaf. If making a loaf without a tin, prove it in a bread basket of the appropriate shape, lined with a piece of coarse material. Then bake the loaves on a greased baking tray.

Imperial (Metric)	American
1 lb 4 oz (550g) wholemeal flour	**5 cups wholewheat flour**
2 tablespoons sea salt	**2 tablespoons sea salt**
1 teaspoon black treacle *or* **honey**	**1 teaspoon molasses** *or* **honey**
1 teaspoon each of the following: sesame seeds, sunflower seeds, porridge oats, ground hazelnuts *or* **ground peanuts**	**1 teaspoon each of the following: sesame seeds, sunflower seeds, rolled oats, ground hazelnuts** *or* **ground peanuts**
1 teaspoon soya flour	**1 teaspoon soy flour**
1 oz (25g) fresh baker's yeast	**2 tablespoons fresh baker's yeast**
13 fl oz (375ml) water	**1¾ cups water**
Juice of ¼ lemon	**Juice of ¼ lemon**
2 oz (50g) hard vegetable fat	**¼ cup hard vegetable fat**

1. Place the flour in a heap on a large pastry board and make a well in the top.
2. In the well, place the salt, treacle (molasses) or honey, all the grains and nuts and the soya flour.
3. In a cup, blend the yeast into about 4 fl oz (120ml/½ cup) of the water and pour into the well of flour. Sprinkle a little flour on top and then leave for 10 minutes until it is slightly foamy.
4. Warm the rest of the water to 74°F/23°C and pour into the well with the yeast mixture. Mix all the flour and water together into a dough and knead well. Gather into a ball and leave covered with a large inverted bowl for 30 minutes.
5. Knock back with the knuckles. Blend in the lemon juice and knead well. Shape the mixture into two balls; elongate a ball, holding each end, then fold the ends into the middle to make a neat oblong shape. Repeat with the other ball of dough.
6. Grease two loaf tins with the vegetable fat, then place the loaves, folded sides downwards, in the tins. Or shape into the type of loaf you wish to make. Leave to prove for 30 minutes in a warm place.
7. Bake in a preheated oven at 425°F/220°C (Gas Mark 7) for 30 minutes. Remove from their tins and leave the loaves to cool on wire racks.

Opposite (clockwise from top right): *Pain au Maïs* (page 182); *Pain aux Bananes au Rhum* (page 184); *Brioches* (page 178); and two varieties of *Pain Bis de Campagne* (above).

Le Pain Brioché

Rich Bread Buns

Makes 1 loaf (1 pound/450g) and 12 small buns
Illustrated opposite page 177.

The oft-quoted phrase of Marie-Antoinette, 'Let them eat cake,' about the shortage of bread in France just before the Revolution is, in fact, a misquote. What she was really saying was, 'If the people are short of bread, give them brioche.' This is because the shortage of flour could be supplemented in a rich and nourishing loaf by the addition of milk and eggs. The French certainly love their bread, and it was the shortage of flour — a ridiculous situation in a cereal-rich country like France — which finally precipitated the French Revolution. These days, every French person can dunk their brioche into their hot chocolate for breakfast, as I do. There is no better breakfast, to my mind!

An enriched dough, such as for brioche, needs extra help to make it good and light. For this reason a mixture of flour, water and yeast is given a while to ferment prior to being added into the main ingredients. This gets the yeast off to a flying start. A baker's ferment, as this first mixture is called, looks rather like very thin pancake batter, but the action of the yeast gives it the appearance of bubbling and boiling, hence the name 'ferment.'

Imperial (Metric)	American
1 lb 2 oz (500g) wholemeal flour, slightly warmed	**4½ cups wholewheat flour, slightly warmed**
½ oz (15g) baker's yeast	**1 tablespoon baker's yeast**
4 fl oz (120ml) mixed milk and water	**½ cup mixed milk and water**
1 oz (25g) raw cane sugar	**2 tablespoons raw cane sugar**
1 tablespoon sea salt	**1 tablespoon sea salt**
4-5 eggs, beaten	**4-5 eggs, beaten**
6 oz (150g) softened butter	**¾ cup softened butter**
Extra milk, for glazing	**Extra milk, for glazing**
2 oz (50g) hard vegetable fat	**¼ cup hard vegetable fat**

1. Place a quarter of the flour in a bowl. Place the yeast in a cup.
2. Heat the milk and water to 78°F/25°C and stir half of it into the yeast; blend well. Stir this mixture into the smaller quantity of flour. Leave to ferment for 15 to 20 minutes, by which time it should have doubled in volume.
3. Place the remaining flour on a large pastry board and make a well in the top. In the well place the sugar and salt, with the rest of the warm milk and water to dissolve them slightly.
4. Add some of the beaten egg, then begin drawing the flour into the liquids, adding more egg if it seems to be getting stiff. Beat the dough for a good 10 minutes to achieve a soft, pliable texture — 'plastic' as it is known in culinary terms.
5. Add the softened butter and knead it in well. (This can be done in an electric mixer with a dough hook, if preferred.)
6. At this stage add the ferment, either by hand or in a mixer, making sure it is completely kneaded into the dough. Leave the dough in a clean bowl, covered with a clean cloth and dusted with a little flour, for 1½ to 2 hours.
7. Grease a 1½ pound (650g) bread tin or large brioche tin with vegetable fat, and grease 12 small, fluted brioche moulds likewise.
8. Weigh out 1 pound (450g) of the dough and shape to fit the tin. Brush the top with milk and leave to prove for a further 35 to 45 minutes in a warm place, until it has risen above the edge of the tin.

9 Divide the remaining dough into 12 equal pieces, then break off about a quarter to each piece. Place the larger pieces of dough in the brioche tins, making a dent in their tops. Then shape the smaller pieces into pear shapes and place these on top of the larger pieces, with the pointed end fitting into the dent — like miniature cottage loaves.
10 Brush the little buns with milk (mixed with any left-over egg if you have some) to glaze. Leave to prove in a warm place for 20 minutes.
11 Preheat the oven to 400°F/200°C (Gas Mark 6). Bake the buns for 15 to 20 minutes, and the loaf for 35 minutes. The heat could be lowered to 375°F/190°C (Gas Mark 5) once the buns have been removed, if the top of the bread looks to be getting too brown. Remove the buns and bread from their tins to cool on racks.

Note: The loaf could be baked in a large brioche tin, in which case, follow the shaping instructions for the little brioches to make the traditional 'cottage' top for your brioche.

Les Petits Pains de Pommes de Terre

Potato Cakes

Makes 16 cakes

These little scone-like cakes combine mashed, floury late-season potatoes with wholemeal flour and butter to make a tasty snack. They use only baking powder to help them rise, as yeast is not needed for this light and quickly cooked mixture. They are delicious fried, but to keep calories a little lower they are very good baked in the oven like normal rolls or scones.

Imperial (Metric)	American
1 lb (450g) wholemeal flour	**4 cups wholewheat flour**
1½ oz (45g) baking powder	**3 tablespoons baking powder**
½ lb (225g) butter	**1 cup butter**
2 lb (900g) boiled floury potatoes	**2 pounds boiled floury potatoes**
½ pint (300ml) cooking water from potatoes	**⅓ cup cooking water from potatoes**
Sea salt and freshly ground black pepper	**Sea salt and freshly ground black pepper**
2 fl oz (50ml) vegetable oil for griddle *or* **1 oz (25g) hard vegetable fat for baking tray**	**¼ cup vegetable oil for griddle** *or* **2 tablespoons hard vegetable fat for baking tray**

1 Sieve the flour and baking powder together, returning sieved bran to the bowl.
2 Rub the butter into the flour, to the consistency of fine breadcrumbs.
3 Mash, and then sieve, the potatoes, and stir in the reserved potato water.
4 Stir the mashed potato mixture into the flour to form a batter. Season to taste. Shape the mixture into rounds about 3 inches (7cm) in diameter and 1 inch (2.5cm) thick.
5 Either heat the oil in a pan and shallow fry the cakes until golden on both sides or bake on a greased tray at 400°F/200°C (Gas Mark 6) for 15 to 20 minutes. Serve hot or cold, as a snack or with a green salad as a light meal.

Variation:
For a more substantial dish, use less water and replace with one or two beaten eggs.

Le Pain Bénit

Sweet Bread Loaf

Makes a 3 pound (1.4 kilo) plaited loaf

It is customary in France to offer a slice of sweet bread during church services on Sunday. This bread is often donated by the local baker. My grandmother used to make her own special Sunday bread, which we had for *goûter* — a snack — in the afternoon. This rich bread, with its decoration of dried fruits and almonds, was always a great treat.

Imperial (Metric)	American
1½ oz (45g) fresh baker's yeast	**3 tablespoons fresh baker's yeast**
1 pint (600ml) milk, warmed to 78°F/25°C	**2½ cups milk, warmed to 78°F**
1¾ lb (775g) strong wholemeal flour	**7 cups strong wholewheat flour**
2½ oz (65g) raw cane sugar	**½ cup raw cane sugar**
1½ oz (40g) sea salt	**3 tablespoons sea salt**
1 teaspoon honey	**1 teaspoon honey**
4 oz (100g) butter, softened	**½ cup butter, softened**
Juice of ¼ lemon	**Juice of ¼ lemon**
3 oz (75g) glacé cherries, halved	**6 tablespoons glacé cherries, halved**
3 oz (75g) citrus peel	**6 tablespoons citrus peel**
3 oz (75g) angelica, chopped	**6 tablespoons angelica, chopped**
2 oz (50g) flaked almonds	**4 tablespoons slivered almonds**
1 oz (25g) vegetable fat	**2 tablespoons vegetable fat**
1 beaten egg plus 2 tablespoons milk, to wash loaf	**1 beaten egg plus 2 tablespoons milk, to wash loaf**
2 fl oz (60ml) clear honey, to glaze	**¼ cup clear honey, to glaze**

1. In a bowl, combine the yeast and the warm milk, and disperse the yeast well. Sprinkle with 2 tablespoonsful flour and leave for 12 minutes until the mixture is foamy.
2. Put the flour into a large bowl and make a well in the top. Sift the sugar and salt together into the well. Then add the fermented yeast and the honey and beat the mixture together into a dough. Knead well.
3. When the mixture is well kneaded, draw it into a ball. Dot the top of the dough with the butter, cover with an inverted bowl and leave to prove for 45 minutes.
4. Knead the dough again, so that the butter is well blended into the dough. Add the lemon juice and half the dried fruits and nuts, and give the dough another quick knead to blend them in, then cover again and leave to prove for a further 20 minutes.
5. Divide the dough into 3 equal parts. Roll each part into a pointed 'sausage' shape, about 9 inches (23cm) long. Join the strands at one end and plait into a neat loaf, joining the other ends when you have finished plaiting.
6. Grease a baking tray with vegetable fat and place the loaf on it.
7. Brush the loaf with the egg and milk wash. Leave to prove for 35 to 40 minutes, by which time it will have doubled in size.
8. Glaze the loaf again with egg and milk, and bake at 400°F/200°C (Gas Mark 6) for 35 minutes.
9. Heat the honey very gently and, as soon as the loaf is removed from the oven, brush it with melted honey to give it a lovely glaze, and decorate the top with the rest of the fruit and nuts.

Le Pain d'Épices

Honey Bread with Aniseeds

Makes 1 large, square loaf

Once a year the Amiens Fair takes place, and at this typical French event you can sample dozens of varieties of the wonderful *pain d'épice* at the stalls which line the fairground. This honey bread, flavoured with spices, is not so sweet as you might first imagine, and is best eaten at tea time with lashings of good French butter. It is not as spicy as its Jamaican 'cousin' gingerbread, since we prefer the subtler flavour of aniseeds blended with a little ginger and other spices. This is an unyeasted bread which uses a combination of soda and cream of tartar to give it lightness.

Imperial (Metric)	American
1 lb (450g) clear honey	**1⅓ cups clear honey**
½ lb (225g) wholemeal flour	**2 cups wholewheat flour**
½ lb (225g) rye flour	**2 cups rye flour**
¼ teaspoon each of: ground cloves, ground cinnamon, ground ginger and aniseeds	**¼ teaspoon each of: ground cloves, ground cinnamon, ground ginger and aniseeds**
1 level teaspoon cream of tartar	**1 level teaspoon cream of tartar**
2 eggs, beaten	**2 eggs, beaten**
1 level teaspoon bicarbonate of soda	**1 level teaspoon baking soda**
4 fl oz (120ml) warm milk	**½ cup warm milk**
2 oz (50g) hard vegetable fat	**¼ cup hard vegetable fat**
4 oz (100g) raw cane sugar	**⅔ cup raw cane sugar**
3 tablespoons milk	**3 tablespoons milk**
3 tablespoons water	**3 tablespoons water**

1. In a saucepan, heat the honey until almost boiling.
2. Mix the two flours together in a large bowl, and stir in the spices and the cream of tartar.
3. Bring the honey to the boil and pour it onto the flour, beating hard to form a dough.
4. Stir in the beaten eggs.
5. Dissolve the bicarbonate of soda (baking soda) in the warm milk and blend this mixture into the dough.
6. Grease a 3 pint (2.5 litre/2 quart) square baking tin and pour the dough into it. Leave to rest for 1 hour.
7. Bake in a preheated oven at 400°F/200°C (Gas Mark 6) for 20 minutes on the middle shelf, then reduce the heat to 350°F/180°C (Gas Mark 4) for a further 20 minutes.
8. While the loaf is baking, boil the sugar, milk and water together in a pan for 5 to 8 minutes to form a thick syrup. As soon as the loaf is removed from the oven, brush the top with this syrup to form a glaze. Cool the bread on a wire rack.

Variations:

If you cannot obtain rye flour, or wish to vary the loaf, all wheat flour could be used. If you like, the top of the spice bread could be decorated with pieces of citrus peel, glacé cherries or angelica after baking.

This loaf is best left in an airtight tin for 2 days before cutting, as this gives the flavours time to develop and mature.

Le Pain au Maïs

Cornmeal Bread

Makes 1 loaf, 2 pounds (1 kilo)
Illustrated opposite page 177.

Bread made with cornmeal needs the addition of wheat flour, otherwise it would be too heavy. Corn was only introduced into France in the sixteenth century, but now it is grown extensively in all regions. The problem which a diet high in maize can cause, the disease pellagra, is due to the fact that corn is lacking in niacin — but this is not likely to worry us in the West so much as in the poor, Third World countries which are often dependent on corn as their staple food. In most countries, corn will always be used more for animal fodder than as a food for people, but a loaf such as this one, where corn and wheat are correctly balanced to produce a substantial, flavoursome bread, makes a very pleasant change.

Imperial (Metric)	American
5 oz (150g) cornmeal	**⅔ cup cornmeal**
8 fl oz (250ml) boiling water	**1 cup boiling water**
2 teaspoons sea salt	**2 teaspoons sea salt**
1 tablespoon honey	**1 tablespoon honey**
2 tablespoons corn oil	**2 tablespoons corn oil**
1 oz (25g) fresh baker's yeast	**2 tablespoons fresh baker's yeast**
1 teaspoon raw cane sugar	**1 teaspoon raw cane sugar**
¼ pint (150ml) tepid water	**⅔ cup tepid water**
1 lb 2 oz (500g) wholemeal flour	**4½ cups wholewheat flour**
1 oz (25g) vegetable fat	**2 tablespoons vegetable fat**

1. Place the cornmeal in a large bowl. Pour on the boiling water and leave to soak for 15 minutes. Then stir in the salt, honey and oil.
2. Place the yeast in a cup with the sugar. Stir in the tepid water and add a pinch of flour. Leave to ferment for 15 minutes, by which time it should be foamy.
3. Stir the yeast ferment into the cornmeal. Reserve 2 oz (50g/½ cup) flour and then add the rest to the cornmeal mixture, mixing well. Knead the mixture to a smooth dough on a large, floured pastry board. Knead very well, punching and stretching the dough to really elasticate the gluten in the wheat flour (the cornmeal is low in gluten).
4. Roll the dough into a ball, cover with an inverted bowl and leave to prove for 45 minutes.
5. 'Knock back' the dough and knead again, then shape it into a ball.
6. Grease a 3 pound (1.5 kilo) round loaf tin. Place the dough in the tin, brush with a little milk and leave to prove again, in a warm place, until the dough has risen to the top of the tin in a dome shape. Sprinkle with the reserved flour.
7. Bake in a preheated oven at 400°F/200°C (Gas Mark 6) for 35 minutes, until golden brown and, when tapped on the base, has a hollow sound. Cool on a wire rack.

Note: This loaf freezes well, as do many breads. It should be well wrapped before freezing, and should not be refrozen once defrosted. Even just wrapped in polythene and stored in a bread box, this loaf will keep well for several days. The loaf can also be baked in a round tin, and sliced cake-like, if preferred.

Le Pain d'Amandes au Kirsch

Almond Bread with Kirsch

Makes 1 small loaf

Almonds are widely cultivated in the South of France and are often used there to produce one of the most delicious bread-cakes ever invented — the famous *pain d'amandes*. Many countries produce almonds and it is certainly the case that this nut is the most important in the world from a gastronomical point of view. It is used in a wide range of dishes, not just breads and cakes, and is the basis for liqueurs as well. Its flavour enhances and complements others like no other nut. There are two types of almond: the bitter and the sweet. The bitter almond is an acquired taste, and contains prussic acid, which makes this type of almond poisonous in large quantities. For this recipe I have used ground sweet almonds, of the type most readily available.

Imperial (Metric)	American
7 oz (200g) softened butter	**1 cup softened butter**
2 oz (50g) soft wholemeal flour	**½ cup soft wholewheat flour**
5 oz (150g) raw cane sugar, powdered in a grinder	**1 cup raw cane sugar, powdered in a grinder**
4 oz (100g) ground almonds	**1 cup ground almonds**
3 eggs, beaten	**3 eggs, beaten**
1 pinch sea salt	**1 pinch sea salt**
3 fl oz (90ml) Kirsch	**⅓ cup Kirsch**

1 Take a 9 inch (23cm) cake tin, 2 inches (5cm) deep and grease it with 1 ounce (25g) butter. Then line it with non-stick baking paper and grease that with a further 1 ounce (25g) butter. Coat the butter with ½ ounce (15g) flour.

2 Beat the rest of the butter and the sugar together until pale and fluffy. Then add the ground almonds and the rest of the flour. Beat the mixture well.

3 Blend the beaten eggs into the mixture until completely smooth, then add a pinch of salt and the Kirsch. Mix all the ingredients together thoroughly.

4 Pour this mixture into the prepared mould and smooth the top level with a palette knife.

5 Bake in a preheated oven at 375°F/190°C (Gas Mark 5) for 40 minutes.

6 Unmould the bread onto a wire rack. Sprinkle with Kirsch once cool. Wrap in foil and keep for 2 days before eating.

Le Pain aux Bananes au Rhum

Banana Rum Bread

Makes 2, 1 pound (450g) loaves
Illustrated opposite page 177.

The French West Indies influenced France quite considerably with regard to the use of bananas in cooking. As I have mentioned before, it is my opinion (and one which is shared by many, particularly residents of regions where bananas are grown) that bananas are not at their best until their flesh is dark and soft like a sort of jam. If you don't like the thought of eating them raw when they reach that state, do not throw them away but try making this rich, sweet bread which uses really ripe bananas to great advantage. Once you have tasted them like this, I am sure you will be converted.

Imperial (Metric)	American
½ lb (225g) wholemeal flour	**2 cups wholewheat flour**
½ oz (15g) bicarbonate of soda	**1 tablespoon baking soda**
½ oz (15g) baking powder	**½ ounce baking powder**
1 teaspoon sea salt	**1 teaspoon sea salt**
Juice and grated rind of 1 lemon	**Juice and grated rind of 1 lemon**
3 fl oz (75ml) peanut oil	**⅓ cup peanut oil**
2 eggs, beaten	**2 eggs, beaten**
2 large ripe bananas, flesh mashed	**2 large ripe bananas, flesh mashed**
2 fl oz (50ml) clear honey	**¼ cup clear honey**
4 oz (100g) chopped, pitted dates	**¾ cup chopped, pitted dates**
2 oz (50g) ground peanuts, roasted	**½ cup ground peanuts, roasted**
1 oz (25g) desiccated coconut (slightly toasted, if liked)	**⅔ cup desiccated coconut (slightly toasted, if liked)**
2 tablespoons French Negrita black rum	**2 tablespoons French Negrita black rum**
1 oz (25g) hard vegetable fat	**2 tablespoons hard vegetable fat**

1. Stir together the first four ingredients in a large bowl
2. Beat together the next five ingredients to a creamy consistency. Stir into the flour mixture until well mixed.
3. Add the chopped dried fruit and nuts, and stir in the rum.
4. Grease two 1 pound (500g) loaf tins with the vegetable fat and pour in the loaf batter.
5. Bake at 325°F/170°C (Gas Mark 3) for 1 hour, on the middle shelf of the oven. Turn out onto a wire rack to cool.

Le Pain au Carvi

Rye Bread with Caraway Seeds

Makes 1 large loaf

Rye comes second to wheat in popularity as a breadmaking grain. It has a very distinctive, slight sour taste, which many people find appealing but which it is useful to mellow with wheat flour if you have not tried it before. Rye withstands cold better than wheat, and has more gluten than barley. Rye bread also keeps better than bread made with wheat flour alone. These facts probably account for the number of traditional recipes which blend the two flours, 'stretching' the more scarce and luxurious wheat with rye. The aromatic flavour of caraway seeds goes particularly well with rye bread, making an especially flavoursome loaf, an ideal accompaniment to dishes such as *Le Dragon Rouge* (page 65).

Imperial (Metric)	American
1 oz (25g) baker's yeast	**2 tablespoons baker's yeast**
1 pint (300ml) water, warmed to 78°F/25°C	**2½ cups water, warmed to 78°F**
8 oz (225g) rye flour	**2¼ cups rye flour**
1½ lb (675g) wholemeal flour	**6 cups wholewheat flour**
3 tablespoons sea salt	**3 tablespoons sea salt**
1 tablespoon malt extract	**1 tablespoon malt extract**
1 teaspoon caraway seeds	**1 teaspoon caraway seeds**
1 oz (25g) hard vegetable fat	**2 tablespoons hard vegetable fat**

1. Blend the yeast into half the warm water. Place the rye flour in a large bowl and stir in the yeast liquid. Leave for 1 hour, covered, to ferment.
2. Place the wheat flour in a large bowl and make a well in the centre. Add the salt and the malt extract, then stir in the rest of the water. Add half the caraway seeds and mix well into the stiff dough.
3. When the ferment has doubled in size, blend it into the wheat flour dough. Knead by hand or with an electric mixer fitted with a dough hook, for 5 minutes. Roll the dough into a ball, cover with a cloth or an inverted bowl and leave to prove for 40 minutes.
4. Lightly grease an oblong loaf tin or a baking tray and shape the loaf accordingly. Brush with a little milk and sprinkle with the remaining caraway seeds. Leave to prove for 30 minutes.
5. Bake at 425°F/220°C (Gas Mark 7) for 30 minutes. When golden-brown and hollow-sounding when tapped on its base, turn the loaf out onto a wire rack to cool.

Les Croissants Conil

French Filled Croissants

Makes 18 Croissants

These croissants are made with a yeasted dough which has been 'laminated' with butter. The pastry is turned, as for puff pastry, to make it especially light. It is then filled with a delicious rum-flavoured almond and peanut mixture and rolled into the traditional crescent shape. This recipe has been so successful that my son Christopher is now selling them in his shop.

Imperial (Metric)	American
1 lb (450g) strong wholemeal flour	**4 cups strong wholewheat flour**
½ teaspoon sea salt	**½ teaspoon sea salt**
1½ oz (45g) raw cane sugar	**¼ cup raw cane sugar**
½ oz (15g) fresh baker's yeast	**1 tablespoon fresh baker's yeast**
8 fl oz (225ml) warm milk	**1 cup warm milk**
1 egg, beaten	**1 egg, beaten**
¾ lb (350g) French butter	**1½ cups French butter**
For the filling:	For the filling:
4 oz (100g) butter	**½ cup butter**
2 eggs, beaten	**2 eggs, beaten**
2 oz (50g) ground almonds	**½ cup ground almonds**
2 oz (50g) ground toasted peanuts	**½ cup ground toasted peanuts**
2 oz (50g) wholemeal flour	**¼ cup wholewheat flour**
4 oz (100g) raw cane sugar, powdered in a grinder	**⅔ cup raw cane sugar, powdered in a grinder**
2 tablespoons dark rum	**2 tablespoons dark rum**
For the glaze:	For the glaze:
1 egg, beaten	**1 egg, beaten**
2 tablespoons milk	**2 tablespoons milk**
2 oz (50g) raw sugar apricot jam	**2 tablespoons raw sugar apricot jelly**
2 oz (50g) flaked almonds	**½ cup slivered almonds**

1. Sift the flour and salt together in a bowl. Stir in the sugar.
2. In a cup, stir the yeast into the warm milk. Blend in the beaten egg and then mix this into the flour to form a dough. Knead the dough thoroughly, roll it into a ball and place it in a polythene bag to rise for 10 minutes.
3. 'Knock back' the dough by pummelling it with the knuckles to get rid of the air. Shape it into a ball again.
4. Shape the butter into a 6 inch (15cm) square. Chill for 10 minutes.
5. Roll the dough into a 12 inch (30cm) square. Place the butter on the dough square and fold the edges of the dough over it to cover it completely.
6. Dust with flour and roll the dough out to an oblong about 18×9 inches (45×23cm). Fold the two sides to meet in the centre of the dough, then fold in the centre like a book. Chill for 15 minutes.
7. Repeat the rolling and folding process, then refrigerate again while you prepare the filling.
8. Combine all the filling ingredients together, beating until light and fluffy.

9 Roll out the pastry dough to an oblong 18×12 inches (45×30cm). Cut triangles with a 4 inch (10cm) base, 6 inches (15cm) from base to tip (see diagram). You should make 16 triangles, with trimmings at either end. Re-roll the trimmings and cut a further 2 triangles.

10 Spread a little of the filling onto each triangle, to within ¼ inch (5mm) of the edges. Roll up carefully from the base to the point, pressing the edges to seal in the filling. Curve the roll into the traditional crescent shape, with the curves pointing away from the direction of the tip of the triangle.

11 Brush the croissants with a mixture of beaten egg and milk. Place on a lightly greased baking tray and cover with polythene or loose cling film. Leave to prove and rise for 20 minutes.

12 Preheat the oven to 425°F/225°C (Gas Mark 7) and bake the croissants for 15 to 20 minutes until golden.

13 As soon as the croissants are removed from the oven, brush with a little beaten egg, milk, or warmed apricot jam, and sprinkle with almonds. And there you have the best croissants in the world (or so our customers say)!

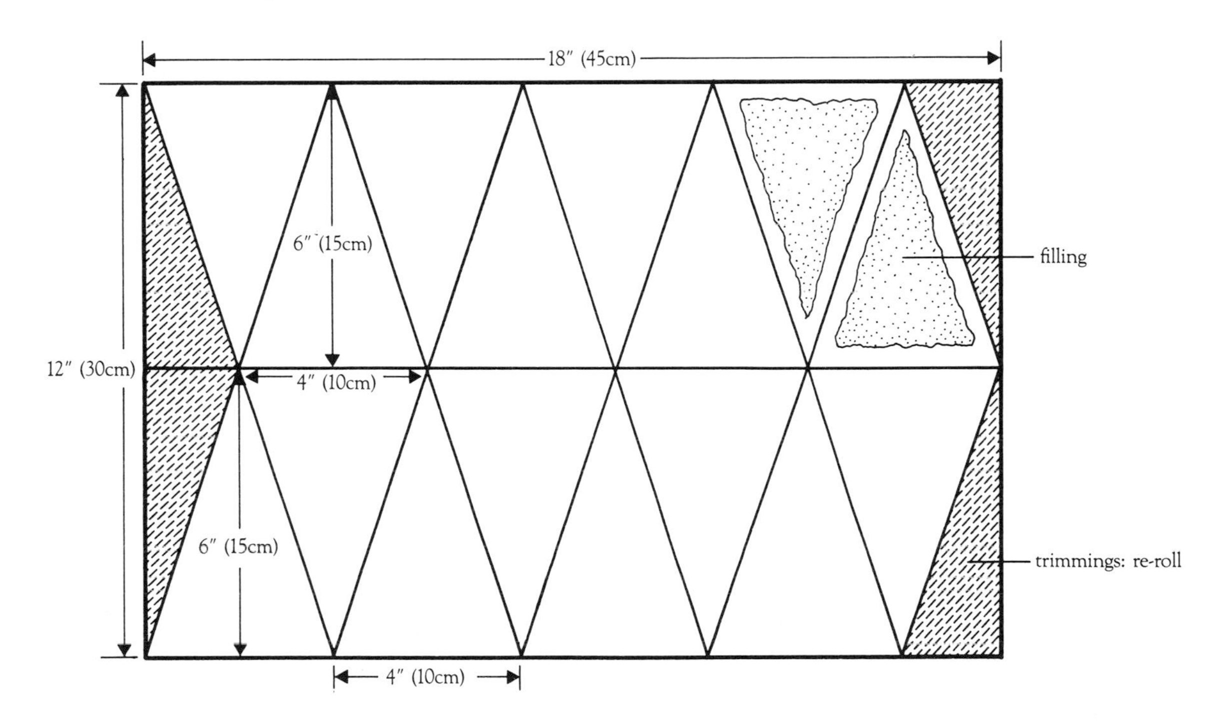

Le Pain de Saint Antoine aux Flocons d'Avoine

Oatmeal Bread with Cheese, Fruit and Nuts

Makes 1 large loaf
Illustrated opposite page 177.

As in some earlier recipes, this bread is baked without the use of yeast, a chemical raising agent being used instead. Many breads and cakes are made by this technique in France. Baking powder consists of two ingredients, one acid and one alkaline. When heated together in the presence of liquid they produce carbon dioxide which raises the cake or bread. Because the balance of acid and alkali is correct there should be no aftertaste from the baking powder. However, bicarbonate of soda (baking soda) is alkaline only, and will leave an unpleasant aftertaste unless balanced with an acid such as cream of tartar, in the case of this recipe, or sour milk as in some soda breads.

Imperial (Metric)	American
½ lb (225g) wholemeal flour	**2 cups wholewheat flour**
2 oz (50g) soya flour	**½ cup soy flour**
1 tablespoon cream of tartar	**1 tablespoon cream of tartar**
1 teaspoon sea salt	**1 teaspoon sea salt**
½ lb (225g) oatmeal	**1½ cups oatmeal**
½ tablespoon bicarbonate of soda	**½ tablespoon baking soda**
1 pint (600ml) milk, warmed to 84°F/29°C	**2½ cups milk, warmed to 84°F**
3 fl oz (90 ml) water, at same temperature	**⅓ cup water, at same temperature**
4 oz (100g) honey	**⅓ cup honey**
4 oz (100g) seedless raisins	**⅔ cup seedless raisins**
1 oz (50g) hard vegetable fat	**2 tablespoons hard vegetable fat**
For the topping:	For the topping:
½ lb (225g) curd *or* cream cheese	**2 cups curd *or* cream cheese**
4 oz (100g) ground peanuts	**1 cup ground peanuts**
2 oz (50g) minced stoned dates *or* dried apricots	**⅓ cup minced pitted dates *or* dried apricots**
2 tablespoons brandy	**2 tablespoons brandy**

1. Combine the first four ingredients and sift them together into a bowl, adding back the bran from the wheat flour. Stir in the oatmeal.
2. Stir the bicarbonate of soda (baking soda) into the milk and water to dissolve.
3. Warm the honey slightly, to about the same temperature as the milk, and stir it into the flour mixture. Mix well.
4. Stir the milk and water into the mixture, ensuring that it is thoroughly mixed.
5. Stir in the seedless raisins.
6. Grease a 3 pint (2.5 litre/2 quart) capacity round baking tin and fill with the bread dough. Bake in a preheated oven at 400°F/200°C (Gas Mark 6) for the first 10 minutes, then turn down the heat to 375°F/190°C (Gas Mark 5) for a further 35 minutes. Turn out onto a wire rack and leave to cool.
7. While the bread is cooling, prepare the topping by creaming together all the ingredients. Cut the loaf into slices, spread each slice with topping and serve.

Index